LIVING NEAR THE DEAD

Sidestone Press

LIVING NEAR THE DEAD

THE BARROW EXCAVATIONS OF RHENEN-ELST: TWO MILLENNIA
OF BURIAL AND HABITATION ON THE UTRECHTSE HEUVELRUG

edited by David Fontijn

Published by Sidestone Press, Leiden
www.sidestone.com

ISBN 978-90-8890-055-6

Photographs cover:
Cover design: K. Wentink, Sidestone Press
Lay-out: P.C. van Woerdekom, Sidestone Press

Contents

Preface: why this book?

D. Fontijn

The answer to the question posed in the title can be simple. In August 2006, the University of Leiden, aided by the National Heritage Agency *RCE*, carried out a small five-day excavation of two prehistoric burial mounds. It is a legal and moral obligation for any archaeologist to report the results of such a research to others. On second thoughts, however, this answer leaves open many questions: to whom exactly should we report our results? To professional archaeologists, to Dutch academic colleagues, to heritage instances, to the wider public, to the international academic world? In the Netherlands, archaeological reports should confirm to the norms laid down in the *KNA*, which is a very helpful tool guiding authors to meet report publication standards, as is the peer review system linked with it. If we were only to follow those guidelines in reporting this excavation our five-day excavation could have done with a good but much more modest report in Dutch, instead of the more voluminous English book that you have now in your hands. There are several reasons why we decided to act otherwise.

The first is that the excavation, small as it was, attracted many visitors and received much publicity in the regional and national press. There were sizeable articles in the *NRC* and *AD* newspapers, and *RTV West* made a documentary on the excavation on regional television. All this interest on the part of the main public clearly shows that we could not confine ourselves to the production of a scientific report only: there should be an accessible "report" for interested non-archaeologists as well. As we do not believe that a compromise between both is viable – a scientific report in Dutch which is also interesting for laymen- we were to make two books: a book for archaeologists with all the scientific results (the one you are reading now), and an attractive low-price publication for a non-archaeological public (*Op de rand van de Rug* by E. van Ginkel and Y. van Koeveringe). We are happy that both could be produced simultaneously and are grateful for the finances made available for the publication of the latter book by the Province of *Utrecht*.

The second reason is that this excavation was done for purely scientific reasons. It was a non-commercial University excavation, a rare occurrence in Dutch archaeology. Excavating heritage that does not seem to be immediately threatened makes reporting on its results a special responsibility. As much as possible, we have tried to go into all the details, paying attention to practically all finds done, and including all the amateur finds from the immediate environment in our argument. Particularly the latter proved to be a very time-consuming, yet rewarding task as the results shown in this book hopefully demonstrate. Unfortunately, the complete destruction of one entire barrow of this group after our excavation ended (see Chapter 8), showed that even this seemingly "safe" barrow group was not as unthreatened as was thought.

The third reason to write a book on an excavation in the Netherlands in such an extended form and in English is of an "academic" nature. It has both to do with what we found and with our ideas on the publication of fieldwork. To start with the former: nowadays, barrow excavations are rare in Northwest Europe and therefore tend to be a subject of special interest not only to the Dutch, but also to students of prehistory from other countries. Also, the excavation described here uncovered rare *in situ* finds of the Early Bronze Age period, as well as closed find

PREFACE | 11

complexes of the Middle Bronze Age *Hilversum* pottery phase. Because of its supposed links with English, Belgian and North French pottery styles, there is a keen interest on good *Hilversum* pottery finds on the part of Bronze Age archaeologists from those countries (see Theunissen 1999). Another argument to publish an excavation report in English is that it allows archaeologists from outside the Low Countries to evaluate and check our conclusions. With the increasing formalization of academic competition, the use of "quality measurements" and citation indices, there is a growing tendency to publish brief articles in peer-reviewed international journals. Although this is a positive development, there is a risk that the time-consuming task of the publication of fieldwork results suffers from this. Excavation reports often are considered as of less importance in the academic rating system than articles in international journals. In our view, this can and should never be decided *a priori*. We are of the opinion that fieldwork is fundamental, primary archaeological research and should be appreciated and published as such. We hope that the present publication of what actually was a very small excavation does justice to this claim.

Chapter 1

Introduction – Problem and Research Aims

D. Fontijn

This chapter describes the research aims of the excavation campaign and the broader problems of the archaeology of barrow landscapes to which it aims to be a contribution. Realizing that this excavation was the first fieldwork since decades that was carried out for mainly scientific reasons, it is necessary to start by making clear why we decided to carry out new barrow fieldwork in the first place (section 1.1). Then, the special nature of barrow landscapes of the central Netherlands, the *Utrechtse Heuvelrug* and the *Veluwe* are charted (section 1.2). It will be argued that there is a general lack of knowledge on these prehistoric burial mounds, and this applies particularly to the c. 150 still-existing barrows of the *Utrechtse Heuvelrug*. However, the latter region – especially the eastern part or the *Elst-Rhenen* area (Fig. 1.1) – is promising for new barrow research for several reasons. These will be

Fig. 1.1 Location of Elst, municipality of Rhenen in the Netherlands.

set out in section 1.3. I will go on to argue why two barrows of the easternmost *Elsterberg* barrow cluster were selected for excavation (section 1.4). Section 1.5 lists the specific research aims of this excavation. The chapter will close with a general description of the environment of the excavated barrows and introduce the structure of the rest of the book.

1.1 Barrow landscapes on the ice-pushed ridges in the southern part of the Central Netherlands

In the modern landscape of the Netherlands, many examples of prehistoric burial mounds, or barrows, can be found. They are particularly numerous in the centre of the country, at the *Veluwe* (province of *Gelderland*) and the *Utrechtse Heuvelrug* (province of *Utrecht*). The *Archis*-database of the National Heritage Service (*RCE, Rijksdienst voor het Cultureel Erfgoed*) records 1492 barrows for this part of the Netherlands, of which 450 are located within the province of *Utrecht*. Many barrows are to be found in areas that have now become natural reserves such as the *Utrechtse Heuvelrug* (Fig. 1.2).

Barrows are usually seen as 'burial places' for prehistoric individuals, but there are reasons to believe that there is more to them than just that: they must have had great social and ideological significance to prehistoric communities at large (Fontijn 2007b). Burial mounds are the first truly ubiquitous type of prehistoric monument in the north European landscape, laying out the main monumental structure of landscape for ages to come (Anthony 2007; Bogucki 1999). Barrows underwent long histories of re-use for burial and other prehistoric practices in prehistory. Everywhere where people built burial mounds, they became focal points for land orderings of much later times. Later prehistoric barrows (Bronze and

Fig. 1.2 Digital Elevation Model of the ice-pushed ridge of Utrechtse Heuvelrug, with the location of prehistoric barrows (red). North is up. 1. Elsterberg barrow group; 2. Amerongen; 3. Leersum, 4. Elst; 5. Rhenen; 6. Veenendaal. Map based on the AHN, used with permission under license of the Province of Utrecht.

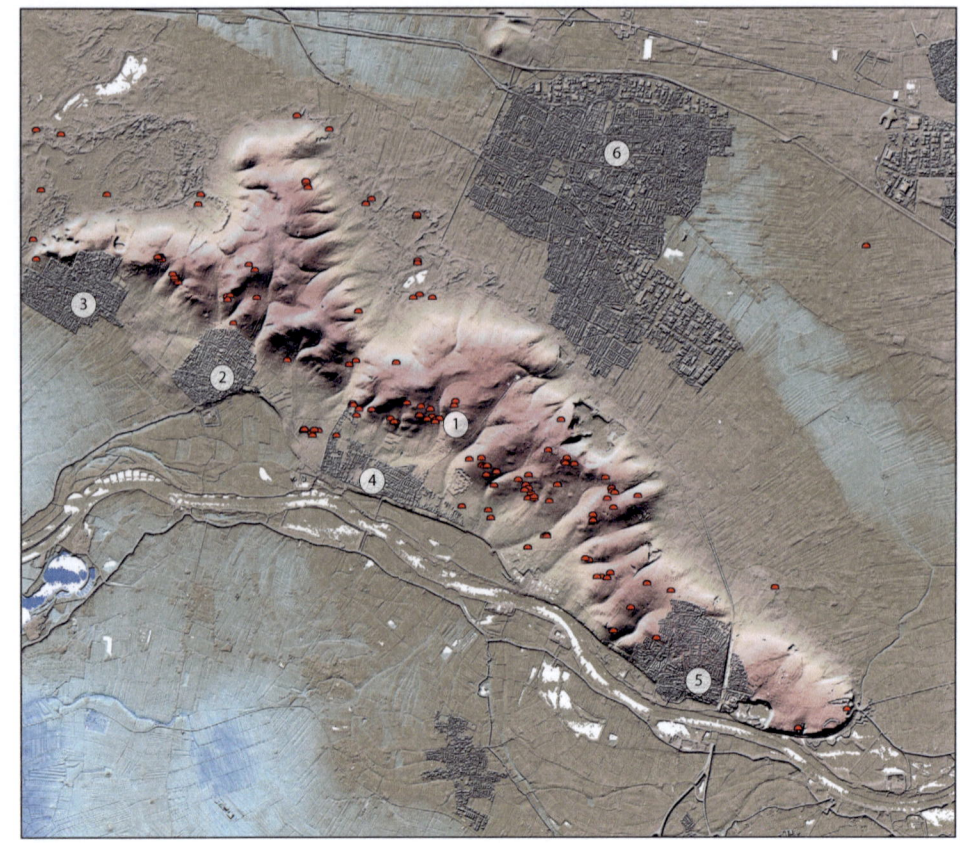

Elevation in metres NAP

Iron Age) seem to have been preferably built close to older ones, leading to the formation of impressive "barrow landscapes" (Fontijn 1996a; Theunissen 1999), but burial mounds were relevant in land organization of historical periods as well (Meurkens 2007; Roymans 1995; Waterbolk 1980).

Extraordinary burials of international significance have been found in the Central Netherlands, like the rich Bell Beaker graves with smith tools in Ede-Wageningen and Lunteren (Butler/van der Waals 1966). They are not only the earliest identified metalworkers in continental Northwest Europe, their rich burial inventories also show that metallurgy was held in high esteem. Such "smith-chieftain" graves appear to be a highly special identity in Early Europe. Less than 2 % of all Bell Beaker burials and less than 0.2 % of all Single Grave Culture burials in Europe have metalworker's implements (Bertemes, 2004, 144-6). The Central Netherlands are also one of the few regions in Europe to document the transition of Single Grave Culture to the Bell Beaker culture: a continuous sequence of a special type of burial for almost 900 years (Van der Beek/Fokkens 2004). In addition, important developments in the Bronze Age are also documented here (epitomized by so-called "Wohlde" warrior graves as those from Bergsham and Putten (Glasbergen 1954, 146; Fontijn 2002, 221-3; 227-9; app.5.6).

True barrow landscapes have been preserved in places, including remarkable aligned barrow groups, like the kilometers-long barrow rows at Epe-Vaassen or the alignments at the Ermelose Heide (Arnoldussen/Fontijn 2006, Fig. 10; Bakker 1976, Fig.11). Such alignments represent a form of land ordering and organization that is unknown from any type agrarian landscape that existed before, but its formation is only badly understood (Bogucki 1999, 227-8). The same holds true for the seemingly extensively dispersed barrow groups. Unlike the later urnfields, such barrow groups rarely have more than ten burial monumens and they lack a clear "focus". They seem to be scattered in an area limited by natural boundaries in what seems to be an arbitrary manner and cannot really be considered as a nucleated cemetery (cf. Garwood 2007). They can be found everywhere where barrows are known but are particularly well-known from the *Utrechtse heuvelrug*, in the areas that are defined by dry valleys (*cf.* van Heeringen 1999, Fig. 2). What steered this remarkable form of spatial organization?

1.2 The significance of the *Utrechtse Heuvelrug*

Many barrows have been preserved on the ice-pushed ridges of the *Utrechtse Heuvelrug* (Fig. 1.2) and the *Veluwe*, but research intensity differs considerably from place to place. An intriguing cluster of very rich and important Late Neolithic barrows can be found on the southern part of the *Veluwe*-ice-pushed ridge, ranging from *Ede, Wageningen* to *Oosterbeek-Arnhem*, with *Lunteren* at its north. This is the area which is home to the rich Bell Beaker smith graves mentioned above. Useful survey and inventory work of amateur archaeologists in the environment of Arnhem has recently shown that the ice-pushed ridge of Arnhem-Oosterbeek is also very rich in burial mounds, and has some very interesting monuments (Houkes/Mittendorf 1996).

The nearby ice-pushed ridges of the *Utrechtse Heuvelrug* (from *Rhenen* to the west; Fig. 1.2) is separated from the Ede-Wageningen ice-pushed ridge by a valley of some 4 km (the low-lying *Gelderse vallei*). Densities of barrows on this *Utrecht* ice-pushed ridge are wholly comparable to those at the Ede-Arnhem ridge. However, remarkably enough, barrows of the *Utrechtse Heuvelrug* were much less investigated. Only 4 % of the mounds have been excavated (source: *Archis*-database). Although *Utrecht* has a sizeable number of barrows, they are only poorly known, certainly when compared with those from the province of Noord-Brabant

(77 % excavated, some 139 barrows) or Gelderland (17 %, some 164 barrows). The few excavated Utrecht barrows include Leusden-Den Treek (Modderman 1955), Soesterberg (Bursch 1934), Zeist-Dijnselburg (Kok 2007) or Maarsbergen (Lanting/van der Waals 1971). The fact that very special finds were done makes clear that the *Utrecht* barrows are just as interesting as their counterparts at the *Veluwe*. A case in point is the Ha C chieftain's grave of *Rhenen-Koerheuvel* (Van Heeringen 1999; Fontijn/Fokkens 2007). Another special case is the long barrow with intact mound, known as *Unitas 5* of the *Elsterberg* group under study here. Although long barrows are known from many periods[1], it is very rare to find examples where the mound itself is still largely preserved [2]. Stray finds of Beaker pottery (both Single Grave Culture and Bell Beaker Culture) suggest that the *Utrechtse Heuvelrug* was also inhabited in the 3rd millennium BC, and we have all reasons to expect that many of the unexcavated *Utrecht* barrows date to that same period (see Chapter 2 and 3). Parallel to the situation at the nearby ice-pushed ridge of *Ede-Wageningen*, we may ask ourselves whether the *Utrecht* barrows display the same special categories of graves like Bell Beaker "smith" graves, and the continuity from Single Grave to Bell Beaker culture.

There are several characteristics that make the *Utrechtse Heuvelrug* a promising region for new research of barrow landscapes. First, the barrow groups at the *Utrechtse Heuvelrug* has many examples of that remarkable category of "extensively dispersed" barrow groups, but contrary to those of *Veluwe*, the environment close to such barrow groups often has seen extensive archaeological research. This makes it possible to gain insight in prehistoric land orderings in general, which may provide us with an important clue as to the explanation of these "loosely scattered" orderings. Such conditions are particularly met with in the eastern part of the *Utrechtse Heuvelrug* (municipality of *Rhenen*). Large-scale excavations of the *Archeologisch Diensten Centrum* company (ADC) and the excavation unit of the University of Leiden *Archol BV* at *Rhenen-Remmerden* yielded the traces of several Middle Bronze Age longhouses close to a barrow group[3] (Meurkens/Van Hoof 2005 and 2007). This makes it possible to shed more light onto the organization of landscape around barrows, and to deal with the question why barrow "cemeteries" were organized in such a way. Interestingly, the area just beneath the ice-pushed ridge in this same *Rhenen* micro-region is also increasingly being excavated. Recent excavations like those at *Elst-'t Bosje* by *Archol BV* (Meurkens 2009a) provided new information on the prehistoric use history of the lower-lying terrain close to the barrow groups. This makes it possible to check whether ice-pushed ridges were separate burial landscapes, with people living in the low-lying area beneath them (as has been suggested for the barrows of the *Rhenen-Remmerden* site and the *Nijmegen* ice-pushed ridge; Meurkens/Van Hoof 2005; Fontijn/Cuijpers 2002).

Second, unlike the *Veluwe*, the *Utrechtse Heuvelrug*, is also relatively rich in sites dating to the Early Bronze Age (find spots with Barbed Wire pottery). It has even been claimed that a house plan dating to this period was recovered in *Rhenen-Remmerden* (Jongste 2001). The Early Bronze Age (EBA; 2000-1800 BC) is one of the least well-known periods in the late prehistoric Netherlands. Much less barrows can be dated to this period than to the previous Bell Beaker Period.

---

1   Middle Bronze Age: Bourgeois/Fontijn 2008 and Van der Veen/Lanting 1988; Early Iron Age: Roymans/Kortlang 1999.
2   Apart from a small trench dug by amateur archaeologists, this mound has not been excavated.
3   The only other place where large-scale excavation of an ice-pushed ridge with barrows has taken place is Nijmegen (Fontijn 1996a and b; Fontijn/Cuijpers 1999 and 2002). Here, however, the barrows and settlements were disturbed by building activities in the Roman Period, and no traces of houses could be recognized.

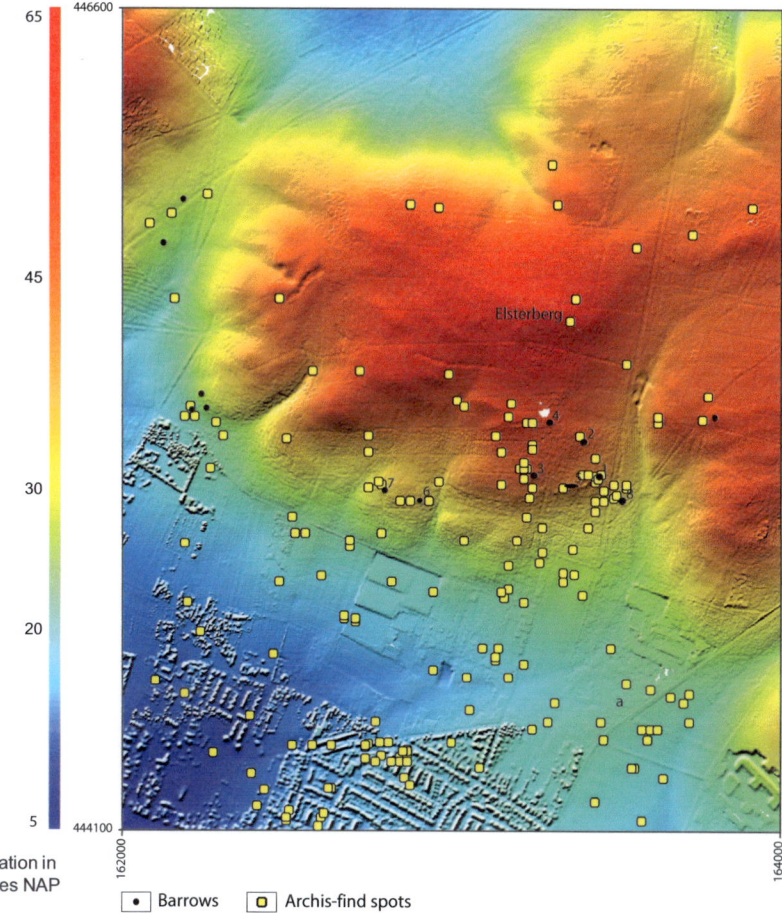

65 446600

45

Elsterberg

30

20

5 444100

Elevation in
metres NAP   162000   164000

• Barrows   □ Archis-find spots

Fig. 1.3 Digital Elevation Model of the Elsterberg. Black dots are barrows, find spots from different periods registered in the Archis database are yellow. North is up. 1.= Unitas 1 mound, 2-7= Unitas 2 to 7; 8= Delfin 190 mound. The flat "blue" plain on which present-day Elst is built is the sandr plain, the hills are ice-pushed sediment. Map based on the AHN, used with permission under license of the Province of Utrecht.

Its burial ritual is badly understood, particularly in the southern part of the Netherlands. However, the *Utrechtse Heuvelrug* happens to be an area where EBA sites are known, including burial mounds. This makes it an interesting region for a further study of this elusive period.

Third, numerous amateur activities as well as the Celtic field project of the province of *Utrecht* and the RCE[4] has yielded a very rich record of information on land orderings, settlement traces and activity areas dating to the Iron Age and Roman Period at and immediately around barrows. Around the barrow group of the *Elsterberg* (Fig. 1.3) that is central in this report, a concentration of Iron Age finds is known that to our knowledge does not have many parallels elsewhere in the Central Netherlands[5]. Celtic fields are known from the *Veluwe* as well (Brongers 1976), but there are large areas on the *Veluwe* where not one has been identified, in spite of intensive research (e.g. the municipality of *Apeldoorn*). It may be expected that the *Utrechtse Heuvelrug* is particularly informative on the later history of barrow groups (Iron Age and Roman Period). Did these field system disrupt the by then age-old land ordering around barrow landscapes? Were barrows destroyed, incorporated, or respected and re-used?

---

4   (*Rijksdienst voor het Cultureel Erfgoed*; Cultural Heritage Agency, formerly know as ROB and RACM).

5   Unpublished research of the RCE and the province of *Utrecht*; information kindly provided by drs. Ruurd Kok.

1.3 Barrow landscapes of *Elst-Rhenen*: a promising research area

If new barrow research on the *Utrechtse Heuvelrug* is to prosper, we need research that focuses on broad developments in barrow landscapes as a whole, as well as detailed case studies of carefully selected sites, dealing with particular problems. Since 2008, research of broad developments is now being facilitated by the N.W.O.-funded "Ancestral Mounds"-project (Fontijn 2007b). This is a multi-disciplinary and internationally oriented project in which a team of scholars of Leiden University studies two main problems:

1. What is the social and ideological significance of barrow graves?

2. What was the significance of barrows as landscape monuments?

This research project mainly deals with barrows from the 3rd and the 2nd millennium BC. It will involve three PhD studies. General chronological developments of barrow groups will be unraveled, and this will for an important part be done on the basis of empirical evidence of the *Utrechtse Heuvelrug*. The impact of the project is not purely scientific. There is an interest on barrows from the part of large estate owners, municipalities, provinces and heritage management agencies for development of cultural tourism and heritage management. New "academic" insights are disseminated towards the large public, for example by means of popular-scientific booklets (e.g. Van Ginkel *et al.* 2009; 2010).

Although many barrows are protected cultural heritage, this is not true for their immediate environment, of which practically nothing is known (Bourgeois/Fontijn 2008). Yet, new research shows that these areas possess many special archaeological features, unlike those preserved at other sites (e.g. long post alignments like at Oss-Zevenbergen, remnants of a ritual ordering of the barrow terrain itself?; Arnoldussen/Fontijn 2006, Fig. 10; Fokkens *et al.* 2006). Although some areas around barrows are protected as well, a recent development, carried out as a result of the so-called *Actualisering Monumenten Register*, is the shrinking of protected areas to 10 m zones around barrows. We are at serious risk here that potentially valuable archaeological terrains are now losing any protection, without their potential being checked. New knowledge on the environment of barrows is therefore badly needed and will be an important part of the 'Ancestral Mounds' project. In this research, there will be a close collaboration with the RCE. The dissemination of knowledge on barrows is another aspect of the academic research. Large estate owners, municipalities or provinces are posing questions on what barrows actually were and what can be told about them to the main public. In several places in the Netherlands, there is an active interest in encouraging cultural tourism around such visible signs of prehistory as burial mounds. Many mounds at the *Utrechtse Heuvelrug* were already made accessible to the main public by Reusink's "barrow trail" (1988), which leads the visitor along many barrows during a walk through the forest. Particularly, there is a vivid interest in reconstructions of the prehistoric environment around barrows. Environmental reconstruction is an important element in the N.W.O. project. But particularly for this research, new excavations should be carried out.

For a number of research questions, the municipality of Apeldoorn is one area suitable for such fieldwork, but in our view, the area around present-day *Elst* and *Rhenen* at the easternmost tip of the *Utrechtse Heuvelrug* is another. An important advantage of the *Elst-Rhenen* area is the relatively high intensity of relevant research here. First of all, it is probably among the best surveyed areas in the Central Netherlands, due to the work of Ms Ch. Delfin and the *Werkgroep Archeologie Rhenen (WAR)*. The number of prehistoric finds from surveys from the forest around mounds is remarkably large – particularly in the *Amerongsche Bos* near *Elst*. This indicates that such a natural reserve may conceal many traces of prehistoric activities. Interestingly, finds have particularly been done around barrow groups (Fig. 1.3). On top of that, amateurs have dug small trenches in a number of barrows in this area (Van Tent 1976), which gives us some preliminary information on the nature and dating of the barrow. An important result of all this activity is that *Rhenen-Elst* appears to be one of the better known areas with sites from the elusive Early Bronze Age. Several sites, settlements and barrows, with Barbed Wire pottery are known[6]. This makes it one of the best places to study barrows and their environment for this particular period. The Celtic field project of the Province of *Utrecht* and the *RCE*, then, has charted and inventoried many of the sizeable Celtic field terrains in *Elst* and *Rhenen*[7]. The nature and size of Celtic fields in this part of the *Utrechtse Heuvelrug* is special, even in a national context. An important by-product of this survey is that it gives us some indications of the size and nature of prehistoric cultural landscapes succeeding the Bronze Age barrow groups. As already remarked above, evidence on the later (Iron Age) history of barrows is scarce elsewhere in the central Netherlands (Van Beek 2009). In addition to this, the environment of the municipality of *Rhenen* is not only unusually rich in relevant prehistoric sites; a number of them have now also been excavated, giving us some insight into prehistoric land use around barrows. All this makes it worthwhile to select barrows of *Elst* or *Rhenen* for new fieldwork: results of barrow excavations can be compared with what we already know about land orderings from adjacent terrains.

1.4 The *Elsterberg* barrow cluster: an unusual group of barrows?

With this in mind, several barrow groups in *Elst-Rhenen* are suitable for study, but not all are available for research. Some are inaccessible National Heritage protected by law. One group on which small fieldwork was possible is the barrow group to the south of the *Elsterberg*, at the southern flank of the ice-pushed ridge, close to the *Driftweg* in *Elst*. In between two dry valleys (see Fig. 1.3), there are several barrows. Although they show some clustering, one can hardly speak of a barrow "cemetery". Rather, they are a good example of the "extensively dispersed" barrow groups mentioned before. If we take the *Elsterberg* as its northern boundary, and the two dry valleys as its western and eastern, and the southern rim of the ice-pushed ridge as its southern boundary, the group consists of several mounds (Fig. 1.3). These are known as Unitas 1 to 7 and Delfin 190 and 191. The code "Unitas" allegedly refers to the *Utrecht* student society: we were told that in the past (1960s?), new members of this society had to remove trees and vegetation from some of these mounds as part of their "initiation rites"[8]. The code name "Delfin" refers to Ms Ch. Delfin-Van Mourik Broekman (1914-), the well-known amateur archaeologist who discovered most of the *Elsterberg* barrows [9]. Some of the Unitas mounds are also known under a "Delfin" code. In order to avoid confusion, we will refer to the barrows using the codification used by Van Tent during his research in 1971.

---

6   Settlement: Rhenen-Remmerden (Jongste 2001; Van Hoof/Meurkens 2005); barrows: Unitas 1 (this book, chapter 2 and 4) and Elst-'t Bosje (Meurkens 2009a), see also Chapter 9 for a synthesis.
7   Unfortunately, the results have not yet been published.
8   Personal communication drs. Ton van Rooijen (province of *Utrecht*).
9   On the impressive achievements of Ms Delfin: Maes/Vroemen 2001 and Van Ginkel *et al.* 2010, 21.

Fig. 1.3 already makes the point that it is hard to speak of a "group"of barrows. By their "unbounded" nature, any definition of such monuments as a group is open to debate. There is a group of six known barrows in the centre (known as "Unitas" 1 to 5 and the "Delfin 190"-mound (Fig. 1.4). The Delfin 191 and Unitas 6 and 7 seem to be in a more peripheral position, but if this reflects a prehistoric reality or is solely the product of selective preservation is unknown. I wish to emphasize that I am using the term 'barrow group' only for practical reasons. Although many barrows are close to each other, it might well be that the prehistoric perception of the right "grouping" of mounds was a much different one. For example, this might have been steered by knowledge on the identity of the dead themselves, and barrows situated on either side of a dry valley might have been perceived of as related, rather than those of the nearby barrows on the plateaus delimited by the dry valleys!

The mounds are not officially protected National Heritage, but they are ranked as having a "very high status", which comes down to the situation that all activities in or around the designated site fall under the jurisdiction of the State, represented by the RCE. Most of the barrows in the "central" part were prospected with excavation in small trenches by the amateur archaeologists of the *Archeologische*

Fig. 1.4 The Elsterberg barrow group in relation to the modern topography of the forest. Drawing by S. Arnoldussen.

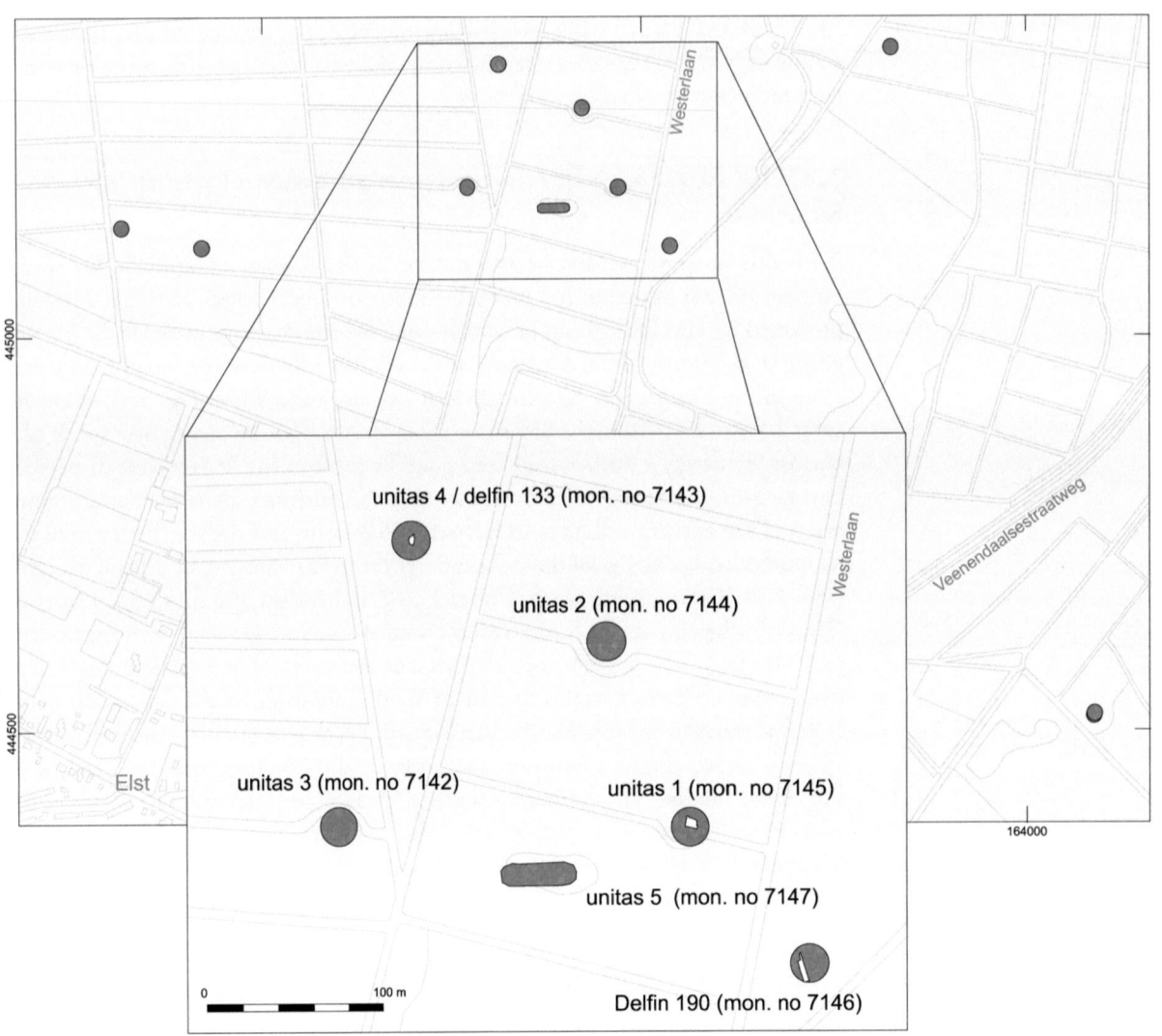

LIVING NEAR THE DEAD

Werkgemeenschap Nederland (AWN[10]). This makes it possible to have some idea of their nature and dating. The Elsterberg group is a rather special one for several reasons. One is the presence of a sizeable long barrow with intact mound, coded as Unitas 5, (see Fig. 1.4). As said before, long barrows with intact mound are very rare in the Netherlands. Another reason is that the *AWN*-fieldwork suggests that at least one of the mounds dates to the Early Bronze Age (the one coded 'Unitas 1'; Van Tent 1976). As remarked in section 1.2, hardly anything is known of burial mounds from this period from the Central and Southern Netherlands. Interestingly, there was also reason to suspect that there is another mound that dates from the period immediately preceding the Early Bronze Age (mound "Delfin 190", claimed to date to the Bell Beaker period; Van Tent 1976). Another unusual feature of this group is the high concentration of pottery finds (sherds) in the immediate surroundings of the mound. Due to the activities of amateur archaeologists, in particular Ms Ch. Delfin, not only the mounds themselves were rediscovered, but also a large quantity of prehistoric artefacts (to be described in Chapter 4 and 5). These date to both the late Neolithic, Early Bronze Age as well as to the later Iron Age. Although such stray finds lack contextual evidence, they indicate that the environment was (intensively) used in all these periods. It is an intriguing question whether they reflect activities related to the burial ritual or the remains of settlements in close proximity to the mounds. On top of that, air photographs of the agricultural fields near the foot of the ice-pushed ridge, show soil traces that might be interpreted as remains of a Celtic field (personal comments R.S. Kok). This implies that an area at less than 100 m from the southernmost mound was used or maybe reorganized for agricultural activities at a large scale in a later phase of the prehistory. It is an intriguing question whether the older barrows themselves might also have been integrated in such land orderings.

Summing up, for both the barrows (their nature and dating) and the environment there are indications that we are dealing with a somewhat unusual group of barrows. In particular, the available evidence begs the question as to the organization of the landscape around these mounds. The concentration of finds near barrows is rather uncommon on the ice-pushed ridges and it makes one wonder as to the developments by which it came about. Is it simply the result of the intensive surveys by knowledgeable amateur archaeologists like Ms Ch. Delfin? Or are we dealing with an unusually long and intensive use history, starting from the moment when the first barrows were constructed, up until the Iron Age? The question of the environment of barrows is particularly acute for the period of the late Neolithic up until the Middle Bronze Age. Established views based on analyses of pollen samples from underneath mounds see Late Neolithic and Early Bronze Age mounds as monuments which were constructed only on small-scale clearings in the forest (Casparie/Groenman-van Waateringe 1980), whereas Middle Bronze Age mounds were built on small heaths. Such views, however, are mainly based on evidence from the northern part of the *Veluwe* and the northeastern Netherlands. For the Early Bronze Age, there are actually very few sites to base an environmental reconstruction on in both the Central and Southern Netherlands, and although the Middle Bronze Age is well represented by mounds from the south, rather few have been sampled in the Central Netherlands (Fontijn 2007). The stray finds around the mounds in the *Elsterberg* cluster at least suggest that the area around these mounds was more intensively used than established views would have it. At any rate, burial mounds claimed to date to both the Late Neolithic and

---

10 The *AWN* fieldwork is briefly mentioned by Van Tent 1976, but the results were not published extensively. We found documentation on Unitas 1, 2, 3 and 5, and Delfin 190. Thanks are due to drs. Ton van Rooijen (province of Utrecht and dr. Liesbeth Theunissen (*RCE*) for their help.

Early Bronze Age present us with an opportunity to test such an idea by taking new palynological samples of them. Of great importance is that the owner of a part of the area on which some of the barrows are situated, *Staatsbosbeheer*, is also interested in such questions. Such information could be used for reconstructing part of the prehistoric vegetation around these mounds. This might make the barrows more attractive for visitors of the forest.

1.5 Research questions and reasons for selecting the Unitas 1 and Delfin 190 mounds for research

Within the framework of the broader question of the environment around barrow sites and the land organization that went with it, we formulated the two following research questions

1. *What was the original vegetation around the burial mounds of the Elsterberg group in the period from the Late Neolithic Bell Beaker phase up until the Middle Bronze Age and how did it change?*

2. *What can be deduced from the vegetation and archaeological evidence on issues like the organization and nature of the cultural landscape around the mounds of this group?*

In order to answer these questions, pollen evidence should be obtained from mounds with secured datings in the Bell Beaker phase, the Early Bronze Age and the Middle Bronze Age. On the basis of the data of the earlier amateur excavations, Delfin 190 (Bell Beaker mound with Middle Bronze Age addition) and Unitas 1 (Early Bronze Age) were detailed for excavation (Fig. 1.5). Both mounds have large undisturbed parts from which pollen samples can be taken and on the basis of earlier excavation, it might be expected that datable finds (pottery sherds) are present. They are only 90 m apart and pollen data from both mounds may inform us on one and the same environment. Potentially, a combination of

Fig. 1.5 Digital Elevation Model of the Unitas 1 mound (left) and the Delfin 190 mound (right) as measured by our excavation team, and measurement points used during the excavation.

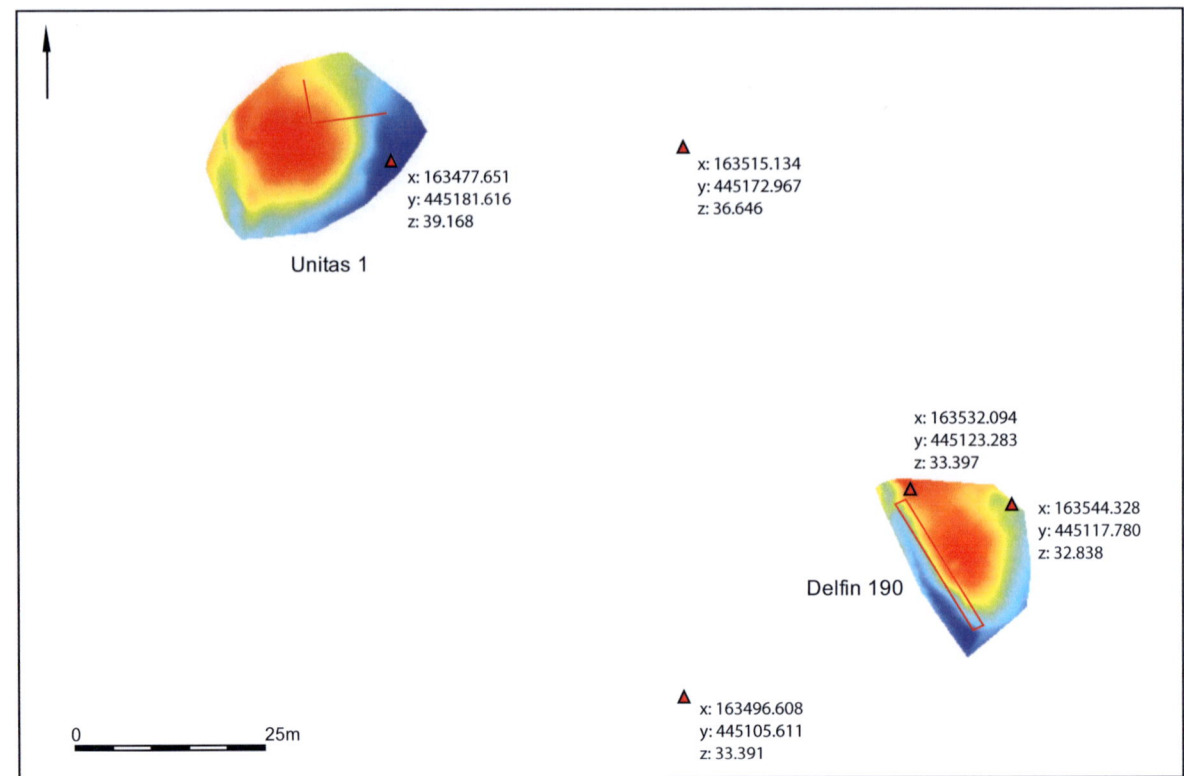

Unitas 1

x: 163477.651
y: 445181.616
z: 39.168

x: 163515.134
y: 445172.967
z: 36.646

x: 163532.094
y: 445123.283
z: 33.397

x: 163544.328
y: 445117.780
z: 32.838

Delfin 190

x: 163496.608
y: 445105.611
z: 33.391

0   25m

environmental evidence from both mounds provides us with the rare opportunity to chart environmental developments from the Bell Beaker phase though the Early Bronze Age up until the Middle Bronze Age.

To structure the research, several sub-questions were formulated for each individual mound[11]

Mound Delfin 190 (the easternmost mound of the "group", situated along a dry valley and expected to be a Bell Beaker mound with an Middle Bronze Age addition)

- Can the mound periods as observed during the earlier research be recognized?
- If not, which mound periods are observable and how do they date?
- What was the local vegetation at the time of the construction of the mound?
- What was the local vegetation during later mound periods?
- Is the soil type underneath the mound in line with what the original vegetation as can be reconstructed on the basis of pollen coming from this mound? (e.g. brown Podsolic soils and forest vegetation?)

Mound Unitas 1 (more or less in the centre of the "group", expected to date to the Early Bronze Age)

- What is the stratigraphical position of the Early Bronze Age Barbed Wire Beaker sherds: material deposited or left on the ancient surface or material that is part of the mound itself)?
- Is the mound's primary dating in the Early Bronze Age warranted?
- Is there evidence for other mound periods?
- Is the "pit-like" feature observed by amateurs in their excavation part of a ring ditch?
- If so, to which mound period should it be related?
- If not, how is this feature to be interpreted?
- What was the local vegetation at the time of the construction of the mound?
- What was the local vegetation during later mound periods (if present)?

Further questions related to field and excavation methods and Heritage management (to be carried out in collaboration between the National Heritage Agency *RCE* and the Faculty of Archaeology)

Since the excavation provides us with the rare opportunity of a scientific barrow excavation, it was decided to use it as a test case for a few methodical issues. Also, we welcome the opportunity to re-evaluate the value of the mounds as Archaeological Heritage. The additional research questions are

- How do the results of the prospective penetrologger device relate to the structure and stratigraphy of the mounds as observed during the excavation?
- How do the results of the prospection with corings relate to the stratigraphy of the mound as observable during the excavation?
- Is it viable to use systematic sieving during barrow excavations? Does sieving result in better results than manual digging?
- Since pottery sherds may contain ferric inclusions, is it possible to use metal detectors for prospecting the location of sherds in the mound before digging starts?
- Has the condition of the mounds deteriorated since the 1970s? Are they still to be seen as mounds worthy of the label "site of very high status"?

---

11 All research questions were part of the written scheme of investigation (WSI, Dutch *Programma van Eisen*; Fontijn 2006).

1.6 General characteristics of the research area

1.6.1 Geology and soils

The *Elsterberg* barrow cluster is situated at the ice-pushed ridge of the *Utrechtse Heuvelrug*, some 2 km north of the present course of the river Rhine. This conspicuous ridge of hills originated during the *Saalien* glacial, some 150000 years BP, and forms the western edge of river sediment pushed forward by land ice. The eastern edge is formed by the nearby hills of the Veluwe (the ice-pushed ridge of *Ede-Wageningen-Arnhem*). The front of the ice-pushed ridges was eroded by the Rhine later in the Pleistocene. The ice-pushed ridge on which the *Elsterberg* mounds were built consists of non-morainic fluviatile sediment which has been distorted and placed diagonally by push force and pressure of the ice (Verbraeck 1984: coded *Gm0*). These are Middle or Early Pleistocene fluviatile formations, consisting of coarse to fine sand, including cobbles and occasionally loamy/clayey layers. In places, they are covered with glaci-genetic (Formation of *Drenthe*; coded as *Dr7* by Verbraeck 1984)) and/or periglacial deposits (Formation of *Twente*)[12]. Obviously, the hills on which the barrows were built are of a rather heterogeneous nature: both coarse sand, gravel, and fine-grained sand surface. The ridge to the north of present-day *Elst* was formed during the earliest expansion of the ice in the *Saalien* (phase a; Verbraeck 1984, 92-93; fig. 30). The ice-pushed deposits surface up until some 250 m south of the southernmost mound that we excavated, Delfin 190. A gentle but conspicuous slope, more or less coinciding with the modern edge of the forest south of Delfin 190 marks the transition of the ice-pushed deposits to fluvioglacial ones (Formation of *Drenthe*). These deposits consist of moderately coarse sand to very coarse sand, including cobbles. This is material that was eroded from the ridges themselves by streams of melting water and re-deposited at the foot of the ice-pushed ridges during the *Saalien* glacial. These fluvioglacial deposits, also known as *sandr* sediment, mark the edge of the ice-pushed ridge to the lower lying river valley of the Rhine with a steep ridge, a few meters higher than the modern backswamps, or *uiterwaarden* (clayey to sandy deposits of the Holocene *Betuwe* Formation). The fluvioglacial deposits have a more gentle slope than the ice-pushed ridges themselves (1 °). The river Rhine eroded a significant part of this system of ice-pushed ridges and *sandr* deposits during the later part of the Pleistocene, which created the steep southern ridge of the *sandr* deposits adjacent to the present river bed. Because of their southern exposure, the *sandr* deposits between *Elst* and *Rhenen* were used for tobacco plantation in the 19th century (Brombacher/Hoogendoorn 2000, 35).

Of great importance for later spatial subdivisions of the ice-pushed ridges are the so-called dry valleys. During the last ice-age, the *Weichselien,* streams of melting water eroded deep gullies (with slopes varying between 1 and 8 °, the walls of the valley have slopes of 30 ° at most; Brombacher/Hoogendoorn 2000, 37-9). Our barrow cluster is more or less defined by two such valleys. running NNE/SSW (Fig.1.3). The largest valley runs immediately to the east of Delfin 190 and can be followed all the way down into the present/day town of *Elst* (near *Elst 't Bosje*). A smaller western valley runs more or less from the ice-pushed ridge south into present-day *Elst*.

North of the barrow cluster, the area is higher reaching 62.5 m *NAP* (the so-called *Elsterberg*, or "hill of Elst" itself; Fig.1.3). North of the *Elsterberg*, the slope declines to reach levels of 8 to 9 m NAP at present-day *Veenendaal*. At its northern foot, slope wash processes and gelifluction caused the formation of gravel and

---

12   Verbraeck 1984.

coarse sand deposits during the periglacial conditions of the subsequent ice age, the Weichselien. These periglacial sediments are covered by a broad swath of eolian cover sand (Formation of *Twente*; Verbraeck 1984).

Both on the ice-pushed ridge and on the extensive fluvioglacial deposits, Podzol soils developed, classified as *holtpodzol*, gY30, in the Dutch system of soil classification[13]. These soils, traditionally known as "brown Podzol soils"[14] are characterized by a Humus top soil of less than 30 cm. They lack the leached-out or eluvial A2 or E horizon that characterizes Humus Podzol soils. Mean levels of ground water are deeper than 80 cm or even 120 cm[15].

1.6.2 Concise history of the area

With the dawn of the historical periods, the *Elsterberg* barrows gradually became part of much different landscapes than in prehistory. As visible markers of a remote past, the burial mounds might have been relevant in Medieval or Post-Medieval landscapes in their own right. For this reason, I wish to pay at least some attention to the later history of the area, and to find out how later reclamations and land use might have affected the barrows in question.

When the Roman emperor *Claudius* made the Rhine the official northern boundary of the Roman empire, the *Elst-Rhenen* area effectively became part of *Germania libera*, just to the north of the *limes*. Both historical and archaeological sources show how this zone, just outside the Roman borders gained in significance particularly since c. 200 *AD*. The tribal confederation known as *Franci* is located precisely in this area, and the excavation of large rural settlements as *Ede-Bennekom* neatly illustrate the growing importance of the ice-pushed ridges just north of the Rhine in the 3rd and 4th century AD (Van Es *et al.* 1985). It is not entirely clear whether comparable settlements also existed in Elst but the presence of a late Roman-Early Medieval cemetery near the foot of the ice-pushed ridge makes this very likely (Heidinga 1988, Fig. 11; Elst 't Woud[16]). It is an intriguing question how these people perceived the many prehistoric barrows of the *Elsterberg* cluster nearby. A small excavation of mound "Unitas 3" allegedly yielded the find of a "native Roman" urn in one of the barrows of this group, apparently a secondary interment (Van Tent 1976). Such a find suggests that these prehistoric mounds were valued by the "Germanic" inhabitants as well[17].

The *Rhenen* region probably became the residence of an Early Medieval (Frankish or Frisian) elite probably from the fifth but certainly in the 9th century when it was an important chiefly center in the Frankish empire (Heidinga 1988). The *Elst* cemetery already mentioned is one of those that were established in the 4th/5th century and remained in use for several centuries. Some of them could become very extensive, like the *Rhenen-Koerheuvel* cemetery on the ice-pushed ridge some kilometers to the east of the *Elsterberg*, which is claimed to have some 1000 burials (Blijdenstijn 2007, 89). Such large funerary areas were built in a landscape that was already dotted with dozens of much older barrows. It is again interesting

---

13   *Bodemkaart van Nederland* 1:50.000 *Blad 39 West Rhenen en Blad 39 Oost Rhenen,* 1973, *STIBOKA.* gY30 means: Moder Podzol, developed in coarse sand (median sandfraction>210 μ) with gravel at less than 40 cm underneath the surface, loam fraction not generally defined.

14   German: *podsolierte Braunerde.*

15   Ground water level class VII in the Dutch system of waterlevel classification. Source: *Bodemkaart van Nederland* 1:50.000 *Blad 39 West Rhenen en Blad 39 Oost Rhenen, 1973, STIBOKA.*

16   *Archeologische Kroniek Provincie Utrecht* 1980-1984, 9-13.

17   We retrieved pottery sherds from this mound in the *provinciaal Depot* in Utrecht (see section 4.7; Fig. 4.5), which we dated to the Roman Period or Late Iron Age. Nothing is reported on their find context. They represent two different pots, perhaps these are the finds meant by Van Tent? In general, it proved to be difficult to differentiate native Roman Period pottery and Late Iron Age pottery (see Chapters 4 and 5).

to find out if there were spatial links created between these Early Medieval cemeteries and the ubiquitous ancient prehistoric barrows. In the case of the *Elsterberg*, there is so far no indication that this was the case, nor are there indications that the area around the mound was settled. It is likely that the lower-lying areas were preferred as settlement grounds.

Rhenen lost its supra-regional significance in the Late Medieval Period, but a town developed which became one of the few cities *de jure* on the *Utrechtse Heuvelrug* between 1230-1258 (Blijdenstijn 2007, 95). At the northern flank of the ice-pushed ridge, a defended settlement or castle was built, a forerunner of the later *Prattenburg* estate on which some of the mounds of the *Elsterberg* barrow group are situated (idem 85). In the Late Medieval Period, the *Elsterberg* terrain largely became a heath area, just like most of the ice-pushed ridge. This remained so until the end of the 19th century. Military maps from 1839-1859 show the *Elsterberg* region as an extensive heath[18].To our knowledge, the *Elsterberg* barrows were not depicted on any of the 19th century maps.

Although a few roads crossed the ridge (like the *Galgenweg* or *Veenendaalse Straatweg*; Blijdenstijn 2007, 89), there were no important routes leading along the barrows themselves. A route along the western ridge of the *Elsterberg* bears the name "*Galgenweg* (gallow's road)". This makes one wonder if one of the more western barrows at the *Elsterberg* served as a location for gallows. The role of barrows for the construction of gallows is well attested in the Southern and Northern Netherlands (Meurkens 2007).

It is only within the period from 1880 to 1900 that major changes were taking place in the landscape: the heath was forested again for large-scale production of wooden posts for the upcoming coal mining industry in the south of the Netherlands. It might be expected that plowing for tree-planting might have damaged both the mounds and soil features around them. Another industry which left its marks on the local landscape are the tobacco plantations, located at the *sandr*-deposits adjacent to the southern flank of the ice-pushed ridge. These were situated nearby, just east of *Elst*, and not in immediate range of the *Elsterberg* group (Blijdenstijn 2007, 111-3). It was probably in relation to this tobacco industry that a large ditch was cut through the western part of the Delfin 190 mound (see chapter 3)[19].

The western part of the barrow group became situated in a forest known as the *Amerongsche Bosch*, whereas the eastern part remained part of the *Prattenburg* estate. New roads were created to facilitate the transport for the forest industry between 1900 and 1940. Many of the barrows were now no longer isolated, but became easily reachable via pathways and sand roads. The current north-south road, known as *Westerlaan* (a sand road) which runs in between Delfin 190 and Unitas 1 is the official boundary between the *Staatsbosbeheer*-area (west of the road: Unitas 1) and the *Prattenburg* estate (east of the road: mound Delfin 190).

With the growth of the village of *Elst* after the Second World War, people came to be living very close to the barrows, and the forest became an important place for recreation. The easy access of the area and the fact that the well-known amateur-archaeologist Ms Ch. Delfin lived nearby is one of the reasons that this barrow cluster was re-discovered and has yielded such a surprising large number of finds. During her many surveys, Ms Delfin rediscovered several of the mounds, which

---

18 *Topografische en Militaire Kaart van het Koninkrijk der Nederlanden, Kaartblad 39-II 1839-1859, 1:50.000.*

19 According to the Prattenburg estate forester, Mr G. van Heyningen, such a ditch was necessary to transport water which was collected in a loam pit nearby towards the tobacco plants.

are named after here since. Confusingly, some mounds were re-named with the "Unitas"-code and they are known under this heading in the *Archis* Archaeological Database.

1.7 Organization of this book

In what follows, the results of the excavation are described. For pragmatic reasons, discussions of features and finds are discussed in separate chapters. Chapter 2 and 3 describe the features of the mounds Unitas 1 and Delfin 190 respectively. Key finds will be mentioned but their description and dating are central to the two following chapters 4 and 5 (finds from Unitas 1 and Delfin 190 respectively). In chapter 6, the pollen evidence will be discussed, whereas chapter 7 described the results of the methodical experiments with the penetrologger and corings at this site. Chapter 8 deals with the sad story of the Unitas 4 mound that was destroyed two years after our excavation ended. The conclusions and implications of the excavation will then be set out in chapter 9, where a tentative outline of the history of the barrow group will be sketched. The last chapter, 10, then, will discuss the future of this barrow group: how special is this dispersed group of barrows, and how might it best be preserved for future generations?

Chapter 2

Burial mound "Unitas" 1: an Early Bronze Age barrow with traces of Iron Age activities

Q. Bourgeois, D. Fontijn

2.1 Introduction

One of the barrows selected for excavation is the one known as "Unitas 1", or site 39-E-10[20] in the *Archis* Database codification. It measures *c.* 14 by 14 m and has a height of 0.93 m (Fig. 1.5). A small excavation carried out in 1971 indicated that this barrow was one of those rare examples of mounds dating to the Early Bronze Age. We carried out a modest re-excavation to check whether this dating was correct, and to prepare a profile from which pollen samples could be taken.

This chapter will first describe the environmental position of Unitas 1, as well as its condition of preservation prior to the 2006 research (2.2 and 2.3). Then, we will discuss results of the 1971 excavation in this mound, and relevant amateur finds that were done immediately around Unitas 1 (2.4). We will continue by describing and discussing results of our own excavation. We chose to excavate this mound in a way which differed from how it was done in the past. Therefore, we will pay much attention to introducing the chosen excavation strategy and set out why it seems to us the most appropriate way of excavating this mound (2.5). This includes the description of an experiment where we sieved a sample of the mound construction material. Section 2.6 and 2.7 will describe the relevant archaeological features. We will first provide the reader with general information on the mound's stratigraphy as deduced from the 2006 excavation results (2.6). The recognized features and associated finds are then described from top to bottom (2.7). Our findings are summarized in section 2.8.

2.2 Environmental setting, local geology and soils

The barrow is built on non-morainic ice-pushed fluviatile sediment (Verbraeck 1984, coded G<u>m0</u>) of which the characteristics are described in the previous Chapter (section 1.6.1). As already remarked there, lithologically, we are dealing with heterogeneous sediment. Our excavation and the corings done by the *RCE* (Chapter 7) showed that the subsoil of the barrow consists of coarse sand containing many cobbles, interspersed with sand layers of a finer grain fraction. In the top of the mound and around it, a Moder Podzol soil (*holtpodsol*) is observable (coded gY30 in the Dutch classification, see section 1.6.1). It is noteworthy that the soil underneath the barrow was vaguer than outside, and that in the soil covered by the mound, an a-horizon could not be observed. The mound lies just north of the remarkable long barrow Unitas 5 (monument nr. 7147; see Chapter 1, Fig.

---

20   CAA-number 26538/27205; monument number: 7145.

1.4), and some 100 m south-east of Unitas 2 (monument nr. 7144). Unitas 1 is in the *Staatsbosbeheer* area. At the time of the 2006 excavation the mound was situated within an open space in the forest, with a dense pine forest immediately to its south (see Fig. 2.1 and Fig. 2.3). The dense forestation impeded an adequate assessment of the mound: it is, for example, likely that the foot of the mound is to be found in the forest. The size of the mound registered here and in *Archis* (14 by 14 m) may therefore be somewhat too small. In 2008, the forest surrounding it was considerably thinned out.

Fig. 2.1 The Unitas 1 mound, just before the excavation. View from the east. Note the dense forestation just around the flanks of the mound. Photograph by Q. Bourgeois.

2.3 State of preservation before the 2006 excavation

This part of the ice-pushed ridge was a heath up until the beginning of the 20th century *AD* [21]. For this reason, it might be expected that the terrain suffered from sod-cutting or levelling. Traces of clearly decapitated soils were not detected at the top of the mound. An inspection report by the *ROB* (now *RCE*), dating to 1987 however, shows that the southern part of the mound was disturbed by digging activities (sand extraction?). The mound is accessible via an – unofficial – path which leads over the barrow from the main N-S road (the *Westerlaan*). As this path is frequently being used by mountain bikers, the top of the mound has been damaged in places. It should be emphasized that mountain biking is formally forbidden on such unofficial tracks, and the foresters try to stop this as much as possible. The pits and hollowed-out top were re-filled with white sand during a restoration carried out by the *RCE* in 1987. The refilled parts were indicated on a map. From it, it can be learnt that the southern half of the mound was the most damaged part. The depth of the disturbances do not seem to have been checked by corings or test trenches.

---

21   *Grote Historische Atlas van Oost-Nederland 1830-1855*, map 96.

2.4 Earlier Research

2.4.1 The AWN-excavation of 1971

A small trench (5 m by 1.2 m) was dug into the north-eastern part of the mound during a one-day excavation of the *AWN* in 1971 (Fig. 2.2). The fieldwork was carried out under supervision of drs P. van Tent, the then provincial archaeologist. It is not exactly recorded how the trench was dug, but there is one drawing of the surface which indicates that – at least one – artificial horizontal level was created. Here, traces of a ditch or pit appear to have been visible. This ditch may have its counterpart in the depression of the old surface indicated by the excavators in their drawing of the profile.

The north profile of the trench was drawn. Soil discolorations are indicated, but not interpreted in terms of soil horizons, or lithological layers (*e.g.* different mound construction phases or "mound periods", *cf.* Theunissen 1999, 38-39). Black and white photographs taken during the excavation and stored with the documentation are few and generally hard to re-interpret. However, during this excavation some important finds were done. No less than four sherds of the rare Barbed Wire pottery were found in this one trench, according to the find list. Our own study of these sherds shows that this is correct (see section 4.3 for a description of these finds). Mention has also been made in the find documentation of

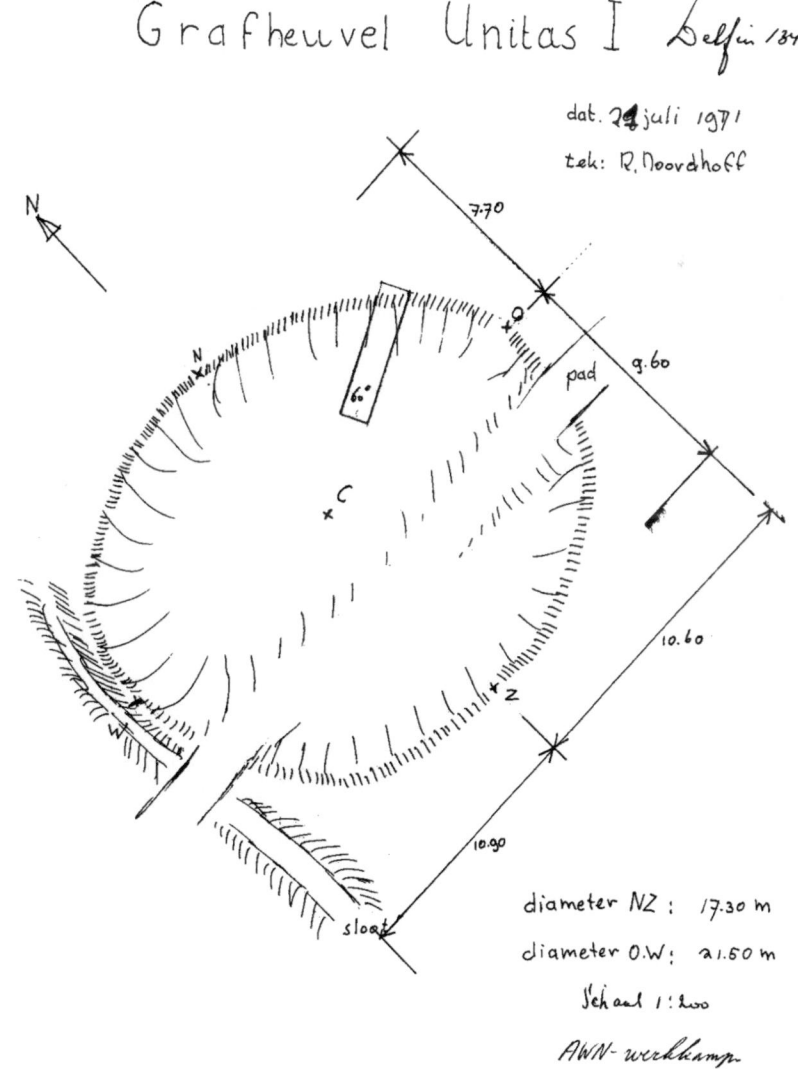

Fig. 2.2 Drawing, recorded in the 1971 excavation documentation, showing the position of the trench in the mound.

eight other sherds of what probably is pottery dating to the Iron Age or native hand-made pottery of the Roman Period[22]. The height of these finds was recorded in m *NAP* (Dutch Ordnance Datum), and the finds are shown projected in the drawing of the profile. This drawing gives the impression that the Barbed Wire sherds were found in stratigraphical positions different from those of the "Iron Age" sherds. The Barbed Wire sherds are shown both in the mound itself and underneath it, whereas the "Iron Age" sherds are only located *in* the mound. This information is confusing: are we dealing with Barbed Wire sherds deposited on the original surface, pre-dating the building of the mound, or were they included in the material with which the mound was built? In the latter case: how then are we understand the position of Iron Age sherds in that same mound?

Deposition of Barbed Wire sherds on the surface covered by mounds is known from Early Bronze Age burial ritual (Lohof 1991, 68-70). But if this is the case how then do the "Iron Age" sherds fit into the stratigraphical picture? Judging from the profile drawing on which they are projected, they appear to have been found at low positions in the mounds as well (like the Barbed Wire sherds). Are they intrusions in an older mound, or are all the finds material which happened to be present in the sand or sods with which the mound was built? In that case, the barrow is much younger than the Early Bronze Age. It may be evident that the excavation documents are far from clear on this point and will not help us to further unravel the problems concerning the dating of this mound.

2.4.2 The Pot Beaker in the vicinity of the mound

Another significant find was done many years later, in 1990. After a storm, several trees in the vicinity of the barrow collapsed, and amateurs of the *Rhenen* "*werkgroep*" surveyed the pits that were created by the fallen trees. One of them, the late J. Mom, found a scatter of Pot Beaker sherds within some eight m to the east-northeast of the foot of Unitas 1. He found these sherds among the roots of a fallen tree. Later that year J. Mom, H. Reusink and Ch. Delfin came back to this find spot to dig a small trench[23] at the location of the fallen tree, uncovering even more sherds belonging to the same pot, dating to the Late Neolithic or Early Bronze Age.(see section 4.6 and Van Tent 1997)[24]. Photographs and notes that were stored with the sherds at the *Rhenen* Museum make clear that the sherds were found very close to the mound, and not at a distance of 25 m from it, as is stated in the *Archis* database[25]. Unfortunately, the disturbance by roots made it very hard to recognize any archaeological features (traces or ditches). This Pot Beaker find will be described in detail in section 4.6.

2.5 Excavation strategy of the 2006 excavation

2.5.1 Reasons for excavating a small quadrant

To provide a check on the findings of the 1971-excavation, we opted for a re-excavation of the old *AWN* trench in the hope to find some new fragments of Barbed Wire pottery and to document their stratigraphical position and thus unravel the mound's dating and stratigraphy. To accomplish this, a small quadrant encom-

---

22 Unfortunately, we have not been able to retrieve these finds and we have to base ourselves on remarks made on the lists in the find documentation.

23 This was approved of by the *ROB* (now *RCE*).

24 Van Tent 1997. Van Tent states that the sherds found belong to at least four different pots, but our study of the find shows that this is incorrect (see also *Archis*-number 43550).

25 The sherds and find documentation were kindly made available to us by drs. Bert Huiskes (Museum *'t Rondeel, Rhenen*).

passing the *AWN* trench was planned (Fig. 2.3). Although the exact position of the *AWN* trench was unknown (it was only indicated on a sketch of the mound (Fig. 2.2) and it was not located in the National coordinate grid), the fill of the former trench was easily visible due to the fact that its vegetation was differently coloured.

Why did we choose to excavate a small quadrant? The most obvious and easiest way to create a profile would seem to be by simply digging a small trench at the foot of the mound, like was done in 1971. We want to argue, however, that this can hardly be expected to be helpful in unravelling the mound's stratigraphy as a whole. At the foot of the mound, it may be expected that different construction layers are relatively thin. Also, the effects of secondary podzolisation may obscure subtle differences in the mound's stratigraphy. At the mound's foot, three pedo-logical phenomena are relevant. First, there is the original soil buried underneath the mound. Next, there is the soil which formed in the top of the mound. It should be emphasized that its b-horizon may be some 10 cm underneath the top itself, hence it might merge with the soil horizon which is buried underneath the mound. Third, around the foot of the mound, soil formation will be amplified by the additional flow of humus from downslope the mound (Modderman 1975, 17). At the foot, where the mound is still thin, all these phenomena occur in the same zone, making it very hard to unravel the diverse pedological phenomena, let alone to recognize different mound construction phases. If we want to do that, obviously longer profiles are needed that penetrate deeper in the mound. One solution would be to simply re-excavate the fill of the original trench and extend the profile in southern position. This, however, would imply that we would ex-cavate a new part of the mound by means of a very small trench. Such a trench, however, would be rather unhelpful as its small size hampers a full understanding of features that might come up in its excavated surface. Given the type of soil processes (the *holtpodsol* soils which lack an eluvial horizon) and lithological mate-rial (heterogenous, coarse fluviatile sediment) it must be expected that features like silhouettes of corpses are extremely hard to recognize, and are prone to remain unrecognized in such a small trench.

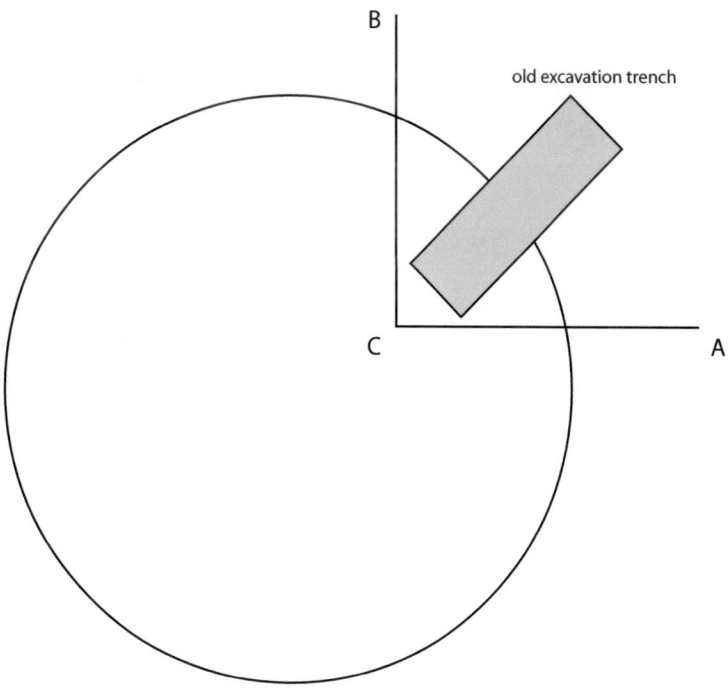

Fig. 2.3 Position of the small quadrant of the 2006 excavation in relation to the position of the former trench of the 1971 excavation. The exact location where the mound flank ends could not be established due to the dense forestation; the drawing only gives a reasonable estimation of its size. A-C indicate the positions of the profile drawings.

For that reason, we abandoned the trench option and decided to excavate a small quadrant of 6.5 by 7.5 m at its largest around the fill of the *AWN*-trench (Fig. 2.3). This would provide us with two long profiles, and enough horizontal space to recognize relevant soil features and to link these to stratigraphy observed in the mound. We refrained, however, from penetrating into the centre of the mound, where the central interment can be expected. Although the central burial would provide us with the best possible means of dating the mound, it would require a much more encompassing excavation than we planned for. We carefully decided to stay out of this part, as additional and properly located finds in the selected quadrant itself would suffice to answer our main questions.

2.5.2 Reasons for excavating in arbitrary horizontal levels

Before we started our excavation, there was no clear view on what would be the best way to excavate mounds like this. Although some 800 mounds have been excavated in the Netherlands, this happened a long time ago. With the exception of the outline of the quadrant method by Van Giffen's (1930, 7), there are no detailed 'best practice' accounts on how mounds were excavated[26]. The question how to excavate barrows revived with the first barrow excavation since the 1980s: the 2004 campaign at *Oss-Zevenbergen* (Fokkens *et al.* 2006). Here, the *Zevenbergen* team experimented with different methods, with varying results (for a discussion see Fokkens *et al.* 2006). They tried to excavate stratigraphically, which meant that layers belonging to one and the same mound period were followed: the original slope of the mound and layers was followed. Although this method was workable, it was very time-consuming and created several problems. One is that it appeared to be very hard to detect the proper stratigraphy in advance, without adequate test trenches. It was particularly difficult to understand subtle nuances in what are pedological rather than chronostratigraphical or lithostratigraphical units, and pedological units are not in themselves relevant units for find collections as they represent a process which works the sediment after people placed it in an artificial mound. On top of that, in the *Zevenbergen* case we are dealing with soil types with much clearer discolorations than here at *Elst* (Humus Podzol soils with a clear eluvial (E) horizon instead of the Moder Podsol soils of Unitas 1). Learning from the *Zevenbergen* experiences, and in anticipation of features that could be expected to be even more difficult to read than in the case of the *Zevenbergen* (due to the fact that we were here dealing with Moder – rather than with the more outspoken Humus Podzol soils), we decided to excavate in artificial, horizontal levels.

One quadrant was measured out (recorded as trench, Dutch *put* 1)[27], and after the topsoil was removed, starting from the top of the mound, three levels were shovelled clean by hand, with distances in between of c. 10-20 cm, right down to the level of the old surface. This way of working implies that the lower each level is, the larger its surface. The first level measured 3 m by 3 m, level 2 was 7 m by 7 m, and level 3 was 7.5 m by 6.5 m (Fig.2.8-2.10). Trees made it impossible to expand the quadrant as a square at level 3, giving the trench an irregular outline (Fig. 2.9-2.10). The entire excavation was done by hand, and each prepared level was systematically checked with a metal detector by Mr André Manders, our skilled metal detectorist. Each level was photographed and drawn. Fig. 2.4 and Fig. 2.7 give an impression of this way of working (respectively showing level 1 and level 3). During the digging and shoveling, all moved earth was also

---

26 See Van der Veen/Lanting 1991, 192 for an account of old barrow excavation practices.
27 As the Unitas 1 and Delfin 190 excavations took place simultaneously, we used one system for the administration of trenches: trench 1 is the excavation in Unitas 1 and trench 2 is the excavation trench in the Delfin 190 mound.

Fig. 2.4 View from the north on level 1 during the excava-tion. Excavating in horizontal levels means that you will have to start at the highest parts of the mound, with a small square trench like shown here, and end up with a sizeable one ranging from centre to flank. Note the dense forestation immediately to the south of the mound. Before these were planted, amateurs found dozens of Late Iron Age sherds at this site beyond the mound. Photograph by D. Fontijn.

inspected with a metal detector. In addition, for a section of 5 m by 50 cm parallel to the north-south profile, all removed sediment was sieved (mesh width 4 mm; see section 2.5.3). Sieving was used as a correction for the manual digging, to see whether small finds were missed. A comparison shows that number and size of finds done during sieving is comparable to what was found during manual digging. In other words: it should not be expected that finds got lost when the ground was not sieved. The exact find spot of each artefact was measured in three dimensions in the national coordinate system using the Sokia 4 B Total Station (measurement error 5 " = 1.5 mgon).

A fourth level, underneath the original surface was only partially dug. It is a 50 cm wide trench in front of both profiles. It was necessary to go beneath the original surface in order to facilitate sampling of pollen preserved underneath the original surface. This trench was extended in one place to the centre of the quadrant, to investigate traces of a ditch fill (feature (S from the Dutch *Spoor*) S19; depicted at Fig. 2.11), which was only visible at this level (see below). An even deeper, fifth level was also only partly dug, in order to inspect feature S21 (see below). Level 1 to 4 were all drawn at a 1:20 scale, and so were both profile sections. Level 5 was photographed but not drawn as it appeared to show natural variations in sediment only. Sections made through features, like the ditch S19 or the post row were also drawn (1:10).

2.5.3 Sieving of mound construction material

Before the excavation it was decided that a pilot with sieving would also be carried out at this site. One trench of fifty centimetres wide along the north-south profile was going to be sampled for sieving. In sections of 50 by 50 cm, ten litres of soil would be sieved over a 4 by 4 mm sieve.

The results of the sieving were minimal. Four tiny sherds, along with three flint flakes were found. Only one flake was an artefact, the other two were frost-cracked pieces (see Chapter 4), while the sherds were tiny, and smaller than one centimetre. Only one larger sherd of coarse-tempered pottery was found. No diagnostic pottery was found.

When contrasting this to the amount of objects found while shovelling, the added value of sieving the soil is limited. Only the sherd of coarse tempered pottery could be used in any way, the small fragments do not tell us much. Furthermore it is very likely that the larger fragment would also have been discovered while shovelling. As a matter of fact, equally small sherd fragments were found by shovelling as well. The total weight of the sherds discovered while sieving does not exceed 50 g, and the one diagnostic coarse-tempered sherd is responsible for the bulk of that (weighing 30 g). All other sherds weigh less than 8 g. The absolute weight of sherds discovered while shovelling is 430 g. A similar trench roughly fifty centimetres next to the sieving trench yielded seven sherds, with a total weight of 117 g, as well as a flint flake. All in all, the sieving experiment shows that carefully shovelling alone does not lead to loss of important finds. Of course, sieving might be expected to lead to finding more smaller artefacts, but in the case of pottery, the fragments recovered will be too small for dating purposes. For flint, it might be more useful, but it must be noted that if the sods of the barrow contain small fragments of flint, they will all be in secondary position. They are likely to represent inclusions in the sand with which the mound was built, and therefore represent replaced material only. In the future, sieving can better be restricted to the levels below the barrow which potentially represent an original prehistoric surface, instead of sieving entire mounds.

2.6 Mound stratigraphy

To make the description of the several features understandable, we will now first give an overview of the general stratigraphy of the mound from the highest to the lowest levels, as could be read off from the profiles we prepared (Fig. 2.5). The mound stratigraphy could ofcourse only be interpreted reliably when the complete profile was prepared during the last days of the excavation[28].

It appears as if the barrow was erected in one single episode. The top of the barrow is covered with a *holtpodsol* soil (1), the bottom part of which shows heavy bioturbation by beetles (2). The mound material itself is very homogenous and shows no traces of sods or other structural elements and has a light-brown hue (3). It is unclear whether sods were used in the construction of this barrow. Their traces might have been erased by soil-formation processes. The mound itself consists of coarse sand, which is also present in the vicinity, but intermixed with relatively few pebbles.

---

28   This matches the results of the prospection with the hand auger by the *RCE* described in section 7.4.1. Their subdivision of the A horizon (in A*h* and/or A*an)* is also indicated on our profile drawings, but we did not use this terminology for the finer sub-division of the top soil in our excavation.

Fig. 2.5 Photograph of the north-south profile at the corner of the quadrant, seen from the east. 1: top of the mound; 2: soil formation in the top of the mound, note the traces of bioactivity (yellow specks); 3: the mound; 4: the (truncated) prehistoric soil underneath the mound; 5: the sub-soil beneath the mound. Photograph by Q. Bourgeois.

The old surface covered by the mound was very hard to distinguish. It could only be visualised by a reddish-brown hue and a rather abrupt transition from the mound with only a few pebbles intermixed to a layer of coarse sand, intermixed with many pebbles (4). In a few places small soil *fibres* were observed just on the transition from the mound to the old surface indicating remnants of a transition of A-, B- to a C horizon. In a few places the distinction between the old surface and the mound material could not be made, and only the transition between the bottom of the Moder Podzol soil (transition B- to C horizon) under the barrow and the unperturbed matrix could be observed. The matrix consisted of coarse sand intermixed with many pebbles, locally consisting of pebbles only and no sand (5). This heterogeneity and the presence of large pebbles is typical for the sediments of the ice-pushed ridges (see Chapter 1). The fact that a distinction between mound material and the top of the original surface was so hard to see, relates to the absence of the original A horizon. This indicates that the original surface was probably truncated before the mound was erected.

2.7 Features and associated finds

We will now discuss the observed anthropogenic features, from top to bottom and mention finds associated with them. The finds themselves and arguments for their dating and function are discussed in detail in chapter 4. Fig. 2.8 to 2.12 give an overview of all recognized features.

2.7.1 General: 'readability' of features

Anthropogenic prehistoric features were very hard to recognize in this mound. Just like in the case of our excavation of Delfin 190 nearby that will be discussed in the next chapter, this is due to the *holtpodzol* soil which developed in this type of sediment, as well as due to the rather heterogeneous ice-pushed fluviatile sediment of which the mound was made. See for example the vague traces of the fill of the ditch S19 in the N-S profile (Fig. 2.6). However, features were even harder to detect in this mound than in Delfin 190. As was described above (see section 2.6), the soil buried underneath this mound was even hardly visible at all. It is noteworthy that Middle Bronze Age pit traces underneath Delfin 190 contrasted quite clearly with the soil in which they were dug, whereas a sizeable and much younger (!) Iron Age ditch in Unitas 1 (S19 section 2.7.3), dug into the mound from above, proved to be very difficult to observe. This is not easily explained, but one factor hampering readability of features in Unitas 1 is the fact that the matrix in which features were visible, was rather heterogenous and exists for an important part of coarse gravel and cobbles at the prehistoric surface. This is in marked contrast to the fine sand layers underneath Delfin 190.

Fig. 2.6 Photograph of the north-south profile, showing the vague traces of the Late Iron Age ditch S19. Photograph by Q. Bourgeois.

2.7.2 Traces of the AWN-excavation trench and a recent ditch

With the topsoil removed, the fill of the *AWN* trench (S1) was easy to recognize, and remained so in all levels (Fig. 2.8-2.10 and Fig. 2.13). Several large sherds were found in the backfill of the trench (4.1.4). At level 3, coinciding with the original prehistoric surface underneath the mound, the trench appeared to have been dug some 20 cm deeper: it was therefore not possible to check the original surface for possible features that might have gone undetected during the 1971 excavation. Another recent feature is the fill of a ditch running north-south through the top of the mound (S20, see Fig. 2.12 and Fig. 2.9 and 2.10).

Fig. 2.7 The preparation of level 3, as seen from the north. Photograph by R.S. Kok.

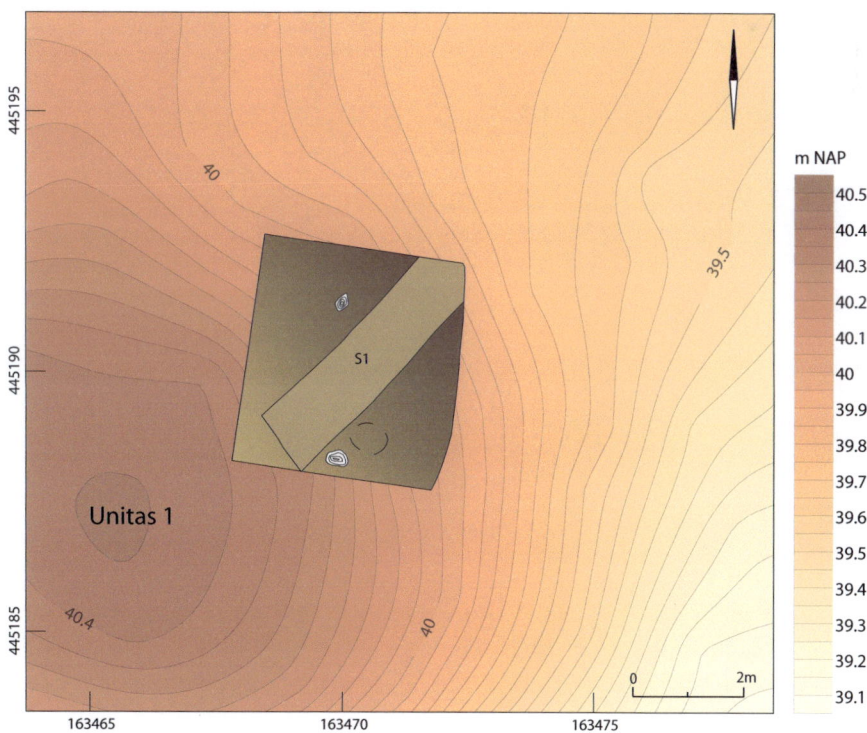

Fig. 2.8 Features recognized at level 1. This level is still situated in the top soil of the mound. The fill of the excavation trench from 1971 (S1) is clearly visible.

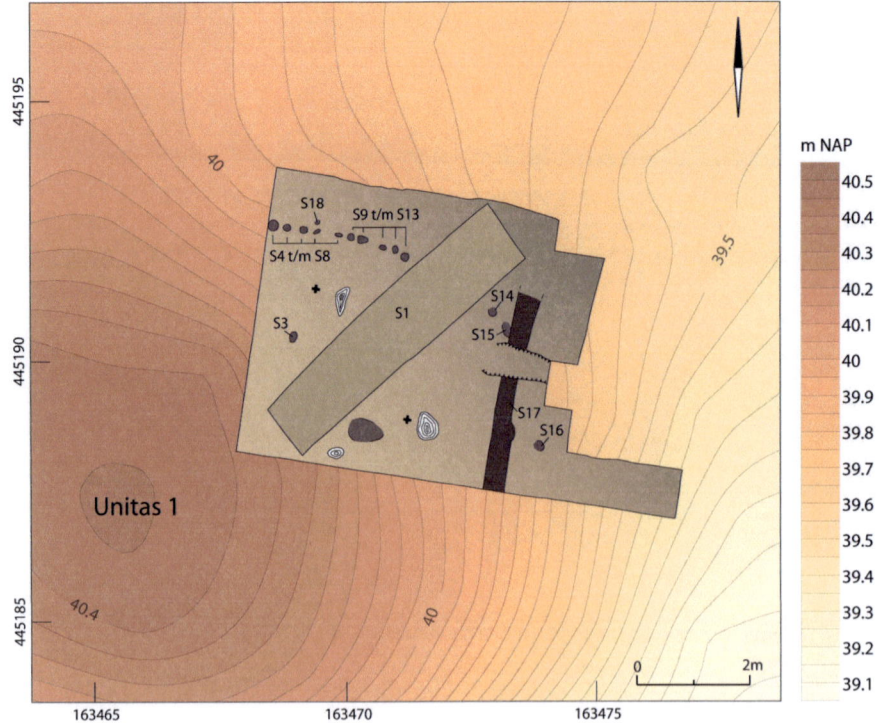

Fig. 2.9 Features recognized at level 2. Apart from the backfill of the 1971 excavation trench, a row of small posts is visible (S4-S13). To the east of the old excavation trench, heavy podzolization may have obscured all post traces. All other features, like the ditch S17, are recent.

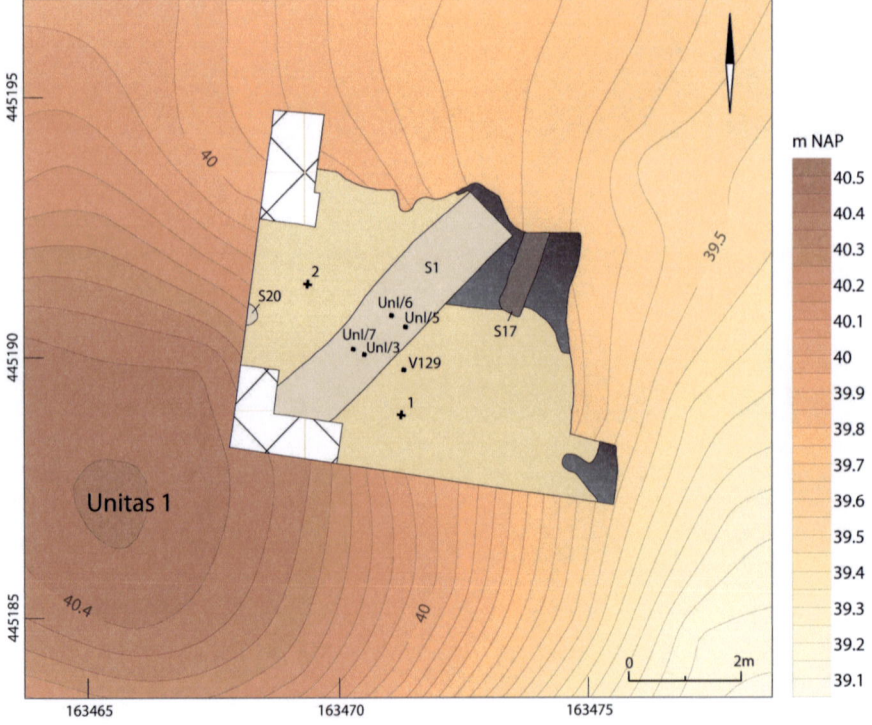

Fig. 2.10 Level 3. This level coincides with the prehistoric surface underneath the mound. It was here that the Barbed Wire sherd was found (V129). The Barbed Wire sherds found by the AWN are indicated as UNI/3 etc. (cf. Fig. 4.2). The darker shades at the rim of the quadrant result from soil formation. The other end of the recent ditch S17 is visible in this podsolized area.

2.7.3 Iron Age ditch (S19)

Already at the second level, three Iron Age sherds were found. Two were found in the back-fill of the *AWN*-ditch and one was found in a sieving segment. By then, it was not possible to relate these finds to an anthropogenic feature in the mound. This was only possible when ten more Iron Age sherds were found at this same place at level 3, more or less coinciding with the original surface. All these sherds can be dated to the (late) Iron Age or Roman Period (see section 4.1 and 4.2). This is exactly the situation that the *AWN* recorded in 1971. Against the

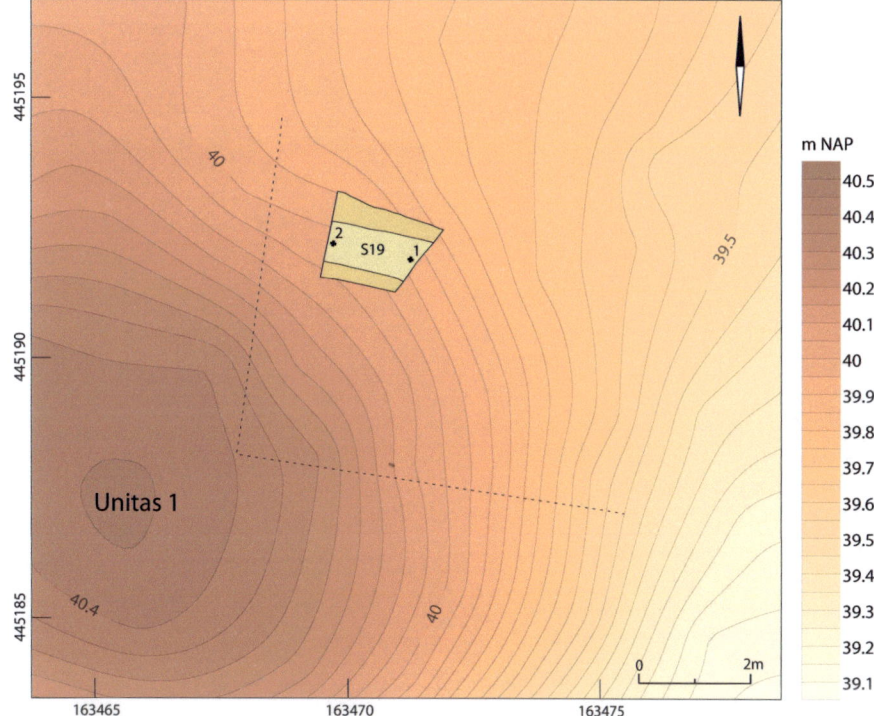

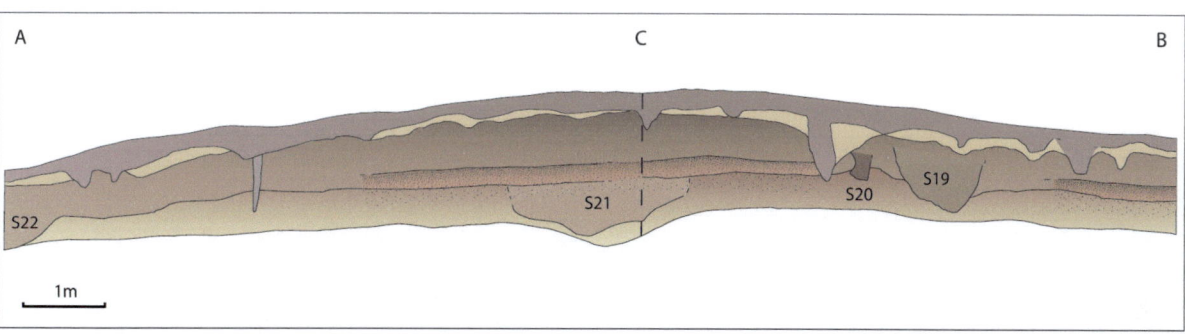

Fig. 2.11 Features at level 4. After the discovery of the ditch feature S19 in the N-S profile, level 3 was deepened locally. Here, at last, the ditch fill became also visible.

Fig. 2.12 N-S (B-C) en W-E (C-A) profile section with recognized features. For soil description, see Fig. 2.5. For orientation of the section see Fig. 2.3.

contrasting background of the original soil, we could now observe the fill of a ditch; the width at level 4 was only 70 cm (Fig. 2.11). With this in mind and with some difficulties, the section of the ditch could now also be detected higher up in the nearby N-S profile (Fig. 2.6 and 2.12). We appeared to be dealing with an east-west oriented ditch, which must have been dug from the top of the mound all the way down to the original prehistoric surface. U-shaped in section, it was filled with light-brown sediment that hardly differed from the material of which the mound was constructed. This explains why it was so difficult to detect. Their coordinates show that the few Iron Age sherds found at higher levels must all have been in the fill of this ditch (see 4.1 and 4.2). At the bottom of the ditch fill, more sherds were found, including a fragment of a tephrite quern (see 4.2). In order to document the ditch, it was decided to dig down to a deeper level at this place and make an additional N-S section through the ditch. The ditch was also observed at this level by the *AWN* excavation and both observations match.

Another ditch (S22), dug from the top of the mound, was observed in the easternmost part of the east-west profile. It had the same light fill as S19 and was also very difficult to detect against the light matrix. Lack of time and the presence of trees prevented us from following this feature (Fig 2.12). It may well be that both features represent one and the same ditch, which delineated the flank of the mound. As S19 is in a straight line, this ditch did not follow the contours of the

mound. If S19 and S22 indeed represent one and the same ditch, we are dealing with a rectangular or square ditch through a mound as is known from some other barrows (*cf.* Texel; Woltering 1994, Fig. 8.3). Fig. 2.11 presents a reconstruction of how S19 and S22 might have been situated. What is remarkable, however, is that the Iron Age ditch was dug *through* the mound, rather than *around* it. We will come back to this in section 2.8.

2.7.4 Traces of a post alignment

Lining the ditch feature on the northern side were several traces (10 in total) of very small posts or stakes (D= ±10 cm; depth 5 to 10 cm), they were only visible on the second level (Fig. 2.9 and Fig. 2.14). They contrasted quite clearly in the matrix, because of their dark-brown hue. The row of posts could be followed right up till the boundary of the former *AWN*-trench. Here however the *AWN*-trench cut through the row. They were apparently not observed during the *AWN*-excavation. They could also no longer be followed on the eastern side of the *AWN*-trench, partly due to the deeper soil formation processes at the foot of the barrow, which erased most of the features here[29], and possibly because a part was shovelled away too roughly. Some features recognized here look like the post traces. It is rather likely that the development of the Podzol on top of the barrow erased these features and that they became much harder to detect on the east-side of the *AWN*-trench (Fig. 2.9). Here the colour of the level was much darker and resembled the colour of the postholes, thus rendering any trace invisible. The orientation of the posts is similar to that of the ditch but the posts seem to be set into the flank of the ditch: they must have been placed into the ditch after it was filled up (*cf.* Fig. 2.9 and Fig. 2.11). It is therefore likely that they were part of the Iron Age ditch boundary which was cut through the barrow.

2.7.5 Mound construction

The section of the mound itself looks very homogenous in colour shades and shows no traces of sods or other structural elements. It is unclear whether sods were used in the construction of this barrow, their traces might have been erased by soil-formation processes. The mound itself consists of coarse sand, which is also present in the vicinity, but it contains less stones than the subsoil underneath and around the mound. The material with which the mound is built is therefore likely to have been acquired from the top of the old surface only, or from an area further away from the mound where the subsoil contained less pebbles. Although a detailed map of local variation in subsoil lithology is not available, such a "pebble-poor" area is nearby. The subsoil of the Delfin 190 mound, for example, contains much less pebbles than the immediate environment of the Unitas 1 mound (see Chapter 3). The Unitas 1 mound might therefore have been built with sods collected at the area where later the Delfin 190 mound would be built.

Another relevant observation, already referred to above, is that the surface covered by the mound lacks an A horizon. This might indicate that the A horizon was truncated before the erection of the barrow, and that a new A horizon did not have time to develop. Similarly the abrupt shift from a gravelly sub-soil to a much less gravelly mound indicates that the A horizon could have been removed prior to mound construction (see above), thus 'cleaning' the area where the barrow was to be erected

Fig. 2.13 Level 1. View to the northeast. Visible is the fill of the trench of the AWN excavation in 1971. Photograph by Q. Bourgeois.

---

29   *cf* the processes described by Modderman 1975, 17.

2.7.6 Implications of the find of Barbed Wire pottery

As already mentioned before, the finds of fragments of a Barbed Wire Beaker brought us to selecting this mound. The problem was, however, that of the four sherds found by the *AWN*, three are reported as lying on the old surface covered by the mound, whilst a fourth one seems to be located in the lower parts of the mound itself (Fig. 4.2). As argued above (section 2.4.1) we are of the opinion that not too much weight should be given to this exception. Even in much better observation circumstances, we found it hard to distinguish between the original surface and the bottom of the mound. These problems must have been much larger in the 1971 excavation, where only a small profile of a tiny trench was available, and where the excavators, as evidenced by the profile drawing, had great difficulty in understanding what they were digging into. Moreover, the position of the sherd was not reported *in situ*. Only its height was recorded, and later on, the sherd's position was projected onto the only drawn profile section. For this reason, not too much should be made out of this sole exception.

Fortunately, we found another sherd of Barbed Wire pottery during our excavation which must have been part of the same beaker (section 4.3; Fig. 4.2). This sherd was found while cleaning the level 3. This level was positioned at approximately the same height as the old surface[30]. On the basis of the *in situ* observations, the new Barbed Wire pottery find can safely be located at or just below the old surface, matching the observations on the position of three out of four of the Barbed Wire sherds found in 1971 (Fig. 2.10). The barrow was thus built on top of this sherd. The sherd was found half a metre to the south-east of the concentration of Barbed Wire sherds found during the *AWN*-excavation.

The scatter of sherds indicates that a Barbed Wire Beaker broke or was deliberately broken before the barrow was erected. Even with our substantially enlarged excavation surface (as compared to the *AWN* trench) and a careful way of digging, in which even very small sherds were found, no more was found than five sherds. It is interesting to note that one of the sherds showed signs of secondary burning while the others did not. This sherd must thus have lain near or in a fire before they got caught underneath the barrow, while the others apparently did not. This and the incompleteness of the beaker suggests that we are dealing with displaced material that was broken elsewhere, rather than with a beaker that was broken on the spot where it was found.

The Barbed Wire Beaker type is something special in the Bronze Age burial ritual. It rarely appears in the grave itself (Lohof 1991, 68-70; Theunissen 1999, 57) and mostly they are found at the foot of the barrow. Some twenty barrows are known to have this type of pottery associated with them. Of these, only two barrows had a Barbed Wire Beaker placed directly in the grave[31]. In some cases the placing of the beakers took place after the barrow was built. For example, at the *Groevenbeeksche Heide* two small Barbed Wire Beakers were placed in a pit dug into the barrow (Modderman 1959; Modderman 1974). In other cases, the pottery was placed on top of an older barrow and covered by a younger mound-period, such as at *Anner Tol* (Tumulus III) for example (Butler, Lanting & Van der Waals 1972). Yet another example shows that a Barbed Wire Beaker was placed on the old surface, sometimes in broken condition. At *Garderen* (barrow 6, Bursch 1933, 75-76), in between the two primary graves, exactly in the centre of the

Fig. 2.14 Level 2. View to the east. Visible are the traces of the post alignment and, in the back, the fill of the AWN trench. Photograph by Q. Bourgeois.

---

30 It was first detected with a metal detector when level 3 was cleaned. Level 3 is approximately situated around the prehistoric surface. It was later dug out. The sherd was thus found a few cm below this level, making it more likely that it was indeed lying at the old surface and not in the mound construction material on top of it.

31 At Gasteren (Van Giffen 1943; Lanting 1973) and at Emmerhout Tumulus III (Lanting 1969; 1973).

mound, a small Barbed Wire Beaker was placed (Bursch 1933, T.IV, nr.9). A barrow at *Aalden* (Lohof 1991, 68; Modderman 1957) had half of a small smashed up beaker deposited on the old surface under the mound, while the other half of the beaker was found in the grave. Here we have an example where a beaker was smashed and where part of its sherds were deposited elsewhere. The Unitas 1 sherds also seem to represent a situation where the sherds found were probably not of a pot that was broken on the spot.

Summing up, sherds of Barbed Wire Beakers are indeed known to be regularly associated with the grave ritual but were often *not* placed in the grave. The smashing up of the beaker and the manipulation of the sherds – in a variety of ways – seems to have been an integral part of the funeral ritual. The Unitas 1 Barbed Wire sherds are most likely to represent the situation where a beaker was broken elsewhere and part of its sherds ended up – or rather – were deposited, at the future site of a barrow. Only new excavations that include the central grave will tell if we might have a situation similar to *Aalden*, where sherds of one and the same beaker seem to have been divided between the grave and the area that would in a later stage of the funeral be covered with a mound.

2.7.7 Implications of the find of two Pot Beaker sherds

Both in the 1971 AWN trench and in our own excavation, a sherd of a Pot Beaker was found. Section 4.4.2 will describe these finds in more detail (see also Fig. 4.3). It appears to be difficult to date both sherds precisely. They might both be older than the Barbed Wire Beakers (Late Neolithic-Bell Beaker phase), or contemporary: Early Bronze Age. Their stratigraphical position is also not entirely clear. They are recorded to have been found close to the transition of the mound to the original surface, or at the original surface. We might thus be dealing with older material which was already lying at this site and came to be covered by the mound, or with material that was part of the lowest layer of sods with which the mound was built. Alternatively, it might also have been intentionally deposited here, just like the Barbed Wire sherds just described. There is even the possibility that the sherd found during the 2006 excavation was part of the fill of the Iron Age ditch S19 (see further section 4.4.2), and with regard to the find administration of the 1971 dig, the same problems of uncertainty on stratigraphical position apply that we already discussed for the Barbed Wire Beaker sherds found then. As there are simply too many possible scenarios we do not think it wise to let these finds play a role in our arguments on dating and funeral ritual.

2.7.8 S21: natural or anthropogenic?

In the centre of the quadrant, on the lowest level a darker discoloration could be observed. In the profile the barrow covered this feature. This feature however was very irregular and gave the impression of having a natural origin. At first the possibility of a grave was examined but there is not a single piece of evidence to support this theory. If it were a grave, it would be rather eccentric in respect to the centre of the barrow. The feature was also highly irregular and could not be followed precisely. The soil underneath the barrow clearly showed the strongly changing sediment layers of the ice-pushed river deposits. Typical to the ice-ridges these are highly changeable over short areas. This might have influenced the soil locally and might explain the irregular feature.

2.8 Conclusions

The purpose of the excavation was to shed light on the dating of the mound, and thus have a good correlate for the pollen analysis. Through careful analysis of the finds the following sequence of actions performed at this site can be established.

We think that it is most likely that the old surface was prepared, probably levelled (vegetation removed) and the topsoil (A horizon) truncated. Then, several sherds of one Barbed Wire Beaker were deposited on the old surface. The sherds probably came from somewhere else and were probably not broken on the spot, since only one sherd was secondarily burnt. We found a sherd from the same Barbed Wire Beaker of which the *AWN* also found fragments and we were thus able to confirm their view on stratigraphical position and dating. Reviewing parallels from other Early Bronze Age burial mounds, we assume that this deposition of pot fragments was an essential part of the burial ritual (cf. Lohof 1991, 68). Since the sherds were deposited at an old, prepared surface, on which no soil regeneration took place, it is very likely that the deposition of the sherds was part of the funerary practices that resulted in the construction of a mound at this place. The fact that the sherds were all found in each other's vicinity is another argument for this hypothesis. The deposition of sherds took place prior to the barrow construction. It remains unclear how the find of two small sherds of Pot Beaker pottery fit into this picture. Both their dating (prior or contemporary to barrow construction) and stratigraphical position could not be reconstructed with certainty. They might both have been inclusions in the barrow construction material, later intrusions or part of the deposition of sherds at the surface during the Early Bronze Age related to the burial ritual.

Then, in all likelihood one or more dead were buried at or in the surface. We do not have any information on this event, as the centre, where the burial should be expected, was not excavated. This prepared funerary area, with sherds and all, then was covered with a mound. No sods could be distinguished in the mound, though this does not mean they were not used to build the mound. It might be that any visible traces of them were erased after three to four thousand years of soil activity. The mound itself was also of a less gravelly nature than the natural subsoil; indicating that a large part of the construction material was not immediately local, but could have come from a less gravelly spot, like the surroundings of the later Delfin 190 mound. Within the sods, little to no finds were discovered, indicating they came from an area without much activity (not from a settlement site). There is no indication for more than one construction phase. As the top of the mound displays a normal soil profile, it is not likely that the mound was considerably levelled in more recent times, as a result of heath cutting activities. Hence, its original height will more or less be similar to its height during prehistory.

At some eight metres from the barrow, many sherds of a Pot Beaker were buried. It is an intriguing, but hard to answer, question to relate this highly remarkable act to the presence of the Unitas 1 mound, and the funerary activities which took place there. A review of Pot Beaker finds in the Netherlands (section 4.6 and Appendix) suggests that Pot Beaker finds are not the straightforward examples of settlement finds that they are usually considered to be. Several seem to be closely linked to burial mounds, though they are not part of the normal burial equipment in the graves under the mound. Unfortunately, this Pot Beaker cannot be precisely dated. It might be (slightly) older than the construction of the mound (Late Neolithic-Bell Beaker Period), or contemporary with it. However, considering the fact that such quantities of sherds of one Pot Beaker are rarely found, its location close to a barrow cannot be a coincidence. Two scenarios are possible. If the Pot Beaker dates to the Bell Beaker Period, then it might represent an intentional deposition of a vessel (with content?) at a zone which already had a specific significance to people. The decision to construct the Unitas 1 mound in this zone, then, might relate to the existing significance of this place. The other option is to date the Pot Beaker to the Early Bronze Age, contemporary to the Unitas 1 mound. In that case, the deposition of this vessel may relate to funerary practices carried out during or after the construction of the mound (e.g. funerary meals).

After almost two millennia after its initial construction, an east-west running ditch was cut through the northern flank of the barrow. Several sherds found in the ditch fill testify to a dating at the end of the Late Iron Age (see Chapter 4). The ditch runs straight, and does not seem to encircle the barrow. It is likely that the ditch connects with a north-south (?) running ditch observed in the east-west profile. As the part where the connection is to be expected could not be excavated, we cannot be sure of this. It might be that we are dealing with a rec-tangular ditch surrounding an older barrow, something already observed at *Texel* (Woltering 2000, 26-7), *Oedelem* (Belgium, Cherretté/ Bourgeois 2005, 263) or *Ursel* (Belgium, Bourgeois 1998, 114-5). What is highly unusual, however, is that it is not a peripheral ditch, but a ditch which cuts through the mound. What might have been the motivation behind the cutting of such a deep (more than 90 cm!) through a by then age-old mound? What might have been the function of such a deep ditch on the higher parts of the ice-pushed ridge anyway? The square Late Iron Age ditches around the *Texel* and *Ursel* mounds also demarcate a much older monument, and may be interpreted as having been dug to demarcate an older monument for ritual reasons (ancestral veneration of older barrows; *cf.* Van der Sanden 1998 on the interpretation of such square ditches as sanctuaries). The relative steep slope of the ditch and the coarse material through which it was dug ensure that it could not have remained open for a very long time. The limited size of our excavation, as well as the lack of data on Iron Age structures in the immedi-ate vicinity preclude any decisive statement on the function of this ditch. We do want to remark that its construction is certainly an unusual one for which a ritual function is a serious option.

Once the ditch was (partially) filled up, a row of stakes was placed into the northern flank of the ditch. The placing of the small posts along the axis of the ditch might indicate that they recognized the original orientation of the ditch and were thus placed not very long after the ditch was filled again. Again, this emphasizes the significance this Iron Age demarcation apparently had, but again, the reasons behind it escape us.

We did not find any evidence that the barrow was used during the late Roman or Medieval Periods. Effectively, the sand cutting activities that slightly disturbed the southern parts of the mound during recent times (20th century) are the only other traces of activities. After the excavation was finished, the quadrant was back filled and brought back to its old state by the addition of new sods of top soil.

Chapter 3

MOUND "DELFIN 190": A MIDDLE BRONZE AGE BARROW BUILT OVER THE TRACES OF A MIDDLE BRONZE AGE A SETTLEMENT SITE

D. Fontijn, Q. Bourgeois, C. van der Linde

3.1 Introduction

The other barrow excavated during the 2006 fieldwork campaign is the one coded as "Delfin 190", also known as site 39-E-11 in the Archis codification[32]. It is situated in the forest on the privately owned *Prattenburg* estate, to the east of the *Westerlaan,* the sand road which forms the border between the *Staatsbosbeheer* and the *Prattenburg* estate. Just like in the case of our research of "Unitas 1", goal of the excavation was to take pollen samples from underneath the mound that could serve as the basis for a reconstruction of the prehistoric environment of this barrow group. In order to adequately date and contextualize the pollen samples, a small excavation of a well-chosen mound section was needed to provide us with a more adequate insight in the dating and development of this mound.

"Delfin 190" was detailed as the second pollen sampling location, complementary to the "Unitas 1" barrow, for the following reasons. First, "Delfin 190" is very close to "Unitas 1" (90 m as the crow flies). This means that pollen from Unitas 1 and Delfin 190 inform us about vegetation on one and the same locality. Second, earlier research suggested that Delfin 190 dates to the Bell Beaker Period (*c.*2500 to 2000 cal. BC). Pollen from this mound might therefore be expected to inform us about the prehistoric environment of this barrow group in a period just *before* the construction of "Unitas 1". Third, due to a disturbance, Delfin 190's flank was already in an exposed position. This made it relatively easy to prepare a section through the mound from which pollen samples could be adequately taken.

This chapter will first describe the environmental position of Delfin 190 (section 3.2), its condition of preservation prior to the 2006 research (3.3), relevant finds from amateur archaeologists around the barrow and a discussion of the results of the 1971 excavation (3.4). We will then describe the excavation strategy designed and followed for this excavation (3.5). As it differs from the way in which barrows were usually excavated in the past, and is also different from the strategy followed at Unitas 1, it will be set out why we decided to excavate in this manner. We will go on by providing general information on the mound's stratigraphy as well as on administrative layers and find units used during the excavation from top to bottom (3.6). This overview will hopefully be helpful for the description and interpretation of recognized archaeological features and associated finds that follows in section 3.7. We will describe the features from

---

32 CAA numbers: 26653/26644; also under *waarnemingen* 43722, 43489, 43490 and 58023.

top to bottom. Interpretation of these features and finds will provide the basis for a new interpretation of the barrow's dating and development described in the conclusive section 3.8.

3.2 Environmental setting, local geology and soils

"Delfin 190" is one of the easternmost mounds of the barrow group under study (Chapter 1). It is built at the gently descending northern slope of the ice-pushed ridge at a height of 33 m NAP, just to the west of the steep-sloped dry valley described in section 1.6.1 (Fig. 1.3). It has an irregular appearance, currently measuring 13 by 9.5 m, with its highest point at some 1 m above the surface (Fig. 1.5). The dry valley which cuts into the ice-pushed ridge and the northern *sandr*-sediment can be followed all the way north through present-day *Elst* to the river Rhine (Fig. 1.3). Just like in the case of Unitas 1, the barrow is built on non-morainic ice-pushed fluviatile sediment (Verbraeck 1984, coded Gm0) of which the characteristics were described before (section 1.6.1). In contrast to the situation underneath the Unitas 1 mound, however, the subsoil of Delfin 190 consists of relatively homogeneous fine-grained sand without cobbles (Fig. 3.9). In the top of the mound and around it, a Moder Podzol soil is observable (coded gY30 or *holtpodsol* in the Dutch classification, see section 1.6.1). The soil covered by the barrow is somewhat vaguer than the one outside it, but better developed and easier to observe than in the case of the soil underneath Unitas 1 (2.2). Apart from the corings carried out by the RCE in and just outside the mound (Chapter 7), additional information on geology and soils was not collected. The mound itself is deforested but on all sides ringed by deciduous and pine trees (Fig. 3.1 and 3.8).

Fig. 3.1 Barrow Delfin 190 before the excavation, seen from the south. People are standing in the gully and indicate the part of the mound that is to be excavated. The irregular shape of the mound is clearly visible as well as the dense forestation on all sides.

3.3 State of preservation before the 2006 excavation

This part of the *Prattenburg* estate was a heath up until the end of the 19th century. It might therefore be expected that part of the original top soil was (slightly) leveled or truncated by sod-cutting that is known to have taken place regularly at heaths. However, in the excavated section, decapitated soils have not been observed, suggesting that the soil disturbances in this part due to heath leveling were only superficial. The fact that the amateur archaeologist Ms Ch. Delfin found prehistoric pottery (see section 3.4.2 below) in and around this mound in the 1970s, however, shows that erosion/disturbance of the archaeological record was taking place by then.

Like the Unitas 1 barrow it is situated in a forest, but Delfin 190 is not accessible via a path or route, and trespassing is officially forbidden. Compared to Unitas 1, the mound's surface is not eroded in places due to regular trespassing or cross country biking. As already mentioned, this mound has a rather irregular form, however. The northern side has a very faint inclination which makes it hard to recognize where the mound ends, whereas the southern side has a steeper slope (Fig. 1.5). This irregularity has been caused by several disturbances. At its western side, the barrow has been cut away by a c. 1 m deep and c. 2 m wide man-made ditch (Fig.3.1). According to the estate-forester Mr G. van Heijningen, this ditch was dug for the water supply of tobacco plantations south of the *Elsterberg* during the 19th century[33]. In the 1980s, the mound was used for sand extraction and further damaged as a result of it. It is not entirely clear whether the flat northern side of the mound also results from such extraction activities or whether it represents the original appearance of the mound. The *ROB* (now *RCE*) superficially mapped the disturbances and refilled the pits with white sand in 1987. They probably also removed some trees from the mound. The barrow has remained deforested until today.

The irregular form of the Delfin 190 barrow is probably the reason that this barrow is hardly visible on the Dutch Digital Elevation map, the *AHN*, in marked contrast to the other barrows of the *Elsterberg* group.

3.4 Earlier research

3.4.1 The AWN excavation of 1971

The mound was discovered by Ms Ch. Delfin in 1970 and recorded as a probable barrow by the then provincial archaeologist, drs P. van Tent. To check her interpretation and to get some indication of its dating, amateur archaeologists of the *AWN (Archeologische Werkgroep Nederland)* carried out a one-day excavation in the summer of 1971, just like they did at Unitas 1 and some other mounds of this barrow group. This excavation was done within the framework of an "*AWN*-summer camp". It was done under supervision of the *ROB*. Provincial archaeologist P. van Tent was in charge. We inspected the original find documentation at the *RCE*, as well as the finds mentioned in the find list.

According to the documentation, the *AWN* dug a small trench (5.5 by 1.2 m) manually at the foot of the eastern part of the mound (Fig. 3.2). It is not recorded which method of excavation was used. We also did not succeed in retrieving the exact place where this trench was dug: the position of the trench seems not to have been measured in the national coordinate grid. Also, in contrast to the situation

---

33 The ditch is not depicted at the military map *Topografische en Militaire Kaart van het Koninkrijk der Nederlanden, Kaartblad 39-II 1839-1859, 1:50.000*, but it might have been considered too insignifcant an environmental feature for it.

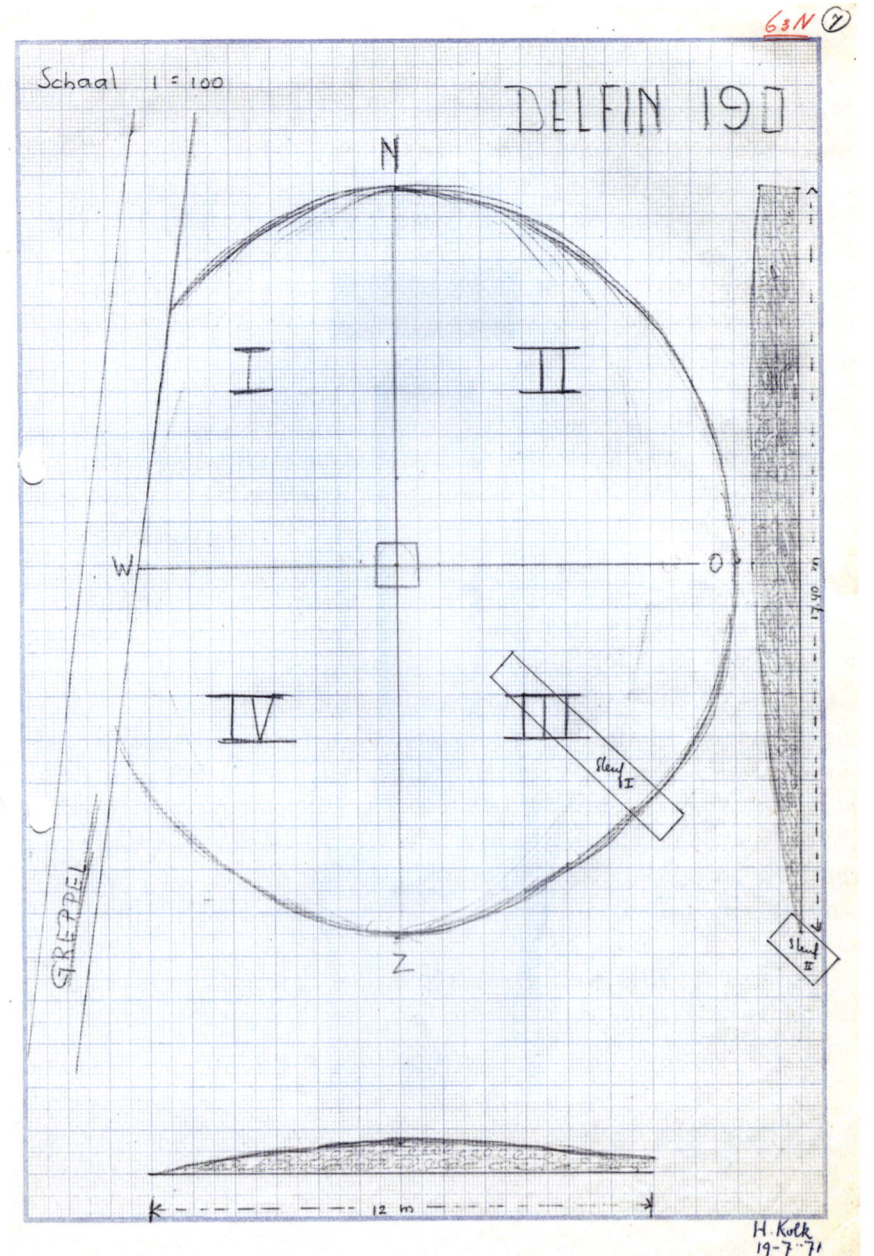

Fig. 3.2 Drawing, recorded in the 1971 excavation documentation showing the position of the AWN trench in the eastern flank of the mound. The gully from which the 2006 excavation was carried out is schematically indicated on the left side of the mound.

at Unitas 1, the original position of the trench could not be recognized on the basis of subtle color shade differences in the shrub vegetation. There are no indications that during the 1971 excavation ground was dug to a horizontal level that was checked for features and finds, before further deepening continued (Dutch: *vlakkenopgraving)*. If it did happen, it was not documented (in day reports or drawings) or such documentation got lost. There is only a colored (1:20) drawing of the east-profile of the trench (Fig. 3.3) and some photographs, which are all, unfortunately, rather hard to re-interpret. The profile drawing describes colors of what are probably soil horizons and mound construction material. The drawing clearly shows an ancient filled-in ditch at the foot of the mound. According to a note on the field-drawing, the ditch was also observed on the horizontal surface of the trench, but this was never drawn. An ancient ditch at the outer rim of a mound might well represent a peripheral ring ditch delimiting the barrow. The

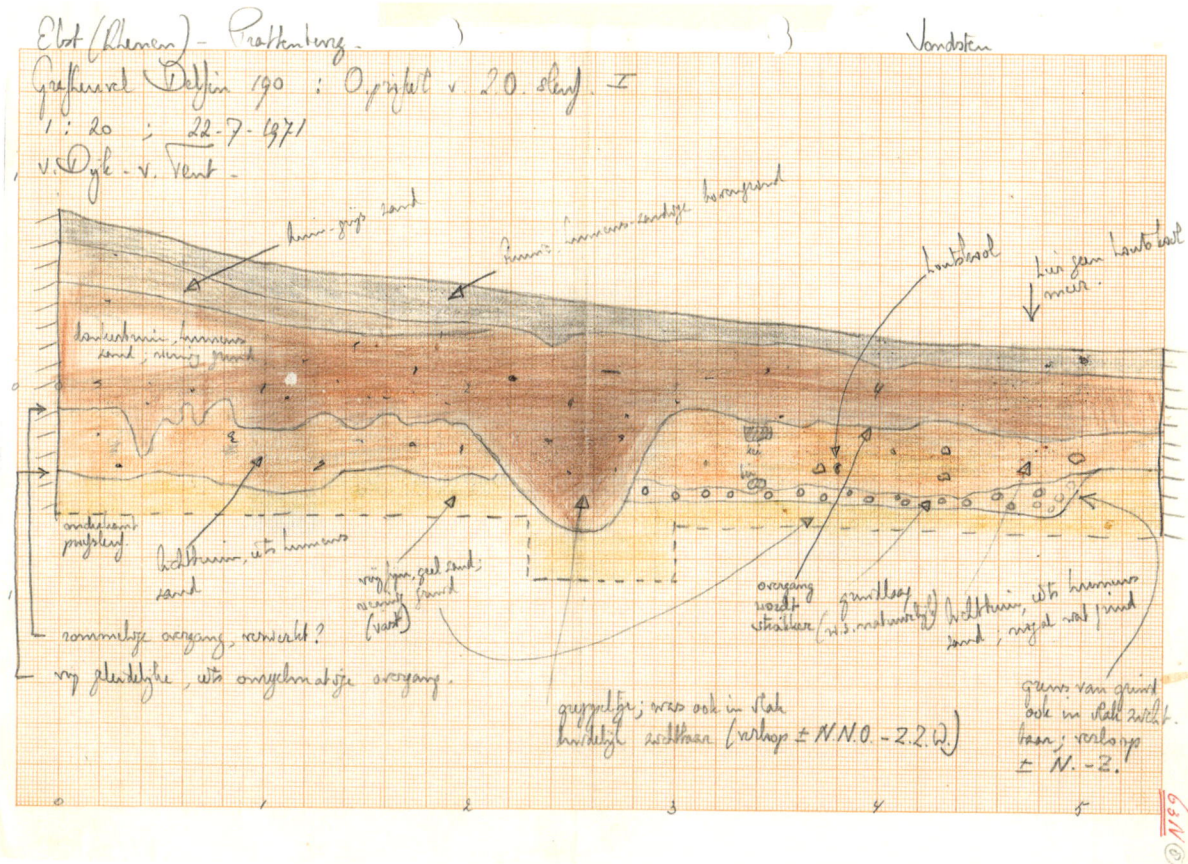

Fig. 3.3 Drawing of the eastern profile made during the excavation in 1971. Indicated is the section of a ditch.

1971 excavation trench is far too small to either confirm or refute such an interpretation. Its stratigraphical relation to the mound itself cannot be checked on the basis of this profile drawing only.

Two sherds of Pot Beaker pottery were found (Fig. 5.8). Both were dated to the Bell Beaker period on typo-chronological grounds, though our review of the dating evidence shows that they might just as well date to the Early Bronze Age (see section 5.6). The height of these finds was measured according to the National Dutch Ordnance Datum (*NAP*). The finds were not projected on the profile (as was done with finds at Unitas 1), and the documentation is not clear on their exact find circumstances, nor on their stratigraphical positioning. The barrow was dated in the Bell Beaker period on the basis of these Pot Beaker sherds, but in retrospect, both its dating and the association between the finds and the stratigraphy of the mound has not been as accurately determined as to warrant this. It cannot be ruled out that these sherds are from a later use-phase, for example as fill of a pit dug into the mound (they would then be *later* than the mound construction). Alternatively, they could also have been part of the material with which the mound was built thus being roughly contemporary with or providing a *terminus post quem* dating for the mound's construction. In all, there was ample reason to check the dating and to get a better insight into the mound's stratigraphy.

3.4.2 Ms Delfin's stray finds in and around the mound

To add up to this confusion, the year before the *AWN*-excavation, Ms Ch. Delfin found undecorated sherds of pottery tempered with coarse quartz together with cremated bone fragments in a depression – a hole dug into the western part of the mound. These sherds can be dated to the Middle Bronze Age (section 5.2 and Fig. 5.3 for a description of this find). As it was found in the mound flank opposite to the side excavated by the *AWN*, it cannot be related to their observations on the mound's stratigraphy. Ms Delfin's find, however, clearly shows that the mound was used for burial during the Middle Bronze Age. Ms Ch. Delfin – and/or other amateur archaeologists – also found several sherds of what must be Iron Age or native Roman Period pottery (section 5.7.2). The precise position of these sherds is not recorded, but was according to the text at the paper bag in which the sherds were stored very close to or on Delfin 190[34]. A few other finds were done at or around this mound. When part of the mound was dug away with a bulldozer in 1983 (for sand extraction), amateur archaeologists observing these destructive activities, again made several interesting finds in the spoil heaps coming from the barrow. These include a rim sherd that can be dated to the Late Iron Age or Roman Period and other Iron Age or Roman Period sherds (see section 5.7.2)[35], but also Middle Bronze Age sherds a few meters to the north from a different pot than the urn found in the mound (see 5.7.2)[36], indicating that more Middle Bronze Age activities took place. Even after the *ROB* restoration finds dating to the Iron Age or Roman Period were done at or around the mound[37]. In addition to this, among Ms Ch. Delfin's finds is also a fragment of a glass La Tène bracelet and another Iron Age/Roman Period sherd, this time found at the sand path close to the Delfin 190 barrow. All in all, due to the work of Ms Ch. Delfin and other amateurs of the *Rhenen* group, we now have recorded an unusual concentration of finds around this mound, indicating its use in several periods of prehistory. Such a concentration is not common around Dutch barrows, and it begs the question how the use history of this mound should be reconstructed.

Summing up, the existing documentation leaves open many questions on general stratigraphy and dating of the barrow, and the amateur finds indicate periods of use that are not recorded by the excavation finds. Additional research was needed.

3.5 Excavation strategy of the 2006 fieldwork

Given the exposed and cut off west flank, we designed an alternative excavation strategy to exploit this particular situation as much as possible. It was decided to use the exposed west flank of the barrow as a convenient starting point for the preparation of a north-south section through the mound.

The digging of the ditch had cut away a part of the barrow, and thereby presents us with a more or less already existing north-south section through the barrow. This section cuts through its flank and bypasses the centre with several meters. It cannot therefore be expected that it gives an ideal impression of the general build-up of the barrow, as an old "core" barrow might be out of reach of this section. Nevertheless, this N-S section was in outline already there and was thought to give us more than enough stratigraphical context for pollen samples to be taken from it, without necessitating substantial excavation and further disturbance to the mound.

The ditch at its deepest point is some 50 cm below the surface of the forest. West of it, no elevation that could be interpreted as remnants of the mound is visible. To the east of the ditch, there is a steep-sloped flank of the mound. We will later on come back to the question if this is really the original flank of the barrow.

---

34   This is the find with the label *Grafheuvel 190*, see 5.7.2.

35   See 5.7.2, under: finds labeled *Prattenburg grafheuvel 190, 163/445, uit opengebulderde grafheuvel 163/445, dec. '83.*

36   See 5.7.2 under: *39 E vondstnr 031-kapotte grafheuvel.*

37   See 5.7.2 under: *Rhenen 39E-132-IJz scherven gevonden na restauratie heuvel (1987).*

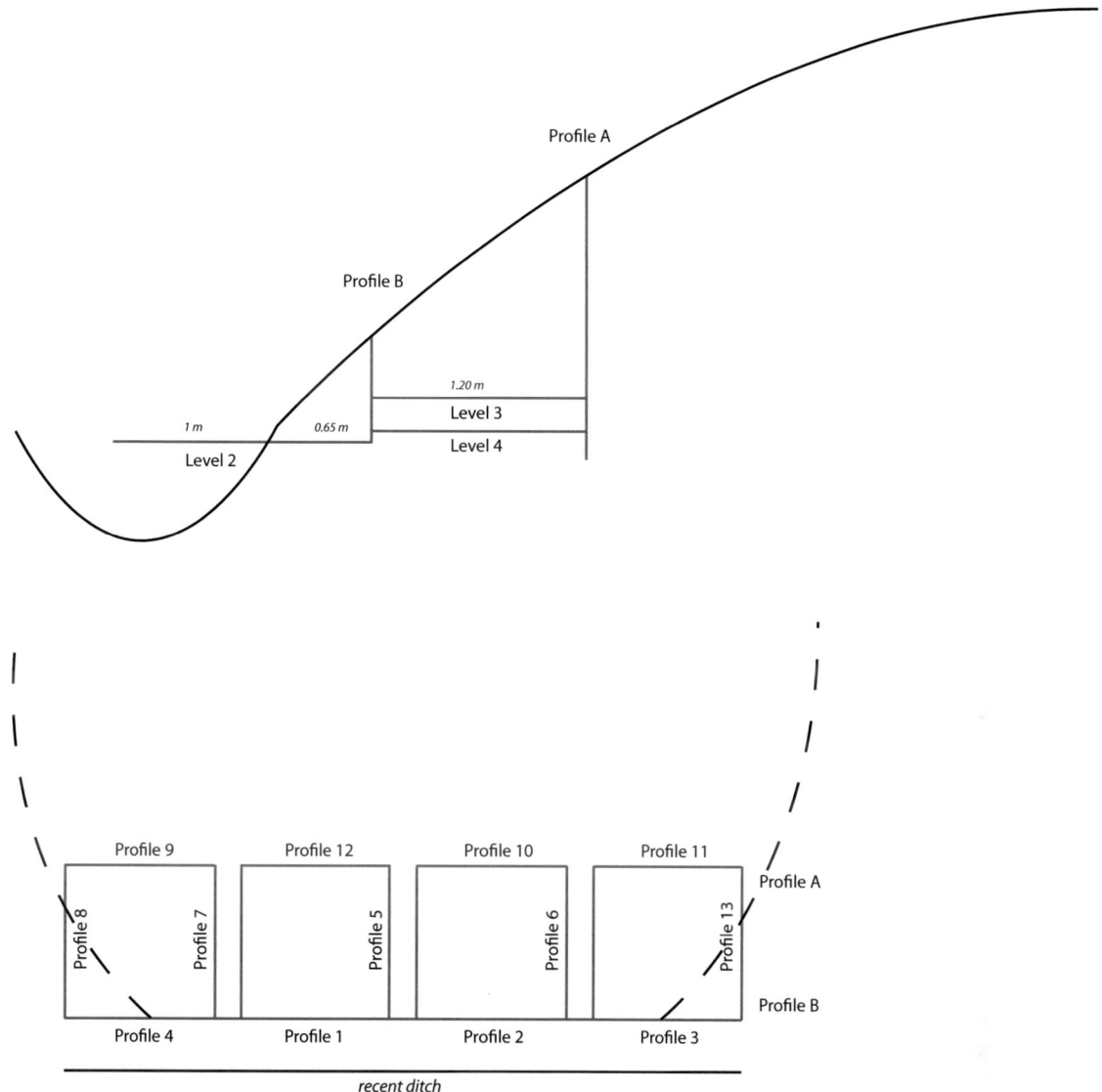

Fig. 3.4 Schematized position of the excavation levels and boxes in the mound, shown in the vertical (upper) and horizontal plane (lower). All profile sections were drawn, and were recorded with a separate number from 1 to 13. These are also indicated here.

In order to get a readable north-south section through this eastern slope, it should be dug away until a vertical section can be prepared of which the stratigraphy could be documented and from which pollen samples could be taken.

In order to adequately record stratigraphy, the planned trench (trench 2) through this slope was organized in four "boxes", separated from each other by a 2 m long E-W profile. In this book they are numbered 1 to 4 from north to south (Fig. 3.5-3.8). These E-W profiles are additional to the planned N-S profile and allowed us to check and detect local changes in stratigraphy. Each separate profile has been recorded with a profile number. These are indicated on Fig. 3.4.

The entire excavation was done by hand. All finds were three-dimensionally measured using the same theodolite as on Unitas 1, the Sokia 4 B Total Station (measurement error 5 " = 1.5 mgon). There was no sieving experiment here like the one we carried out at Unitas 1. It will be indicated when sieving was practiced.

First, the area to be excavated was manually stripped from covering vegetation. On this stripped surface, which still follows the original slope, no archaeological features were detected. It was therefore documented with photographs only as level 1 (Fig. 3.5). Then, inside the gully, a preliminary profile (B) was dug to determine the exact position of the old surface. This appeared to be a very faintly

Fig. 3.5 Photograph taken from the south, from the same position as Fig. 3.1. Here, it can be seen that the topsoil has been stripped everywhere (level 1), and the level 2 has been prepared. The small profile section (profile no. 3 front right) shows the original prehistoric surface underneath the mound as cut by the recent ditch dug through it. Photograph by R.S. Kok.

Fig. 3.6 Excavation box 1, as seen from the west. Detail of level 1 (stripped barrow top soil), level 2 (prehistoric surface uncovered at the bottom of the recent ditch). After recording level 2, a part of it has been dug away to create a small profile (no. 4) showing the prehistoric surface covered by the mound at the intersection of the ditch through the mound. Photograph by D.R. Fontijn.

Fig. 3.7 Picture taken from the north, standing in the recent ditch. Visible from left to right are boxes 1 (partly in front) to 4. One of the excavators is carefully digging down in box 3 to prepare level 3, which is to be located around the prehistoric surface covered around the mound. It can be seen that the top soil has now been removed everywhere and that the position of the prehistoric surface has been located in all small profiles that were created at the intersection of ditch and mound. Photograph by R.S. Kok.

Fig. 3.8 Picture taken from the north, standing in the recent ditch. The excavators have now reached level 3 in all visible boxes (2 to 4), and in front the E-W profile 5 is now being cleaned. Mr G. van Heijningen of the Prattenburg estate (front right) inspects the progress. Photograph by L. Theunissen.

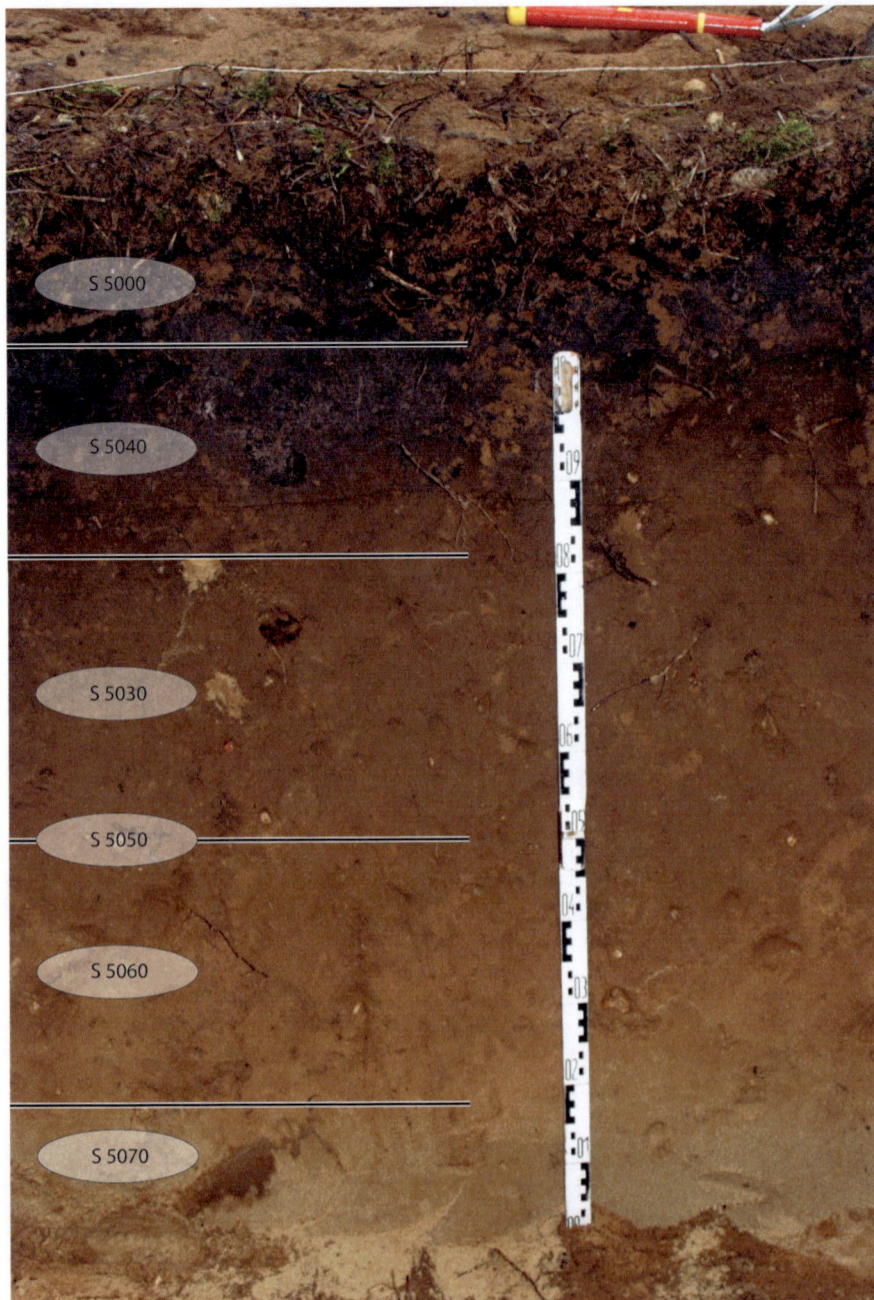

S 5000

S 5040

S 5030

S 5050

S 5060

S 5070

Fig. 3.9 Profile section through the mound (profile 12). S5000: vegetation layer on top of the mound; S5040: Moder Podsolic Soil formed in the top of the mound; S5030: the mound; S5050: prehistoric surface; S5060: prehistoric soil covered by the mound; S5070: sub-soil underneath the mound. Photograph by Q. Bourgeois.

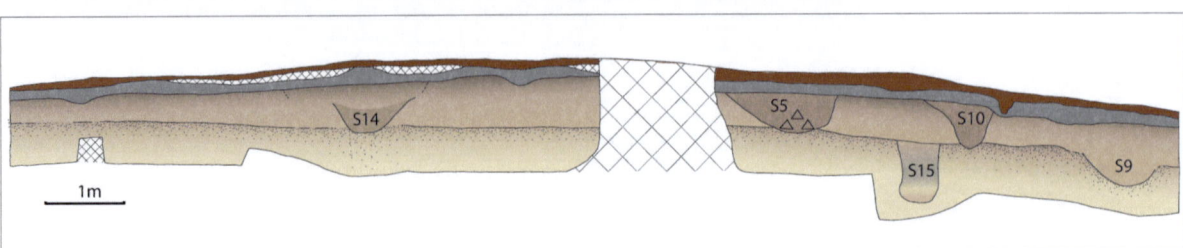

1m

S14

S5

S10

S15

S9

developed Moder Podsolic soil (Dutch: *holtpodsol*; Fig. 3.6). In front of this profile an additional – this time horizontal – surface was prepared in each box at the same level (Fig 3.5-3.6). This is documented as level 2. All of them were photographed. In addition to this, the cleaned surface of level 2 of the southernmost box was also drawn, as this was the only one where an archaeological feature was observed (Fig. 3.11: S4).

Fig. 3.10 North-south profile A (9-11, see Fig. 3.4) with indication of the most important features and the disturbed area (hatched).

Having determined the nature and exact position of the original soil underneath the barrow, made it easier to plan the further excavation of the N-S trench and to recognize the original soil itself underneath the mound. The four boxes were dug out in such a way that there was each time a flat, clean horizontal surface on which potential features could be recorded. In the end a flat clean surface was prepared in each box at the height of the old surface underneath the mound. This is level 3 (Fig. 3.7-3.8 and Fig. 3.17). All were photographed. Two were also drawn (in box 2 and 4), as they displayed traces of archaeological features (Fig. 3.12). In the southernmost box 4 an extra fourth level was prepared to clarify the horizontal stratigraphy of several archaeological features (Fig. 3.13). This fourth level was also photographed and drawn.

We opted for excavation in horizontal, artificial layers rather than following stratigraphical layers for reasons outlined in the previous chapter (section 2.5.2). Digging was done manually with shovels and, sometimes, with trowels. We did not sieve the mound material here as we did in Unitas 1 (section 2.5.3), apart from the location where cremation remains were found (section 3.7.2). Our metal-detectorist, Mr. A. Manders, was continually present. He surveyed each level before it was excavated. No metal was found in the process, but with his detector he was able to indicate the presence of most sherds, and even some stones *before* the actual digging took place. The position of all finds was measured three-dimensionally using the national coordinate grid .

Of the three to four artificial horizontal levels (Dutch: *vlakken*) created, only those that did display features were actually drawn (1: 20). All E-W sections and the entire N-S profile were drawn (1: 20). Unfortunately, a small part of the N-S section collapsed: it appeared to be internally weakened by a disturbance just below the excavated part (*cf.* Fig. 3.10). Here a former depression was filled-in with white sand during the *ROB* restoration.

3.6 Mound stratigraphy and excavation administration of mound `layers´ and finds

A concise description of the mound's stratigraphy is as follows (see also Fig. 3.9 and section 7.4.2[38]). The entire top of the barrow is covered by a layer of leaves and grass (administrated as S5000). Underneath that was the top of a Moder Podsolic soil which developed on top of the barrow (labeled S5040; (coded gY30 in the Dutch classification, see section 1.6.1)). We will later on return to the question whether the soil which developed in the slope that forms the transition of the large ditch to the mound, was formed at the same time as the soil at the top of the undisturbed part of the mound.

The mound itself had a dark brown to brown hue and became gradually lighter downwards (labeled S5030). In the top of the mound the B horizon of the old Moder Podsol soil on top of the barrow is still visible, gradually fading to the bottom of the mound. The barrow consists of mostly sand intermixed with only a few pebbles. The old surface underneath it was clearly visible in most profiles (labeled as S5050) but in places it was bioturbated by beetles. The soil covered by the mound can also be characterized as a Moder Podsolic soil (Dutch: *holtpodsol*). It was administrated as S5060. It is less pronounced as the soil which was formed on top of the barrow. It had a light-brown hue that gradually became more yellowish

---

38 There is a good match between the results of the prospection of the mound with the hand auger by the *RCE* and our interpretation of the profile section. We did not use the same terminology for the subdivision of the top soil as the *RCE* did (sub-classes like A*an* or A*h*) but the same horizons are indicated on the profile drawings.

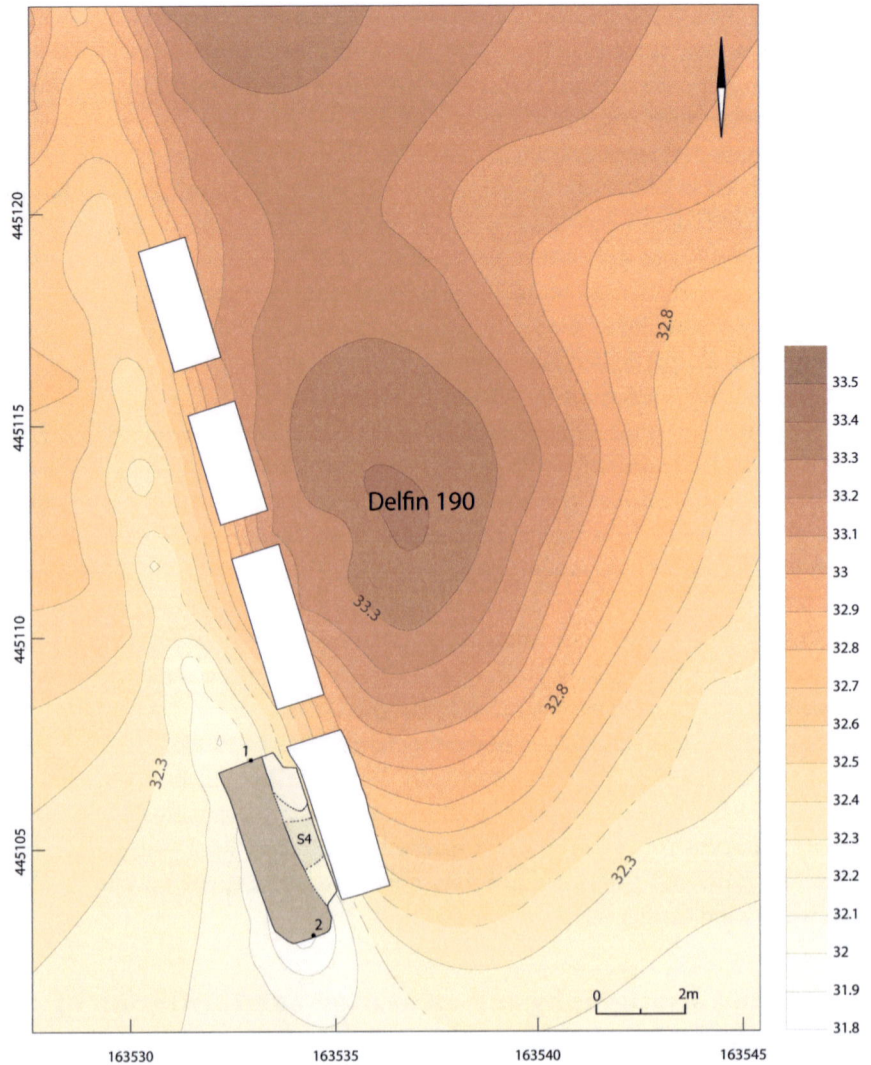

Fig. 3.11 Plan of features found at level 2 (created at the intersection of the ditch and the mound). Visible is the dark fill of the ditch. The only prehistoric feature recognized is S4 in box 4, which could later be linked to S9 at level 3 (ring ditch).

downwards and faded into the sandy matrix of sub-soil (labeled S5070). This soil profile is complete (including an A horizon) and is much better visible than the soil that was covered by the Unitas 1 mound (section 2.2 and section 2.8).

3.7 Features and associated finds

3.7.1 General: 'readability' of features

The *holtpodsol*, the type of soil that developed in this type of sediment lacks a grey leached-out or eluvial horizon (E horizon) and as a whole does not have clearly separated horizons at all. Rather, it is characterized by a faint light brown shade of which the boundaries cannot be precisely pinpointed. As might be expected, the sediment of which the mound was constructed consists of material from the ice-pushed ridge, and is, by its very nature, heterogeneous. Fine sand, patches of loam, gravel and even boulders have been found in it. This lithological heterogeneity and the less outspoken soils make it in general much harder to recognize archaeological features than in the case of barrows built out of cover sand sediments on Humus-Podsol soils like at Oss-Zevenbergen (Fokkens *et al.* 2006). Faint traces are particularly hard to recognize at the surface and might be easily missed while digging down (*cf.* 3.14-3.15 and Fig. 3.17). The same applies to the situation at Unitas 1, with two differences. The first is that the soil covered by

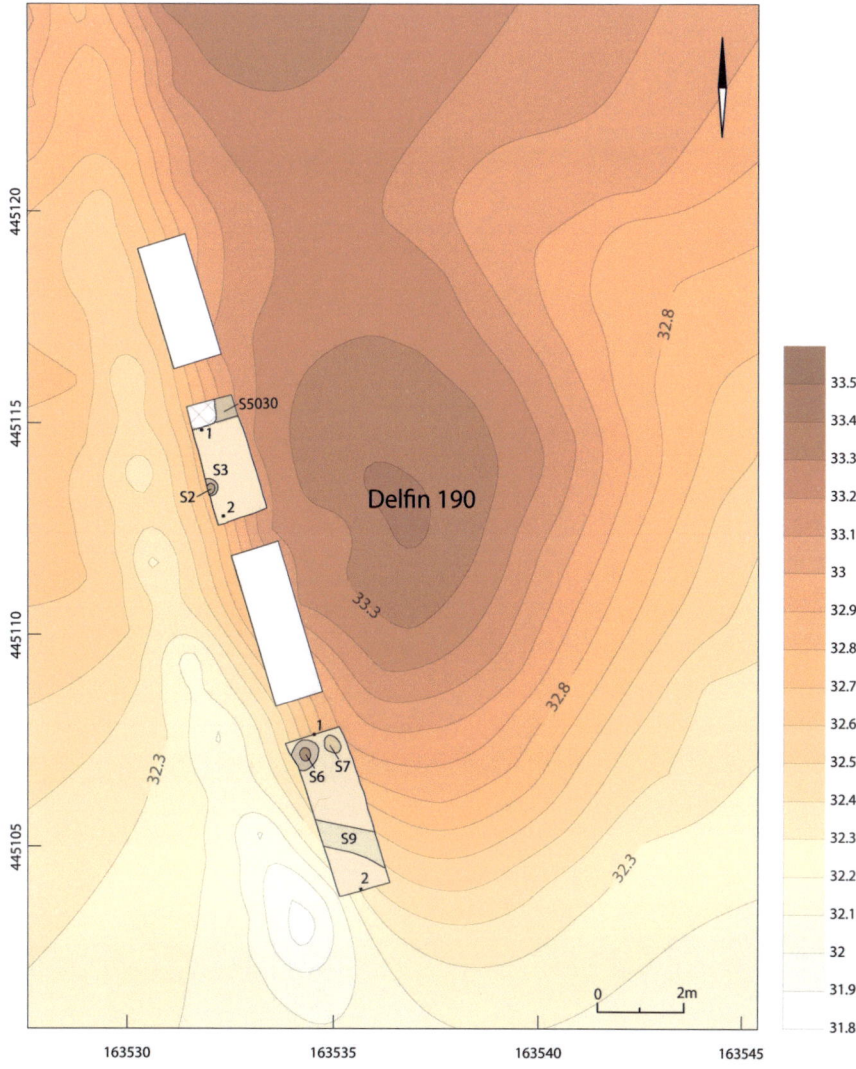

Fig. 3.12 Plan of features recognized at level 3 (created around the prehistoric surface covered by the mound).

the mound was better observable in the case of Delfin 190. The second is that the lithology in the excavated part underneath the Delfin 190 was not as heterogenic as it was in the case of Unitas 1. This made it easier to distinguish archaeological features underneath the mound. In retrospect, the chosen strategy in which several horizontal levels were created to be inspected for potential archaeological features like secondary graves was the best way to detect such faint traces.

3.7.2 An urned cremation burial dug into the mound

While deepening excavation box 3 towards the old surface (level 3), several small fragments of cremation remains (bone fragments) and pottery sherds were found close to the N-S profile. They were inside the fill of a pit, the cross-section of which was visible in the N-S profile itself (administrated as feature S (from the Dutch *Spoor*) 5; see Fig. 3.10). Although the surface was shoveled clean to look for traces of the horizontal extension of this pit, no convincing traces could be identified. This relates to the fact that traces are very hard to read here due to the later discolorations of the ground by the B horizon of the soil which formed at the top of the mound. The sherds are of a single hand-made undecorated quartz-tempered pot that will be described in detail in section 5.2. It can be dated to the Middle Bronze Age (Fig. 5.3).

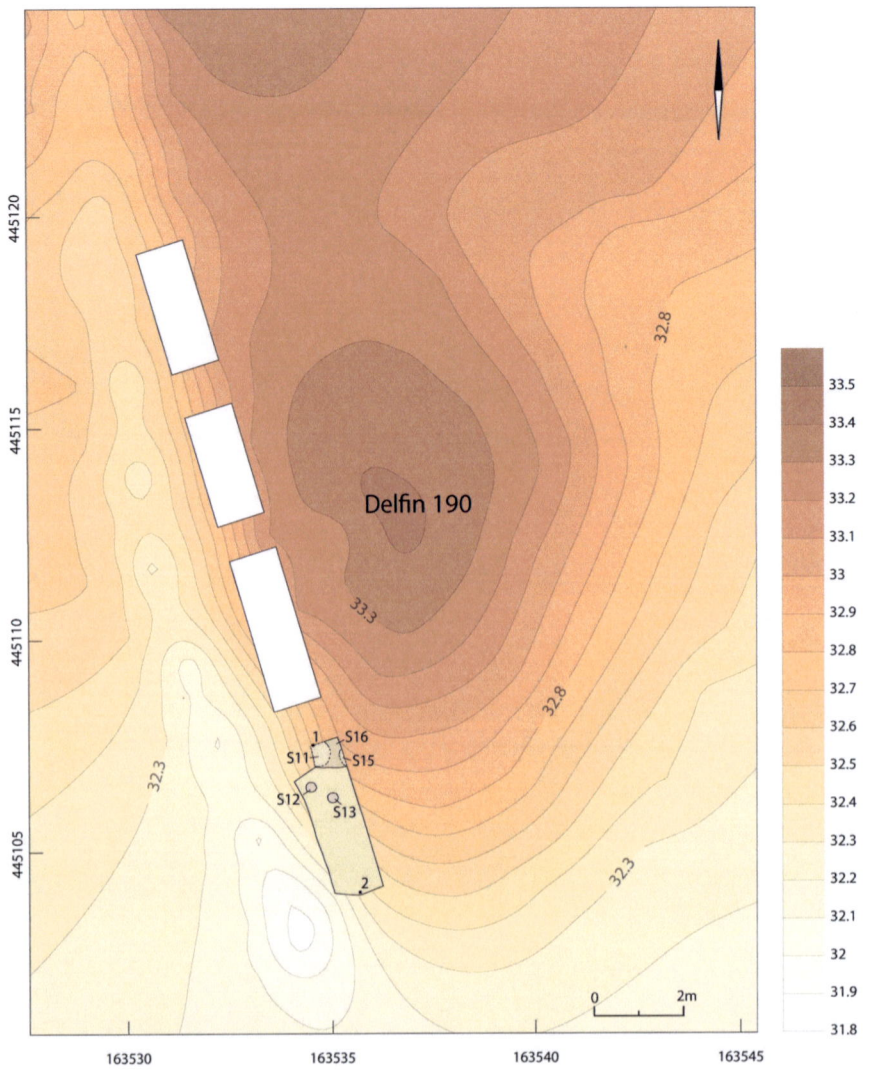

Fig. 3.13 Plan of features recognized at level 4 (c. 10 cm below the prehistoric surface covered by the mound).

In the profile section, the grave pit had a grey-brown fill, the observed part is 50 cm deep and had a diameter of at least 1.4 m. As it is partly in the unexcavated part of the mound, its precise shape cannot be determined. The profile clearly shows that it was dug into the mound from the surface. The sherds are from the same pot, and cremation remains and sherds must have been deposited at the same time. We assume that the pot served as an urn for the cremated remains. The entire fill of the excavated pit was sieved (mesh width of 4 mm), and yielded

Fig. 3.14 Profile 12. Picture taken from the west. Vaguely visible is S14, dug into the top of the mound to the left. Note that the presence of this pit fill resulted into a marked – and much better visible – dip in the b horizon below. Photograph by Q. Bourgeois.

Fig. 3.15 Profile 11. Picture taken from the west. Visible are S10 (left; dug from the top of the mound), the fill of what probably was the mound's ring ditch (S9, to the right). The top of pit fill S15 (not dug out yet) is vaguely visible in the left corner. Photograph by Q. Bourgeois.

cremated bone[39]. We assume that more sherds and bone fragments are still in the unexcavated profile section itself. As remarked in section 3.4.2, Ms Ch. Delfin also found sherds and cremated remains in a disturbance in the top of the mound in 1970. A comparison of these sherds and those found by us showed that they are similar (section 5.2). Although no sherds of both finds could be refitted, we assume that they belong to one and the same urn. When visiting our excavation, Ms Delfin herself told us that she found these sherds and cremation remains somewhere in the part that we were excavating. At that time, we still had not told her of our find!

This Middle Bronze Age urn with cremated remains must be interpreted as a burial that was later dug into the surface of the mound. Such later interments are very frequent for the Middle Bronze Age (Drenth/Lohof 2005). It provides a clear *terminus ante quem*-dating for the construction of the mound.

3.7.3 Other pits dug into the mound's surface

Next to the pit with the cremation remains, traces of two more pits were found that were also dug into the barrow (S14 to the north and S10 to the south; measuring 90 cm by 35 cm and 90 cm by 55 cm respectively – see Fig. 3.10 and Fig. 3.14). Their fill is comparable to that of the pit with the urned cremation, and soil formation both around and on top of these features shows that we are dealing here with traces of relatively old, probably prehistoric, activities. They did not yield finds, but scattered throughout excavation box 2, six fragments of handmade undecorated grit-tempered pottery was found (see section 5.3.3; find no.12, 17, 18, 22 and 42), of which one was decorated with the *Kalenderberg*-style of decoration (find no.15; Fig. 5.5). Unfortunately, these finds cannot be more precisely dated than to the Late Bronze Age-Iron Age or even Roman Period. The fact that such find concentrations could originate on the top of the mound, suggests that the mound was used for certain activities by that time, the nature of which we can only guess at. It might well be possible that the digging of small pits like S14 and the sherd debris may reflect contemporary or even related activities.

---

39 The bone fragments were inspected by dr Liesbeth Smits (University of Amsterdam) in a quick scan, and interpreted as remains of a human adult. Less than 100 g was collected but bone fragments were also found by Miss Ch. Delfin and the remainer of the grave is still within the mound itself. The determination is not based on the entire content of the grave.

3.7.4 Mound construction

On the top of the excavated slope, a *holtpodsol* soil had formed (see 1.6.1 and Fig. 3.9). This topsoil contained a number of sherds, all of which can be dated to the Iron Age or Roman Period, as well as a few flint flakes and a flint thumb scraper (S5040; for description of the finds see section 5.1). These finds lack a clear context, and there are indications that sherds were secondarily moved. One sherd displays gnawing traces of a mouse, evidencing disturbance by bioturbation. The other reason to be cautious is that the top of the mound might represent a spoil heap of mound construction material that was removed and dumped when the ditch was dug in the 19th century AD. This is not very likely, however, as nothing in the way of an additional layer of excavated material on top of the mound is visible in the profiles. Alternatively, the material may represent (Iron Age/Roman Period) activities taking place on the top of the mound (section 2.7.5). This would be in line with the many amateur finds of Iron Age/Roman Period sherds found at and near the mound long before our excavation took place (section 3.4.2 and see section 5.7 for a description of these finds).

Within the mound itself, no sods could be distinguished. This is not to say that no sods were used in the build-up of the mound, but it is likely that sods were cut from ground with poorly developed soil, hence making them hardly recognizable when stacked to form a mound. Also, secondary soil processes (they are within the B horizon of the modern soil formed at the top of the mound) might have erased any traces of them. The mound construction material consist of sand intermixed with a few pebbles. This reflects the lithology immediately around the mound, and it seems therefore likely that the material with which the mound was constructed was obtained in its immediate vicinity. The mound material is similar from top to bottom and there is no evidence for different mound construction layers.

Several prehistoric sherds and a few flint flakes were found in the mound construction material (S5030; finds to be described in 5.3). A number of them can be dated to the Middle Bronze Age period, a few of which can be placed in its earliest phase, the *Hilversum* pottery phase (5.3.2). Other finds date to the Late Bronze Age, or (late) Iron Age or Roman Period (5.3.3). For the Middle Bronze Age sherds and flint flakes, it is likely that they ended up here as inclusions in the mound construction material. The Iron Age/Roman Period sherds must be interpreted as later intrusions, transported vertically by bioturbation (tree roots, digging of mice), following the erosion of the steep slope of the mound that resulted from the digging activities carried out for the construction of the ditch (see further 5.3.4).

As the A horizon of the soil profile covered by the mound has been preserved (in contrast to what seems to be the case for Unitas 1) the old soil was not truncated before the erection of the mound.

3.7.5 A peripheral ditch (S4 and S9)

In the southernmost excavation box, traces of a 95 cm wide and 45 cm deep filled-in ditch were observed. The ditch was dug in from the same height as the prehistoric surface, and is located around the edge of the mound. The ditch fill was first discovered on the cleaned surface of level 2 (Fig. 3.11) where it was recorded as S4. Later, it could be continued at level 3 in the adjacent box 4, where the ditch fill was recorded as S9 (Fig. 3.12). Hereafter, we will refer to the ring ditch feature as S9.

It is marked by a vague light grey discoloration, which makes that it hardly contrasts with the light subsoil (see Fig. 3.15 and Fig. 3.17). Its color is different from that of the pit fills that were found underneath the mound in the same excavation box to its west, which contrasted much better (S6 and S7; see 3.7.6). The interpretation of this feature as a ditch fill could be corroborated when the N-S profile section was inspected. The ditch fill was examined for finds. Three very tiny sherds (< 6 mm) and two flint flakes were found, as well as several tiny specks of charcoal (see section 5.4). As these sherds are tempered with quartz, it is likely that they are fragments of Middle Bronze Age pottery. Their small size precludes any further determination. These charcoal fragments have not been selected for C14-dating. They do not derive from posts placed in the ditch, and their C14-age would at best substantiate a *terminus post quem*-dating.

In view of its position around the edge of the mound, we may interpret this feature as the remnants of a peripheral ditch that is known from many other barrows (Drenth/Lohof 2005, 440). Its cross-section, width and depth are comparable to the ditch segment that was observed during the *AWN* excavations at the eastern part of this mound (Fig. 3.3). To find indications whether the traces the *AWN* had seen indeed are to be interpreted as a ring ditch was one of the question we had when we started (section 1.5). Both ditch fills are situated around the place where the constructed mound ends, but it should be emphasized that in both cases, it is not entirely clear whether the ditch is situated just *outside* the mound (as a true peripheral structure), or is situated just *underneath* the mound (as a ditch pre-dating the construction of the mound – an intermediary structure, cf. Drenth/Lohof 2005, 440). In the latter case, it might have been a temporary structure related to the funerary ritual (*cf.* Lohof 1991, 56), or a feature of earlier occupation at this site like the pit traces that were found underneath the barrow in the neighboring northern excavation box (see below, section 3.7.6). The latter explanation is less likely, in view of the fact that the discoloration of the ditch fill differs from those pre-barrow pits. Also, a ring ditch, be it underneath or outside the mound, is a common feature of Middle Bronze Age barrows.

A pendant to this ditch (S9) might be expected at the northern side of the mound. No such feature was found in our northernmost excavation box, but it might well be that we have not reached the end of the mound here yet. The irregular shape of the mound makes it very hard to see where the mound ends, particularly in this northwestern corner, probably because of the disturbances caused by sand extraction. We did not have the time or means to extend our trench with a few meters to check where the mound ends and to see if traces of a ring ditch are to be found in the northern section as well.

The excavated ditch fragment does not show the kind of bend that might be expected when we were excavating a *ring* ditch, and its horizontal shape shows that it extends in westernmost position, even west of the gully. If S9 represents a peripheral ditch around a round barrow, then the modern ditch cuts through the mound, instead of bypassing it. Also, it means that the mound originally extended to the west of the gully. Nowadays, there is not the slightest elevation to be seen to its west, implying that the last remains of the mound west of the gully were removed, either with the digging of the modern ditch, or during the sand extraction in the 1980s. This would explain why the mound nowadays has such a remarkable oval shape. Our hypothesis that S9 represents a peripheral structure can be tested by new excavations west of the modern ditch.

In view of its position, its different fill and discoloration, and the fact that the *AWN*-excavation detected a comparable ditch fill at the eastern flank in a comparable position, we see the interpretation of S9 as a peripheral (ring) ditch as the most probable one. However, as emphasized above, there is also reason for doubt and only a more extensive excavation of the site can corroborate or refute this hypothesis.

3.7.6 Features underneath the mound

One of the more interesting discoveries of this excavation is the recognition of several features located *underneath* the barrow. These features were clearly covered by the barrow and are thus older than its construction. The features were first observed on the third level in box 2 and box 4 (Fig. 3.12). In the latter box, they were not very clear at that level, and for that reason we decided to deepen level 3 by 10 cm thus obtaining a fourth level (Fig. 3.13 and Fig. 3.17).

Box 2

In box 2, one pit (S3) containing the traces of a post (S2) was discovered. The pit and post respectively had a width of 80 and 20 cm. The depth of the post traces was 40 cm. In its light brown color, they are comparable to the traces in the southernmost box 4, yet they did not contain any finds.

Box 4: level 3

In box 4 we were confronted with a complex stratigraphy. At the transition of the mound to the prehistoric surface, a contrasting discoloration was observed. The outline of the round pits S6 and S7 was by then not yet visible. In this discoloration, later recorded as S16, a flint barbed-and-tanged arrowhead was found (V88; section 5.5.1; Fig. 5.2). Only a few cm deeper, we recognized the outline of two round pits: S6 and S7 (Fig. 3.12). Around S6, representing traces of a post, a broad discoloration was visible that may have been connected with the discoloration of S16 a few cm higher. In retrospect, it seems likely that once pits S6 and S7 were filled in , there was a slight depression at this place due to soil compaction. Because of this slight dip in the surface, the first layers of the mound are situated somewhat deeper here than in other places. This explains the discoloration. The Late Neolithic arrowhead probably was part of the sods with which the mound was built. Alternatively, it might have been an artefact that had been lying on the surface, and ended up in the uppermost fill of S6 (see below). As the transition of S16 into the top fill of S6 is unclear, we cannot be sure where exactly this arrowhead was located.

The features that became visible are S6 and S7. S6 is a remarkable, large pit containing the traces of a post. Its dark grey-brownish color is in contrast to the lighter colors of both the mound and the substrate. S7 is slightly lighter. The width and depth of the pits are respectively 68 and 38 cm, whereas the discoloration indicating the position of a post in S6 is relatively large: its diameter measures 38 cm. Pit S6 was filled with a remarkably large number of sherds (470 g), burnt loam, charcoal flint and 1.4 kg of (burnt) stones (see section 5.5). They were found in the place where we would expect the post itself, which is highly uncommon and must indicate that the post was removed and its hole filled with debris. All sherds are from the top fill, whereas the flint was all found in the second fill. This indicates that the hole was first partly filled in or silted up, to have debris swept in the last remaining depression, perhaps at a later stage. All sherds can be dated to the Middle Bronze Age. A few provide a key to a more refined dating: they are characteristic for the *Hilversum* phase of the Middle Bronze Age-A, giving us an idea of the time in which the pits were formed and filled. It is also noteworthy that half of the sherds and many of the stones and flint show traces of burning. Detailed information is given in section 5.5 and Fig. 5.4.

Pit S7 has a diameter of 22 cm and a depth of some 25 cm. Its outlines were less well-defined than those from S6. It contained 500 g of fire-cracked stones and only one wall sherd, the fabric of which is comparable to those from S6. It is possible that it was also a posthole feature like S6, but we are not entirely certain of that.

Box 4: level 4

By then, we were of the opinion that we had reached the last level with archaeological traces. However, once we made a section through S6 (excavating its western part), we noticed that there were more traces at a deeper level: we could see a grayish discoloration around the pit of S6. Creating a new level 4, some 15-20 cm deeper, we found two new traces of postholes to the north again with a dark grey-brownish colour (S12 and S13; Fig. 3.13). These represent the bottom of two posthole fills that were apparently not yet visible at level 3 for some reason. S12 has a diameter of 17 cm and a depth of only 5 cm, whilst S13 has a diameter of 23 and a depth of 12 cm. Here, a discoloration indicating the former presence of a (wooden) round post was recognizable (diameter 8 cm). No finds were done in the fill of S12 and S13.

In the zone where S6 and S7 were seen at level 3, at level 4 we now first observed a grayish discoloration identical to S16 noted earlier (interpreted as the depression). Shoveling this discoloration, the outlines of two new large features were found c. 5 cm deeper: pit fills S11 and S15. It is important to stress that these two features are actually situated *underneath* S16, since Fig. 3.13 might give the impression that they intersect S16. S11 and S15 appeared to be two large pit fills both with different layers. How are they to be linked with the traces of S6 and S7 at a higher level? This was not immediately apparent during the excavation. Analyzing the feature drawings and photographs, we now think that S6 and S7 are the remains of two posts placed immediately to the side of two comparable large pits.

S11 is 80 cm deep and has a diameter of 65 cm (Fig. 3.16). It contained a number of burnt and fire-cracked stones and 266 g of secondarily burnt and weathered wall sherds. In fabric, these are comparable to those found in S6, and one of the sherds has a wall decoration typical for the Middle Bronze Age A *Hilversum* phase (see section 5.5.4 and Fig. 5. 4). Although there are five different fill layers, the top and the lowest layers 4 and 5 hardly contain anything other than sand: all finds are concentrated in layers 2 and 3. Again, this indicates that the pit had been open for a longer time, gradually silting up. From time to time, material was dumped into it.

S15, the largest part of which is situated outside our excavation trench, then, is 75 cm deep and approximately 50 cm in diameter (Fig. 3.10). It had four different fills, but just one Middle Bronze Age wall sherd (13 g) and no stones or flint were found.

Conclusion: a *Hilversum*-phase Middle Bronze Age pit cluster

Summing up, we found a cluster of pits and posthole traces. A number (S6, S7, S11) contains Middle Bronze Age sherds of similar fabric. For finds from S6 and S11 typology of some sherds indicates that they date to the *Hilversum* phase of the Middle Bronze Age, c. 1800-1600 BC (see also section 5.5). There were two deep rectangular pits (S11 and S15), both probably flanked by posts. If there was

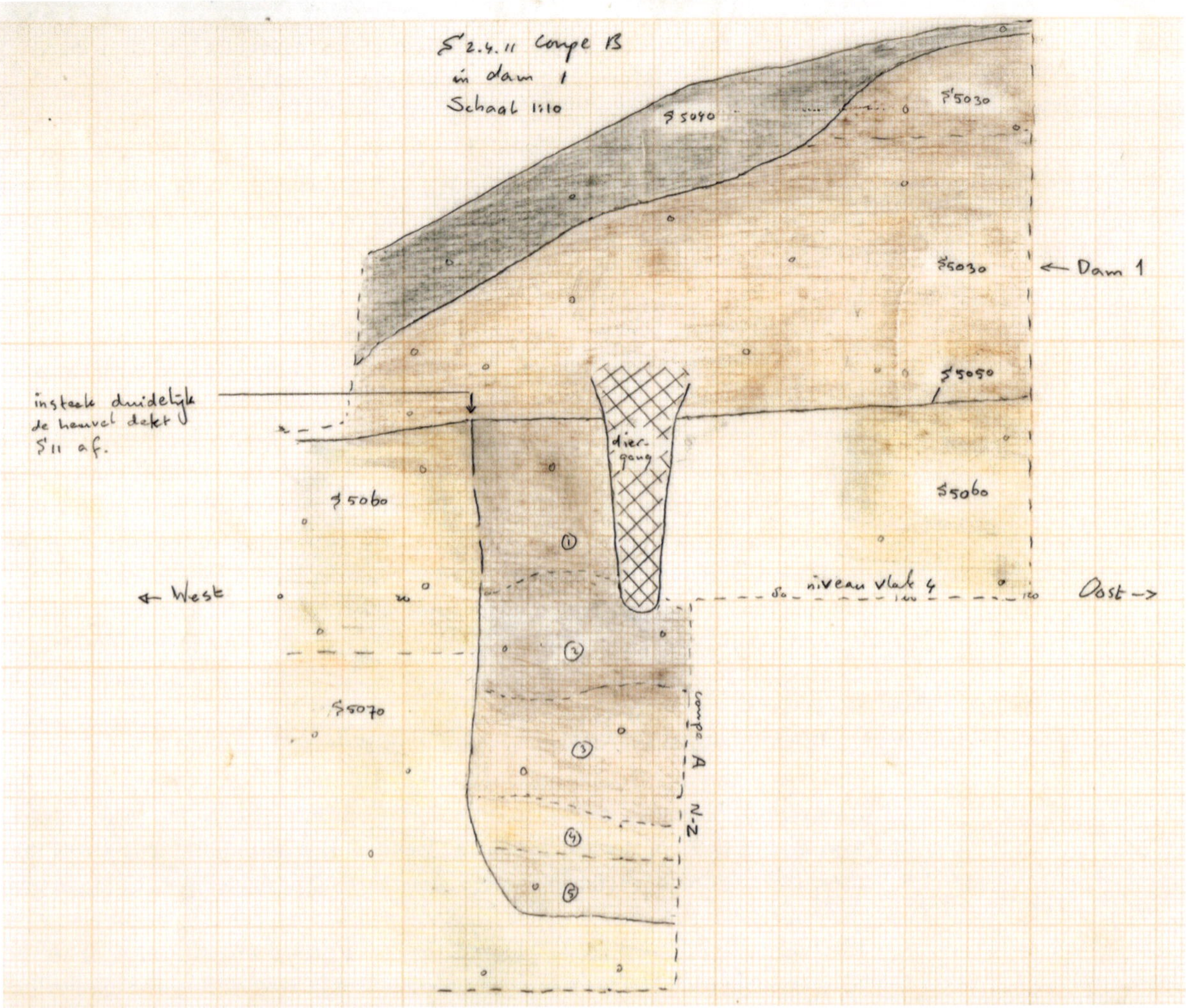

a functional relation between those features remains unclear, but they all date to the same phase and therefore are likely to represent one complex. S6, S7, and S11 contain similar material: non-fitting sherds many of which were secondarily burnt and wheathered, fire-cracked stones and sometimes burnt and unburnt flint. In the case of S6 and S11, we can see that it was not dumped in those pits in one moment, but from time to time. S15 also shows evidence of separate fills. We seem to be dealing with pits constructed for a specific – yet unknown – purpose, that were later on gradually filled in with debris of *e.g.* food preparation ending up in pits. The finds do not reflect *in situ* activities taking place within the pits. The clustering of features on such a small surface is remarkable, but the limited size of the excavation precludes any further interpretation of these traces in terms of a structure. Yet, they indicate a specific activity area that we would expect on a settlement. The traces of a post in the northern box 2 might well be contemporary. At any rate is it also situated underneath the mound. The dating of these features in the *Hilversum* phase of the Middle Bronze Age, is interesting. A recent overview shows that *Hilversum* phase settlement sites are very rare in the Low Countries (Arnoldussen/Fontijn 2006, 307).

It is conspicuous that we have such a dense concentration of pits and posts in such a small area (our box 4 does not exceed 3.50 by 1.30 m). Most features seem to be contemporary and to have had comparable, yet unknown primary functions (two deep rectangular pits, flanked by posts). The larger pits also underwent a comparable process of filling-in: they had been open for a while, gradually silting up, to be used as a dump for comparable material used elsewhere: a mixture of burnt and unburnt *Hilversum* pottery sherds, cooking stones and some burnt and un-burnt flint. Both in primary and secondary (refuse dump) function, we may therefore speak of a similar activity area: a pit and post cluster. With some exceptions (Arnoldussen 2008), Dutch archaeology has not paid much attention to pit clusters at Middle Bronze Age settlements. Yet, particularly in the *Elst-Rhenen* area, we now have more evidence for such pit clusters. At the nearby *Elst 't Bosje* site, a contemporary and comparable *Hilversum* phase pit cluster was recognized (Meurkens 2009a, 49-52, pit cluster 1 and 2; Fig .5.14; see Chapter 9 and Fig. 9.3 in this book). Here, we are also dealing with a dense cluster of pits that are rectangular in section and have a flat bottom. Like in our case, the excavators also argue that they were first used for one particular activity, to end their life as refuse dumps. A few kilometers to the east, at the *Rhenen-Remmerden* site, several pit clusters were recognized at the excavation of a Bronze Age settlement (Van Hoof/ Meurkens 2005, 23). Our pits S11 and S15 are comparable to the "medium" type in the pit shape typology designed for this excavation. Interestingly, here these pits also are rectangular in section, have a flat bottom and separate fills (three in this case). A difference, however, is that the deepest fill of the *Rhenen-Remmerden* pits always seem to contain a dark, charcoal-filled layer, related to the primary use of this pit. This is clearly lacking in the case of pits like S11 and S15 underneath the Delfin 190 mound. At any rate, we now have evidence for the existence of pit clusters on more than one Bronze Age settlement sites in this area. All these sites show that these pit clusters represent a specific activity area within the settlement, and hence a specific structuring of settlement space that is so far rarely known from archaeological literature. The *Rhenen-Remmerden* and *Elst 't Bosje* evidence makes it more plausible that the clustering of pits and posts in box 4 of Delfin 190 represents a similar phenomenon. By the same token, we may expect the traces of a Middle Bronze Age (A) settlement under and around the Delfin 190 mound.

3.8 Conclusion

The main goal of the excavation was to unravel the confusing dating evidence of the earlier excavation and stray finds, which indicated that both in the Late Neolithic, Middle Bronze Age and (late) Iron Age or Roman Period people had been using this mound. On the basis of our own excavation and study of the finds done by amateur archaeologists, we arrive at the following reconstruction of the history of this burial mound.

The site and/or its immediate vicinity might have been used during the Bell Beaker Period. This is suggested by the find of a Bell Beaker arrowhead which we found in secondary position as well as by the find of two Pot Beaker sherds

Fig. 3.16 Original excavation drawing of W-E section through S11 by C. van der Linde. The pit fill S11 is still covered by a part of the mound (profile 6). Clearly visible are the separate fills of the pit.

Fig. 3.17 Profile 3 (the small profile in front) and 11 (the high profile in the back) from the west. The excavation box has been deepened until level 3. The first traces of S6 (situated on top of the pit fill S11) are visible in the front corner to the left of the excavation box. The vague, light fill of the ring ditch S9 is visible in the right of the excavation box. Photograph by Q. Bourgeois.

found in the mound during the *AWN* mini-excavation of 1971, that were either left on the surface covered by the mound or included in the mound construction material. As for the Pot Beaker sherds, it cannot be excluded that they date to the younger Early Bronze Age (see section 5.6). We did not find features dating to either the Bell Beaker period or Early Bronze Age, and in our view the arguments for a Bell Beaker Period dating used by Van Tent (the presence of the Pot Beaker sherds in the mound) do not stand up to scrutiny. Since both we and our *AWN* colleagues only excavated the periphery of the mound, there is still the – so far totally unproven! – possibility that a small core barrow was built here during the Bell Beaker Period, which was extended during the Middle Bronze Age. It might then be that both we ourselves and the *AWN* have only excavated the *later* barrow extensions.

At any rate, all the evidence we found during the 2006 excavation proves that the excavated part of the Delfin 190 mound was constructed much later than the Bell Beaker Period/Early Bronze Age: during the Middle Bronze Age.

During the Middle Bronze Age-A *Hilversum* phase (*c*.1800-1600 BC) there probably was a settlement at this site. This is based on our discovery of traces of pits and posts and postholes dating to the *Hilversum* phase, that were clearly covered by the mound, and thus ante-dating it. The pit fills contained remains of domestic debris, and although the excavated trench is just a very small one, the nature of the finds (debris of domestic activities like food preparation) and features (refuse pits) suggests that the barrow was constructed on a former Middle Bronze Age-A *Hilversum* settlement site. This is in itself a special find, as *Hilversum* settlement sites are relatively rare in the Netherlands (Arnoldussen/Fontijn 2006; Theunissen 1999) .

Later during the Middle Bronze Age, a barrow was built at this site. Building a Middle Bronze Age barrow on a Middle Bronze Age settlement site is not very common (see the recent inventory in Bourgeois/Fontijn 2008). It is therefore an intriguing question what motivated people to locate it here: was a barrow deliberately built upon a farmyard, as has been argued for the case of the barrow of *Geldermalsen-De Bogen* (Bourgeois/Fontijn 2008, 51-4; Meijlink 2008)? As long as nothing is known on the central grave, as well as on character of the settlement on which it was built, not much can be said on this topic.

There is no evidence that the original surface was leveled or truncated (as probably happened at Unitas 1): the construction material (sods or otherwise, this cannot be determined) was directly placed at the old surface, thus sealing off the older Middle Bronze Age settlement features. In view of the lithological similarities between the mound construction sand and the sand in the subsoil surrounding it, the mound was probably built with material from the immediate vicinity. This may explain why Middle Bronze Age sherds, again including *Hilversum* pottery, were sometimes found in it. The part we excavated must have been constructed in one phase; there is no evidence for different construction layers. The mound was probably ringed by a ditch, of which both we and our AWN-colleagues in 1971 uncovered a section. Such ditches are very common around Middle Bronze Age burial mounds. The mound was used for a secondary burial of an urned cremation grave later in the Middle Bronze Age. This is the urn of which one part was found by Ms Ch. Delfin, and the other part by us. The presence of this urn, dug into the mound from the top, provides us with a *terminus ante quem* – dating for its construction. The mound, then, must have been constructed after or during the later phase of the Middle Bronze Age-A *Hilversum* pottery stage (up until *c*. 16th century BC), but before the Late Bronze Age (*c.* 1100 BC). Using Middle Bronze Age mounds as locations for new burials, often not after a long period of time, is very common in the Middle Bronze Age. Lohof (1994, 102) argues that the relative short time interval between the use of barrows for different burials means that people had an adequate knowledge of the deceased who were buried in it.

A number of finds that can be dated roughly to the Iron Age or Roman Period, in some cases more precisely to the Late Iron Age/early Roman Period (Chapter 5) indicates a new period of activity around the Delfin 190 mound after more than a millennium. Although many of the finds lack a clear context, most are consistently found at or close to the barrow. The digging in of two pits into the flank of the mound might be related to these activities. The sherds, and a fragment of a glass La Tène bracelet, are similar to material normally found in settlements. Similar finds were done in and around the Unitas 1 mound and its surroundings (Ch. 2 and 4). We will see later on that the entire *Elsterberg* barrow group saw intensive activity during the later Iron Age/Roman Period.

The barrow seems to have been left alone for at least eighteen hundred years afterwards, until the moment that a large ditch was dug through its western flank, presumably in the 19th century *AD*. This ditch destroyed at least a quarter of the barrow, and we argued that it is largely responsible for the strange shape of the present-day barrow. The steep slope at the transition from the mound to the 19th century ditch thus was formed as a result of these recent digging activities. The moder Podzol soil (S5040) in the top of this steep slope therefore developed quite recently. In 1971 the barrow was excavated by the *AWN*, and some ten years later a large part of the barrow was used as a source of sand for the paths through the forest. The remaining gaps were finally filled in with white sand during a restoration in 1987. After the excavation of the flank of the mound in 2006, the trenches were immediately filled in. Today, the location of our trenches is again overgrown and can hardly be recognized anymore.

Chapter 4

FINDS FROM THE UNITAS 1 MOUND AND ITS SURROUNDINGS

Q. Bourgeois, D. Fontijn, A. Louwen,
P. Valentijn, K. Wentink

This chapter will describe all finds recoverd during the 2006 excavation of Unitas 1. This will be done according to useful archaeological contexts (for example: the fill of ditch S19) that were recognized during the analysis of the features and have been discussed in chapter 2. We will describe them starting with finds from the highest and ending with those from the lowest levels.

In addition to this, we have also tried to retrieve and study as much as possible other artefacts found in or around this mound. These are finds from the *AWN-*excavation of 1971, survey finds from members of the research group of amateur archaeologists of *Rhenen*, the *Werkgroep Archeologie Rhenen* (hereafter *WAR*), including many finds recovered by Ms Ch. Delfin herself, and the special find of the Pot Beaker by Mr J. Mom. These finds were retrieved in the Provincial Depot and the *Rhenen* Museum *'t Rondeel*. Most of the finds lack inventory numbers. We will therefore refer to them with the text written on the attached labels[40].

Finds from our own excavation will be referred to with the administrative find number (Dutch *Vondstnummer,* hereafter: "V"). As we worked with one find administration for the entire excavation of Delfin 190 and Unitas 1, find numbers 1 to 100 were reserved for Delfin 190, and numbers starting from V100 for Unitas 1. Several stored finds appeared to be of natural origin and are not further discussed here. The material was studied by different people, and brought together and edited by D. Fontijn. Flint artefacts, Iron Age/Roman Period indigenous hand-made pottery and positively identified Pot Beaker pottery, Barbed-Wire Beaker and Bronze Age pottery are each described separately. Each author is mentioned in the section heading written by him. All sherds described are of hand-made pottery, unless stated otherwise.

4.1 Finds recoverd from the mound *(by D. Fontijn, A. Louwen, and K. Wentink)*

4.1.1 Finds from level 1 and 2: Iron Age/Roman Period pottery and an unidentified sherd

Four wall sherds were recovered while removing the topsoil of the mound (V101, 102, 104, and 107) (approximately ten centimetres into the mound). None of the finds can be related to a feature. All are potgrit-tempered. Two are too small to allow further determination (V101 and 102). V104 and 107 are two undecorated

---

40 Retrieving these finds was impossible without the help offered by drs Ton van Rooijen (*Utrecht Erfgoed*), drs Bert Huiskes (*Rhenen* Museum), drs Ruurd Kok (province of *Utrecht*), Edwin van Hagen (*WAR*) and drs Mirella de Jong (*Provinciaal Depot Utrecht*). We are grateful to them all.

sherds, of which the latter has a smitten (*besmeten*) [41] surface. The sherds can be dated to the Iron Age or Roman Period on the basis of their tempering material, general similarities in fabric and the presence of a smitten (*besmeten*) surface.

At level 2, three small finds were done that cannot be attributed to a feature. Level 2 is some 10 cm underneath level 1 so they are not very much deeper in the mound than those described above. These three finds were all found by sieving the western strip of ground (section 2.5.3). One is a small hump of burnt loam (V113), another one is a small undecorated wall sherd, tempered with potgrit. This sherd also contains some sand (V112). It is not clear whether this is tempering material or a natural constituent of the clay used. The sherd can be attributed to the Iron Age or Roman Period and is not unlike any of the other Iron Age/Roman Period sherds described above and in section 4.2. A third one is very different (V114). It is a small undecorated wall sherd that is deviant from the rest by its fine mineral temper (smaller than 1 mm and distributed in a clearly larger concentration than in the sherd of V112). It is also different by its yellow color (oxidized on outer and inner side). Comparable light colors and mineral temper are known from the Pot Beaker and Barbed Wire Beaker pottery sherds described in this chapter, but both the dense concentration of mineral temper and its thinness (8 mm) are different. We are not sure how this sherd should be dated.

All finds may have ended up in the top of the mound as a result of activities during that period, and some will have worked their way downwards into the mound as a result of bioturbation (tree roots) and trampling. Iron Age or native Roman Period pottery has also been found as stray finds on its top (4.5.1), in its immediate surroundings (4.5.2), close to the Delfin 190 mound (5.1) and in the highest levels of the latter mound (5.7.2).

4.1.2 Tiny Iron Age/Roman Period sherds, flint flakes and charcoal from level 3

V116, V121, 126 and V127 are all tiny sherds (c. 10 by 15 mm or smaller) found relatively deep in the mound, at level 3. Tempering material is not visible but is probably potgrit. They are similar to the sherds found in the ditch fill of S19 (discussed below). It is likely that these finds also date to the Iron Age or Roman Period rather than any other period of prehistory. They cannot be related to any feature and – considering their small size – it is well possible that they ended up in these positions in the mound's body as intrusions by bioturbation of animals or roots of trees. The same must apply to a small piece of charcoal (originally part of a branch?) found by sieving ground from level 3 (V152).

Two small un-retouched flint flakes were found as well (V125 and V143). They can also not be related to any feature. They are made of typically northern flint that was transported here by the *Saalien* glaciers and can be recognized as such by the rather glassy texture, or the presence of fossilized *bryozoa* (Verhart 2005, 81). Moreover due to glacial activity the nodules of flint found locally are all relatively small and of poor quality [42]. They are un-retouched and lack typo-chronological characteristics. One has been lightly burnt (V125). They might have been part of the material with which the mound was constructed or were included by later processes of bioturbation.

---

41   Before the pot went into the kiln, wet clay was thrown to its outer walls creating a rough irregular surface. This is not the same as a roughened surface, where material is removed in order to create a rough surface. As this practice is not easily translated into English, we will also refer to the Dutch term.

42   From the mound material, eight ice-cracked pieces were collected. None of them are artefacts. They are inclusions in the local sediment and are invariably covered with a distinct glossy patina.

4.1.3 Iron Age/Roman Period pottery attributable to the fill of ditch S19

A concentration of some ten pottery sherds and one flint flake was found in the northwest corner of the quadrant at level 3. As set out in section 2.7.3, at level 4 traces of a ditch fill – S19 – were recognized that was invisible at higher levels and could later on – only with some difficulty! – be recognized in the nearby N-S profile (see section 2.7.3 and Fig. 2.11). The profile made clear that this ditch was dug into the mound from above and thus post-dates it. In retrospect, the 3D-position of the finds with the numbers V117, 118, 120, 123, 124, 126, 127, 130, 139 and 151 shows that the concentration of finds at level 3 must quite probably have been in the fill of this ditch (Fig. 4.1). These "probable ditch fill" finds are nine handmade undecorated pottery wall sherds and one bottom sherd tempered with potgrit, and in one case, with potgrit and small quartz (V120). The latter is also slightly smitten (*besmeten*). One sherd is of the bottom of a pot (transition bottom to wall; V123) The sherds are entirely comparable to those found in what was recognized as the fill of the ditch at level 4 (V142; Fig. 4.1), to be described in the following section. One strange artefact was also located in the fill of the ditch (V122). It appears to be a completely burnt, even melted, fragment of pottery. To transform a sherd in such a way, intense heat is needed. It might have been melted in an oven for iron-production.

The pot-grit temper, the undecorated walls, and the presence of smitten walls are all characteristic for Iron Age or native Roman pottery. As these "probable ditch fill" sherds are very similar to those that are positively identified as situated in the fill of the ditch S19, we assume that the dating of Late Iron Age/early Roman Period of the ditch fill material (see 4.2) is therefore also applicable to the find concentration described here.

An un-burnt flint flake was also part of this find concentration (V119). It has been made of the same local flint that was used for the other flint flakes described in 4.1.2. It is not possible to provide a more precise dating for such a flake, but flint flakes are practically non-existent among Late Iron Age/Roman Period artefacts. It is therefore more likely that it was a much older artefact which ended up here as an inclusion in the mound construction material.

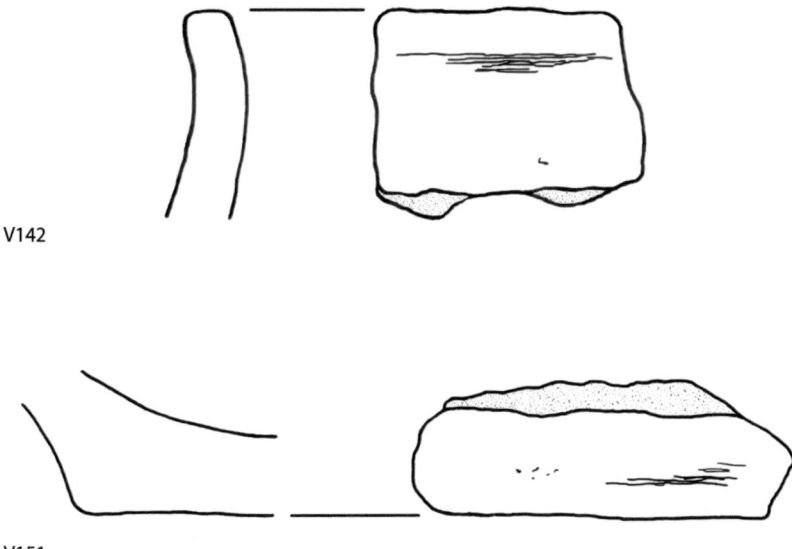

V142

V151

Fig. 4.1 Two sherds from the fill of ditch S19 (V142: rim) and V151 (bottom fragment). Scale 1:1. Drawing by A. Louwen.

4.1.4 Iron Age sherds from the backfill of the AWN trench

In addition to this, we found five wall sherds and one flake in the backfill of the *AWN*-trench (S1): V103 (at level 1), V111 (at level 2), V115 (flint flake level 2),V131 (level 3) and V141 (at level 5). As the excavators of 1971 are not known to have added new sand to fill their trench, they must have backfilled their trench with the soil which came from it. It is therefore very likely that these five sherds are from the part of the mound through which they dug their trench, but were not noticed by them. This implies that these sherds are from the concentration of sherds described in the previous section, which we attributed to the fill of the large ditch S19. We cannot be entirely certain of this, but it is very likely in view of the fact that they are entirely comparable and rather large. All are tempered with pot-grit and undecorated, none is smitten (*besmeten*). The flint flake is made of local flint as described in section 4.1.2. It is un-retouched and lacks typo-chronological characteristics.

4.1.5 Conclusion

The large number of finds from the higher levels of the mound can be interpreted as follows.

There is a clear concentration of finds just below the topsoil and somewhat deeper (10-20 cm deep; level 2. These are practically all sherds dating to the Iron Age/Roman Period. Concentrations of such sherds in the top of the mound is matched by the evidence of Delfin 190 (Chapter 5), and with stray finds at and around Unitas 1. The homogeneity of all these finds and the lack of finds from later periods (wheel-thrown pottery of the Roman Period, Early and Late Medieval Period or younger periods) indicate their integrity. This means that we can refute the scenario that they ended up in the mound as secondarily moved material during Medieval or younger periods (for example relating to activities when the *Elsterberg* area was a heath or during its reforesting in the early 20th century *AD*).

Some very small sherds, found deeper in the mound are also attributable to the Iron Age/Roman Period. We assume that they are from the same find scatter in the higher parts of the mounds, but locally penetrated deeper into the mound due to bioturbation (animals and tree roots[43]). It is unlikely to attribute the – in total – three flint flakes to the Iron Age, since flint was rarely used anymore by that period. It is more probable that they were part of the mound construction material.

A level 3 concentration of Iron Age/Roman Period sherds in the northwest corner of the quadrant can in retrospect be interpreted part of the fill of ditch S19, which was only positively recognized at level 4. It is also very likely that this applies to the Iron Age/Roman Period sherds found in the backfill of the *AWN* trench. In the next section, we will argue that al the sherds attributable to or positively identified as coming from the ditch S19 must be dated to the late Iron Age or Roman Period.

---

43   Before the 1970s, the mound was covered with trees. We noticed that tree roots can penetrate very deep into the mound. In this lithological matrix and these pedological circumstances (Chapter 2), once the tree dies, the roots can decay without leaving any traces.

4.2. Pottery and tephrite fragments from the fill of ditch S19
(by D. Fontijn and A. Louwen)

Several sherds and fragments of tephrite were found in what was recognized as the fill of the ditch at level 4 during the excavation, just below the concentration of sherds mentioned above (section 4.1.3). These finds are administrated as V142. There are at least six sherds that can be individually described (comparable in size to the finds from the concentration at level 3) and a larger part of much smaller fragments (total weight of V142 is 91.3 g). For the larger sherds, it is clear that we are dealing with handmade potgrit-tempered wall sherds, all of which are undecorated. Quartz temper is absent, also among the smaller fragments. None of the larger wall sherds is smitten *(besmeten)*. There is one rim fragment (Fig. 4.1) belonging to a pot with a very faint S-profile. Its rim is undecorated and unfaceted. The outer surface of this sherd is slightly "caked" with some sort of soot.

The sherds are entirely comparable to both the Iron Age/Roman Period sherds from the top levels of the mound (4.1.1), and the level 3 concentration at the location of the ditch (4.1.3) in the dominance of potgrit temper and the absence of wall decoration. This fits best with a dating of the finds in the later part of the Iron Age or in the Roman Period in province of *Utrecht*. Ernst Taayke (2002, 205), who studied the handmade pottery from a large Roman Period site at *Wijk bij Duurstede* which is also in the province of Utrecht, remarks that the pottery he studied is tempered with pottery grit and/or organic material. He does not indicate, however, in which frequency both tempering materials were generally used, although he does remark that there is a trend towards the use of organic material (Taayke 2002, 205). Further to the west (the coastal province of *Zuid-Holland*), there is even an abrupt switch from the use of potgrit to organic temper around the Late Iron Age-Early Roman Period (*cf.* Van Heeringen 1992; Bloemers 1978). If the *Wijk bij Duurstede* pottery study can be taken to be representative of general developments in pottery typo-chronology in the province of Utrecht, the lack of organic material in the pottery from *Elst* may be taken to imply a dating in the Late Iron Age rather than Roman Period[44].

Other indications for dating can be deduced from the pot form. The very faint S-shape is well-known from the late Iron Age (Hulst 1981: I.a.1, nos 5-7). For statistical purposes, there is not enough material for a sound characterization of material, however (100 sherds are needed; Van den Broeke 1987a, 34; Van Heeringen 1992, 10). The number of sherds is even too low if we combine the finds described in section 4.1 and those from V142 (13 large sherds and a number of very small fragments), yet the fact that they all are undecorated, potgrit-tempered and barely smitten remains suggestive for a dating in the Late Iron Age or Roman Period, and makes a dating in the Early or Middle Iron Age less likely.

A third argument for a date in the Late Iron Age rather than the Roman Period is the fact that not a single imported, wheel-made piece of Roman pottery has been found. Roman import pottery north of the *limes* is generally found in settlements north of the Roman boundaries dating to the second and third century *AD* (cf. Van Es *et al.* 1985, 587-594). A dating in the first century *AD* may therefore still be possible, but for the second or third century *AD* we would expect to have found at least some wheel-made pottery. On top of that, handmade pottery from the late second and particularly third to fourth century *AD* differs considerably in form and decoration from what was found in S19. A pottery assemblage found nearby in *Rhenen* is a case in point. It was found along the *Utrechtse Straatweg*

---

44 See also Van Tent 1978 on the *Jutphaas* pottery and on the native Roman pottery of the Utrecht Domplein *castellum* (Van Tent 1989). The number of sherds studied in both sites, however, is much too low to allow generalizations.

27 (Van Es 1968) and dates to the second to fourth century *AD* (based on the imported Roman pottery). This Roman Period handmade pottery is very different in decoration, shape and finish from the finds discussed here, and fits within the so-called "*Uslarien*" tradition (see also Miedema in Van Es *et al.* 1985, 595-609).

Summing up, a dating in the Late Iron Age seems most likely, but as long as there is no well-founded typo-chronology of Iron Age and native Roman pottery in the Utrecht area, we should be cautious in pressing the evidence too hard.

Several small fragments of tephrite were found as well (V150). Tephrite is a volcanic rock type that does not occur in the Netherlands. It has been widely applied in the Netherlands for the production of querns since the Late Bronze Age and Iron Age and Roman Period (Van Heeringen 1985), and is regularly found on settlement sites. V150 contains a rounded rim or bottom fragment and several small fragments of the original grinding surface. This makes clear that we are dealing with quern fragments here. This kind of blue grey tephrite is provenanced in the *Eifel* area. The form of tephrite querns has typo-chronological significance (Van den Broeke 1987, 39, Fig. 10), but the fragments of V150 are hardly informative on the quern's original form.

As remarked in Chapter 2, our *AWN*-colleagues also recognized this Iron Age ditch. According to their find documentation, they found eight sherds in it. Unfortunately we were not able to include these finds in our study as they could not be retrieved at the place where they were reported to have been stored (Provincial Depot).

4.3 Sherds of Barbed Wire pottery found at the prehistoric surface underneath the mound *(by Q. Bourgeois)*

In total, five sherds of Barbed Wire pottery were found in this mound (Fig. 4.2). The *AWN* found four in their trench of 1971, and we found a fifth one during our excavation in 2006. The temper, thickness and decoration pattern of all sherds are identical and it may be assumed that they are part of one and the same pot. None of the sherds fit together, however. As set out in Chapter 2, it was not clear whether the *AWN* Barbed Wire sherds were part of the material with which the mound was constructed or whether they were deposited at the prehistoric surface underneath the mound. As argued in section 2.7.6, the latter option is the most likely one and the deposition of these sherds must be seen as part of Early Bronze Age funerary ritual (just) before the construction of the mound (*cf.* 2.7.6 and 2.8).

4.3.1 The AWN finds

In the *AWN*-trench, one rim sherd (Un I/ 5) and three wall sherds were found (Un I/ 3, Un I/ 6 and Un I/ 7; Fig. 4.2). All sherds are tempered with quartzite and granite fragments (2-3 mm; thickness of sherds : 9-10 mm). The rim sherd shows three perforations five mm below the rim, each a centimetre from one another. The holes were punched through the wet clay from the outside. Afterwards the bulb of clay left on the inside was smoothed out. Five mm below the perforations a first row of Barbed Wire decoration can be seen. In total seven rows, approximately every four millimetre were impressed into the surface. The decoration was impressed with a Barbed Wire stamp (cf. Lanting 1973).

On two wall sherds (Un I/ 3 and 6), a group of five lines of Barbed Wire decoration can be seen, each also approximately four millimetres from one another. Then, on both sherds an undecorated zone one centimetre wide separates at least one more line beneath this. One of these two wall fragments is secondarily burnt

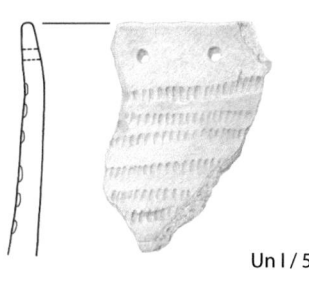

Un I/ 5

Un I/ 7　　　　　Un I/ 6　　　　　Un I/ 3

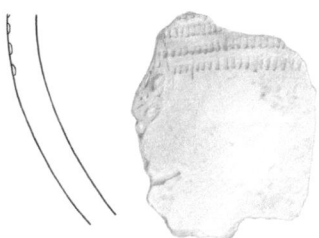

V 129

Fig. 4.2 All Barbed Wire pottery sherds found in the Unitas 1 mound. Scale 1:2. Drawing by E. van Driel.

and shows small hairline cracks all over its surface (Fig 4.2; Un I/ 6). Another, smaller wall fragment (Un I/ 7) only shows four lines of decoration each separated four millimetres from one another. The stamp used for the wall sherds and the rim sherd is identical. All sherds are slightly worn.

4.3.2 The 2006 find

During the 2006 excavation, one more wall sherd was found during clean-shovelling of the level of the old surface underneath the mound (V129; Fig. 4.2). It is a wall fragment from the same beaker, but of a part more towards the bottom than the other ones. Probably, the bottom of the beaker was just below this point. The sherd is 9 mm thick and tempered with quartzite and granite (2-3 mm), identical to what was seen on the sherds from the *AWN*-trench. Only the top half of the fragment is decorated with a short-wound Barbed Wire stamp. The belly seems to have been undecorated. Four lines of a Barbed Wire stamp can be seen, each two mm from one another. An undecorated zone of at least four centimetres separates the last lines of decoration and the presumed bottom of the beaker.

4.3.3 Discussion

Even though the sherds could not be fitted to one another, they must be part of the same pot. The beaker must in all likelihood have had a smooth S-curved profile, similar as the one at *Hulzen* (Modderman 1955, fig. 4.4). The perforations just below the rim are common among Barbed Wire Beakers (see for example Modderman 1955, fig.1.4 and 6 or Modderman 1959). A good parallel for the beaker found during the excavation would be one of the beakers found at *Emmerhout* tumulus III (Lanting 1973, fig.3).

Barbed Wire pottery has always been attributed to the Early Bronze Age (Anonymus 1965-1966, 9; Lanting & Mook 1977, 6). The established view is that the Dutch Early Bronze Age dates to 2000-1800 BC (Fokkens 2001[45]). The most recent dating of the Early Bronze Age is by Lanting and Van der Plicht, who state that it lasted from 2000 BC until approximately 1575 BC (Lanting/Van der Plicht 2001/2002, 152)[46]. Radiocarbon dates, however, do not support such a late end-dating for Barbed Wire Beaker pottery. Rather, an end-date of around 1700 BC is more likely. Three radiocarbon dates have been obtained from other barrows associated with Barbed Wire Beakers[47]. When calibrated these three fall in the period between 2150 and 1700 BC. One of these radiocarbon dates is furthermore backed up by a typo-chronological date of a *grooved ogival dagger* found in the grave of the mound period associated with the Barbed Wire Beaker. These radiocarbon dates are in line with other radiocarbon dates obtained from settlements (Arnoldussen 2008, 380, note 68). Following this line of thought, the barrow was probably erected between 2000 and 1700 BC.

4.4 The Pot Beaker sherds *(by P. Valentijn)*

Two sherds of Pot Beakers have been found during the excavations. Although both were found at the lower levels of the excavation, it proved impossible to determine their precise stratigraphical position (see section 2.7.7).

4.4.1 A Pot Beaker sherd from the 2006 excavation

A wall sherd (V132; Fig. 4.3) different from the Iron Age/Roman Period sherds described above was found at the outer zone of the sherd concentration of level 3 (section 4.1.3). This one was not detected during the deepening to the third level, but only when level 3 was cleared of debris. It is not clear whether it was part of the fill of the ditch of S19, as is assumed for the Iron Age/Roman Period sherds discussed above (4.1.3), or whether it was lying on the prehistoric surface underneath the mound, undisturbed by this ditch. At any rate, this sherd has different characteristics than the Iron Age/Roman Period sherds. It is a potgrit-tempered wall sherd with a deviant grey-yellowish colour and a decoration of impressions made with a fingertip or spatula, in a fishbone-like pattern. With a thickness of 9 mm, such a decoration pattern is best matched by those known from Late

Un I/ 4

V132

Fig. 4.3 The two Pot Beaker pottery sherds found in Unitas 1. The rim fragment was found during the 1971 excavation and the wall sherd (V132) during the 2006 excavation. Scale 1:2. Drawing by E. van Driel.

---

45 In this same article, Fokkens proposes to drop the term Early Bronze Age and to replace it with "Late Neolithic C", which illustrates the fluidity of the chronological terminology.

46 This is not the place for a more encompassing discussion on the chronology of the Bronze Age. We agree with Lanting/Van der Plicht 2001/2002 that the established dating of the Dutch Early Bronze Age (2000-1800 BC) must be criticized, but their alternative is also problematic (*cf.* Arnoldussen 2008). For the present discussion, it is only the dating evidence for Barbed Wire Pottery that counts.

47 The barrow at *Eext Kerkweg* 2 (Lanting 1973, 226 & 264-265); *Eext Eexterhalte* tumulus a (Waterbolk 1957, 23-27) and *Annertol* Tumulus III (Butler & Van der Waals 1972).

Neolithic or Early Bronze Age Pot Beakers rather than from Bell Beakers or All-over-Ornamented Beakers. With regard to its decoration pattern a parallel might be a Pot Beaker found near *Maarn* (Lehmann 1965, no. 15). Unfortunately the sherd is too small to provide a more precise date.

4.4.2 A Pot Beaker sherd from the 1971 trench

The *AWN*-excavators also found a Pot Beaker sherd: a rim fragment (Fig. 4.3). According to their find administration, it was situated on the original surface underneath the mound, the same position as we reconstructed for the Barbed Wire sherds, suggesting that it was also left there or deposited. However, we are not convinced of the accuracy of this stratigraphical observation and we have chosen not to let it play a role in the argument on the interpretation of the mound (section 2.7.7).

The sherd has been tempered with quartzite and potgrit. It has a bevelled rim (Fig. 4.3). About one cm below the rim there is a row of small bumps, which were pinched outward from two sides. This row is followed by three rather broad bands (5-7 mm), separated by v-shaped grooves (2-3 mm deep). In the grooves some possible nail impressions can be seen, which are probably the result of squeezing out the bands. It is hard to assign the sherd to one of the known Pot Beaker types. The sherd has a concave profile, which seems to be characteristic of Neck Pot Beakers (Lehmann 1965, pot number 6, 14, and 15). Also, a decoration in the form of broad bands on the neck seems to be most common on Neck Pot Beakers (Lehmann 1965, pot number 7, 11, and 17). It is therefore likely that the sherd was part of a Neck Pot Beaker, but this is of course not certain. Lanting (1973, 254-7) sees the Neck Pot Beaker as the oldest Pot Beaker type in the typological development.

4.5 Finds without clear context *(by D. Fontijn)*

In what follows, we will describe a number of stray finds, that nevertheless are of relevance for the interpretation of the Unitas 1 mound.

4.5.1 An unprovenanced find from the 2006 excavation

One sherd, (V137), was found on the soil heaps, and unfortunately cannot be contextualized. It is an undecorated potgrit-tempered wall sherd, that would not be out of place among the Iron Age/Roman Period sherds found in the ditch fill S19.

4.5.2 Pre-excavation "footpath finds"

In the Provincial Depot, we retrieved a find of 38 sherds, probably from the find collection of Ms Ch. Delfin, associated with "134" (this is the mound Delfin 134, here referred to as Unitas 1). The find label describes that these are probably Iron Age sherds found after the restoration of the mound. As described in 2.3, a restoration of the mound was carried out in 1987 and we assume that these finds were done as a result of these activities. The label notes that they were found "*op h. pad opp. v*". This probably means that they were found at the surface of the path. This must be the path running on top of the mound that is also drawn on the restoration sketch of 1987. This would mean that these finds were done in the slight gully on the top of the mound that had formed as a result of trespassing and erosion. This footpath is just south of the area we excavated. The sherds are wall sherds or small fragments that do not allow further determination. They include one rim and one bottom sherd. Most are undecorated (this can be said for at least 18 sherds), two are decorated, the rest are fragments too small to allow determination on this topic. There are one or two smitten (*besmeten*) sherds. One decorated wall sherd has an impression of a spatula or nail, the other one probably the impression of a fingertip. All sherds except one are tempered with potgrit. The rim sherd is too small to allow further discussion on pot profile, but it does have a decoration of fingertip impressions on the top of the rim. This is known from Early or Middle Iron Age rather than from Late Iron Age, though this is not as strict a trend as to exclude a dating in the Late Iron Age (Van Heeringen 1992, Fig. 43). Their tempering material, the type of rim decoration, the presence of smitten (*besmeten*) wall surfaces all point to a dating of these finds in the Iron Age or Roman Period. They are rather similar to the sherds found in the top layers of the mound (see 4.1.1) and to those from the ditch fill S19 and the concentration of finds associated with it (4.1.3 and 4.2). In view of their position, they might well represent material from an eroded top layer: the same find concentration observed in our levels 1 and 2 (section 4.1.1). The small number and size of the sherds, their lack of a true archaeological context prevents a positive identification, however.

4.5.3 Pre-excavation finds from a ploughed field to the south of the mound

In the fall or winter of 1990, a storm felled several trees to the south of the mound. The foresters of *Staatsbosbeheer* removed the trees and ploughed the area in order to plant a new pine forest. After the spectacular find of the Pot Beaker in this area (see 4.6), the amateur archaeologists J. Mom and H. Reusink remained active in this part of the forest and they surveyed the recently ploughed field before the new group of pine trees were sown or planted at 28th of December 1990. In the ploughed area, they found some 52 sherds and a few pieces of flint. Their finds are stored in the museum " 't Rondeel" in *Rhenen*, where they were kindly made available to us by its director drs. B. Huiskes. Stored with the find, labelled "find no 201" the finders attached information on the find spot. Coordinates of the site are 163470/445120. It is unsure whether this implies that they were all found at one spot or scattered over a broader area. According to their description, the finds were done on the ploughed field to the west of the central *Westerlaan* sand path, and south of the find spot of the Pot Beaker (and thus to the south of the Unitas 1 mound), and probably around, or including the area of the Long Barrow Unitas 5. Today, there is indeed a dense young pine forest immediately to the south of Unitas 1 and west of the *Westerlaan*, so the sherds must have been found in this area (*cf.* Fig. 2.4)

The flint finds are all natural pieces (determination by K. Wentink), but the sherds are interesting. There is one rim fragment and one bottom fragment. The remainder are all undecorated wall sherds, of which several have weathered breaks; a few show gnawing traces of mice. Practically all are tempered with pot grit and less than half of the sherds has an oxidized outer surface. There is one sherd with quartz temper (3 mm). The rim sherd has fingertip impressions on the top of the rim, which is usually characteristic for Early or Middle Iron Age pottery (Van Heeringen 1992, Fig. 43). The sherds are rather similar in fabric and the lack of wall decoration would fit a dating in the Roman Period or Late Iron Age. The undecorated sherds are comparable to those found in the ditch fill of S19 (section 4.1.3 and 4.2). Although the ploughing must have (severely) destroyed their original archaeological context, the similarity of the sherds suggests that they are from the same context. It is a serious possibility that they represent the same (settlement?) debris of activities that we also found in the top layers of both the Unitas 1 and Delfin 190 mounds.

4.6 A Pot Beaker deposited in the surroundings of the mound *(by P. Valentijn, Q. Bourgeois and D. Fontijn)*

Special finds are sherds of a Pot Beaker found by amateurs in 1990 to the east-northeast of Unitas 1. As set out in section 2.4.2, after discovery of a few sherds between the roots of a fallen tree the find location was investigated by amateur archaeologists by digging a small trench, bringing to light even more sherds. They were disturbed by the roots of the fallen tree and no obvious soil traces could be seen on the photographs from which the sherds could have derived. It is therefore unclear whether the sherds derive from a pot deposited as a whole, which was later heavily disturbed in the process of which sherds got widely spread, or if only part of a broken pot was deposited.

4.6.1 Description

In total 35 sherds of one pot were found. They are tempered with mineral material (3-6 mm). The large number of sherds allows us to reconstruct a large part of the profile of the Pot Beaker (at least up to a length 24.5 cm). There are no sherds from the bottom of the pot. Very few of the sherds, however, actually fitted together. The reconstruction[48] is therefore largely based on apparent similarities of decoration between the sherds and the logical placing of decoration on the sherds within the overall decoration scheme of the pot (Fig. 4.4). This has resulted in a reconstruction of which we can of course never be fully certain whether or not it is correct, but which to the authors seems accurate. From top to bottom the decoration consists of:

- a slightly pinched-out ridge with nail impressions on both sides
- a row of 4-sided bumps
- a small, slightly pinched-out ridge
- a row of vertical bands (2,5 cm long and 1 cm wide) between which v-shaped paired nail impressions can be seen
- a small, slightly pinched-out ridge
- a row of 4-sided bumps
- a pinched-out ridge (2 mm high) beneath which lays a 5 mm deep, wide smoothened groove at the junction of the neck and shoulder
- a row of vertical bands (5 cm long and 1 cm wide) between which at the bottom can be found two v-shaped paired nail impressions
- two times a small, slightly pinched-out ridge beneath which lays a wide smoothened groove with a row of oblique nail impressions at the bottom
- a row of oblique nail impressions
- a row of 4-sided bumps
- a small, slightly pinched-out ridge beneath which lays a wide smoothened groove with a row of oblique nail impressions at the bottom
- a small, slightly pinched-out ridge beneath which lays a wide smoothened groove without nail impressions
- a row of 3- or 4-sided bumps
- a small, slightly pinched-out ridge

---

48   At the *RCE*, an ink drawing of the pot is kept. The reconstruction of the ornamentation patterns on that drawing differs from ours however. After careful study of the sherds, we are of the opinion that the reconstruction on the *RCE* drawing is incorrect.

- a row of 4-sided bumps of which the upper row of nail impressions seem to form a more or less detached row
- a small, slightly pinched-out ridge
- a row of 4-sided bumps
- a row of 4-sided bumps of which the upper row of nail impressions seem to forms a more or less detached row
- a small, slightly pinched-out ridge
- a row of 4-sided bumps. The lines of nail impressions that form the top and bottom of the rows of 4-sided bumps seem to be the result of the pinching-out of the small ridges that lie above and beneath the rows of bumps.

The authors are not certain on the correct placement of the last four rows of decoration, since these are part of a sherd which may have been incorrectly glued to a higher placed sherd by the finders. The rim of the sherd is convex, slightly flattened. The bottom of the pot is missing. Some of the sherds show signs of secondary firing. It appears from the fractures of some sherds that the pot was made using the coiling technique.

Fig. 4.4 Reconstruction of the shape and decoration pattern of the Pot Beaker of which 35 sherds were found by J. Mom in 1990. Scale 1:2. Drawing by E. van Driel.

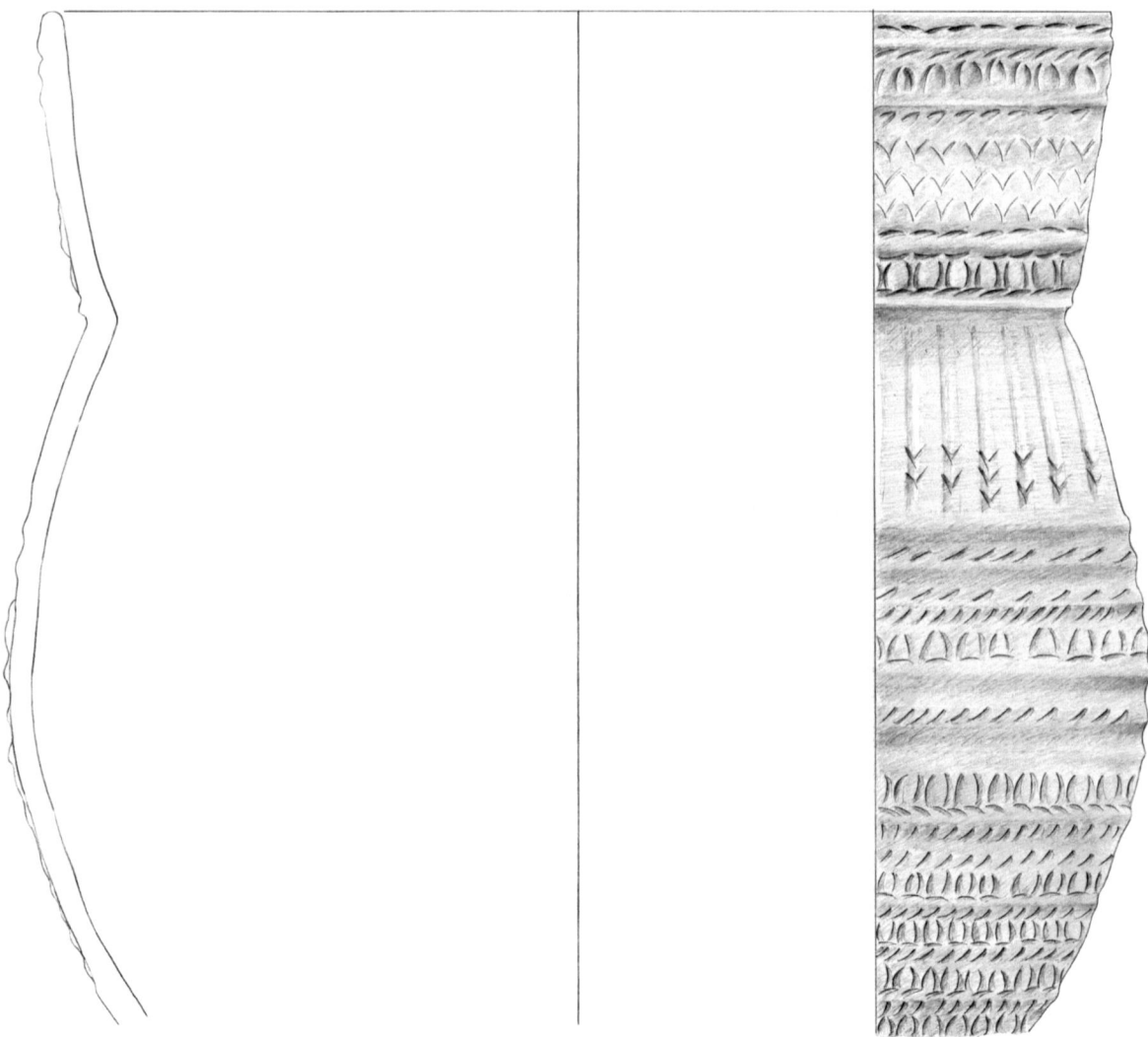

4.6.2 Typology and dating

A typology of Pot Beakers has been made by Lehmann (1965). He distinguishes between three types of Pot Beakers on the basis of the form of the vessels, the type of decoration, and the arrangement of the decoration. These are Neck Pot Beakers (NPB; *halspotbekers*) with a clearly detached cylindrical or conical neck and a break of the decoration at the angular junction of neck and shoulder, Trumpet Pot Beakers (TPB; *trompetpotbekers*) with a wide flaring mouth and decoration applied in continuous zones, and Belted Pot Beakers (BPB; *gordelpotbekers*) with no shoulder but a zone of decoration around the upper part of the body like a belt. The specimen discussed here can be determined as a Neck Pot Beaker, which has, in comparison to the Neck Pot Beakers depicted by Lehmann, a rather complex decoration scheme (Lehmann 1965). Also, the vertical bands on the neck of the pot are not known from the pots depicted by Lehmann.

Lehmann largely refrained from arranging his Pot Beaker types into a chronological order. A typo-chronology of Pot Beakers has been forwarded by Lanting (1973, 254-7). He argues that there is a development from the Neck Pot Beaker to the Belted Pot Beaker (and Beaker Pots of the Bentheimer type) on the one hand, and to the Trumpet Pot Beaker (having characteristics in common with beaker pots with Barbed Wire decoration) on the other. This would imply that our Pot Beaker dates to the earliest phase (contemporary to the Late Neolithic Bell Beaker Period)[49]. Although Lanting's typo-chronology has the benefit of presenting a seemingly logical typo-chronological development, the low number of Pot Beakers found and the absence of absolute dates of the pottery make it somewhat speculative. We therefore do not apply it to our finds, and side with the established view that it is not possible to date Pot Beakers more precisely than the (Veluvian) Bell Beaker period or early on in the Early Bronze Age (Butler/Fokkens 2005, 252-60).

4.6.3 Is there a relation between this Pot Beaker find and the barrow?

This find of a near-complete, rare type of lavishly-decorated large vessel close to a barrow begs the question whether we are dealing with an intentional deposition? This is not an easy question to answer. Pot Beakers are not very common finds in relation to burial mounds whereas they are known in some numbers from settlements (Drenth/Hogestijn 1999, 124-134; Lanting 1973, 258). For that reason they are usually interpreted as settlement pottery as opposed to burial pottery (Butler/Fokkens 2005, 374). However, Butler and Fokkens do suggests that there is something extraordinary with them. In the captions to their plate 26, they remark that Pot Beakers are settlement pottery that is often placed upside down, particularly in the *Veluwe* area "presumably in order to protect votive gifts". In order to get a better insight into possible patterns of deposition, we charted the contextual associations of finds of largely complete Pot Beakers in the Netherlands as described in the inventories of Lehmann (1965, 1967a & b), Lanting (1973 & 2007/2008), Hulst (1965/66 & 1970) and Drenth/Hogestijn (1999) (see appendix). As we are particularly interested in the role Pot Beakers might have played in relation to funerary practices and barrows, we excluded the – rather numerous – settlement finds. The results of this inventory are summarized in the appendix. Of the 30 listed finds, 12 have some relationship with a barrow (14 if we include Pot Beakers found in a pit beneath a mound), whilst another six are reported to

---

49 Recently, Lanting suggested that the Pot Beakers of the Bentheimer type probably need to be placed before the Neck Pot Beakers (Lanting 2007/8, 92-7).

have been found in a Neolithic megalithic grave. Of the barrow-associated finds, five were found near a barrow, whereas nine were found in or under a barrow. The latter category conceals a broad variety of contexts, ranging from sherds from a pit beneath a barrow, sherds at the old surface underneath the barrow before it was built, sherds as part of the mound construction material or as later intrusions.

Beside the place of deposition, it is also interesting to note the way Pot Beakers were deposited. It is remarkable that for many of the Pot Beakers of which a large part of the vessel is found, a part of the bottom up to the entire lower half of the body is missing[50]. At least the neck and often the entire upper part of the body are almost always present. A possible explanation for this, suggested by Louwe Kooijmans (1974, 291-2), may be that Pot Beakers were often placed upside down into the ground, like was the case at the *Driesche Berg* near *Putten* (Lehmann1967a,162-4; Hulst 1970, 28), the *Leusderheide* near *Leusden* (Modderman 1955, 40), *Velp* (Hulst 1965/66; Hulst 1970, 29), the *Hunneschans* near *Apeldoorn-Uddel* (Lehmann 1965, pot 11) , and the *Venenberg* near *Elspeet* (Lehmann 1965, pot 18; Louwe Kooijmans 1967; Hulst 1970, 29). When a pot is placed upside down and the top of the soil is disturbed, for instance by ploughing, the lower part of the vessel will be destroyed. Holwerda and the collector Bezaan also noted that Pot Beakers usually were placed upside down, but it is not known on which finds they based their ideas (Lehmann 1965, 28). Drenth and Hogestijn, mention an interesting German parallel from *Metzendorf-Woxdorf* (*Lkrs. Harburg*), where a human skull was found on a bowl with Barbed Wire decoration, dated to the Early Bronze Age, beneath a large undecorated pot which was placed upside down and was in its form identical to the Beaker Pots with Barbed Wire decoration (Wegewitz 1960 and 1967). Louwe Kooijmans (1974, 291-2) mentions three similar finds. In Llancaichisaf, Glamorgan, Wales a large pot related to the pottery with Barbed Wire decoration was placed beside or over a skull, and in Findon, Sussex a large pot with cordoned rim and Barbed Wire decoration was inverted over a cremation grave. At *Sande*, Germany an undecorated *Riesenbecher* was placed over a late *Schnurkeramik* beaker containing cremation.

A recent find from *Rhenen* itself suggests that even individual Pot Beaker sherds might have been deliberately deposited. At an excavation (2008-2009) that was carried out in relation to the construction of a bicycle path in the southeast in *Rhenen*, archaeologists of the RAAP company found the traces of a pit with Pot Beaker sherds (Schute 2009, 65-74). The excavators lifted the find *en bloc*, and further preparation showed that we are dealing with a careful sorting and deposition of pottery sherds in a pit. The careful research of Schute and his team ruled out that a complete vessel was deposited, as might have been the case next to the Unitas 1 mound. Rather, individual *sherds* were deposited according to a specific logic (e.g. decorated side turned towards the bottom of the pit)[51]. Summing up, Pot Beaker (sherds) are often found in relation to Late Neolithic-B and Early Bronze Age burial mounds, and there is reason to believe that these large, lavishly decorated vessel had a special significance. There are examples where complete

---

50 Lehmann 1965, pot number 2, 4, 6-9, 11-17, 20; Lehmann 1967a, two of the Pot Beakers found at the Poolse Driesten near Putten (p. 165-6, fig. 6 & 9). Of the pot depicted in fig. 6 only a small part of the bottom is missing; Lehmann 1967b, pot number 4.

51 It is not always clear that Pot Beaker sherds had an added significance. The case of the *Nijmegen-Hunerberg* group, where Pot Beaker sherds were found in a pit lined to a ditch of a barrow at least suggests that they were not simply settlement debris. A small excavation of a scatter of Pot Beaker sherds, Bell Beaker sherds and flint in *Ermelo*, however, did not yield any indication on the formation of this find complex (Van Sprang 1993, 81-5). At the well-preserved Early Bronze Age settlement *Molenaarsgraaf*, a few Pot Beaker sherds are found among the other sherds in the settlement debris layer, but nothing suggests that they were deposited in a deviant way (Louwe Kooijmans 1974, 210-20; 290-2).

vessels were deposited in an inverted position, and at least one examples where Pot Beaker sherds themselves were deliberately deposited (though not in relation to a burial monument).

For the Unitas 1 barrow, we now have evidence that Pot Beaker sherds were both contextualized *inside* and *beyond* the burial mound (even though the position of the sherds inside the mound remains unclear). This association cannot be ignored as coincidental, in view of the parallels mentioned above. At least for the Pot Beaker next to the mound, it is very likely that it was intentionally deposited[52]. In both contexts, the broad dating range of the Pot Beaker types found, as well as lack of insight in the precise stratigraphical position of the sherds do not allow us to decide whether the burial of Pot Beaker (sherds) was part of the contemporary funerary rites related to the building of Unitas 1, or whether they testify to earlier activities at this particular place. In the latter case, the burial of many sherds of one Pot Beaker might well have been an expression of the ritual (?) significance of this site before the barrow was built.

4.7 Finds from the nearby mound Unitas 3 and Unitas 5 *(by D. Fontijn and A. Louwen)*

In the process of finding additional information on the environment in the provincial depot, we retrieved sherds that were allegedly found in Unitas 3 (=Delfin 132), the mound at a distance of some 175 m west of Unitas 1 (Fig. 1.4 and 4.5). Nothing has been reported on the find circumstances. In the same field campaign in which Delfin 190 and Unitas 1 were investigated by the *AWN*, Unitas 3 was also inspected. The mound is described as 13 m in diameter and c. 1 m high. The trench was dug into the southeastern quadrant. The mound was already damaged by digging activities. Several sherds were found during the *AWN* excavation, which are all interpreted as "Iron Age" (day report 28th of July 1971). Most finds could not be retrieved by us in the *Provinciaal Depot* unfortunately[53]. Those found have an attached label, which only mentions "Un 3/5/8". On the basis of the finds, the profile of two pots could be reconstructed (Fig. 4.5)[54]. The first find comprises three large rim sherds of one and the same pot. The sherds are rather weathered, particularly on the outer surface. Both rim and wall are undecorated. They are potgrit-tempered and the profile displays a faint S-curved form with a short neck and an irregular rim without facets. Its form displays similarities to the rim fragment found in the ditch fill of Unitas 1 (V142, see section 4.2). The other sherd is also of a potgrit-tempered pot without decoration on the remaining parts. It has a somewhat more outspoken S-shaped profile, with similarities to a rim sherd found in the nearby mound Unitas 4 (see Chapter 8; Fig. 8.5: no 5).

---

52   On top of that, two Pot Beaker sherds were found inside the Delfin 190 mound as well and there is also a stray find from this site (see sections 3.4.1, 5.6, 5.7.2). However, since everything indicates that this mound dates to the Middle Bronze Age, the sherds in the mound are probably in a secondary position (inclusions in the mound construction material). As this material must come from close to the barrow, this at least indicates that Pot Beaker material was lying in the immediate vicinity of that mound as well.

53   See the inventory in the student report *Uitwerkingsverslag 'Barrow-landscapes'-project* by A. van Weerelt and N. van Rijswijk (2007), Leiden University. Another find labeled "39E-132" is reported in section 5.7.5 as possibly found at the Delfin 190 mound because the label refers to sherds found after a restoration (of which we presumed that it took place there). However, there are reasons to doubt the attribution to Delfin 190: the confusing label text may also be read as "39E mound (*Delfin*) 132". Delfin 132 is the other name for Unitas 3.

54   We are not entirely sure whether this is the same find that is mentioned as Un/III/5 in the find documentation of the excavation inventory.

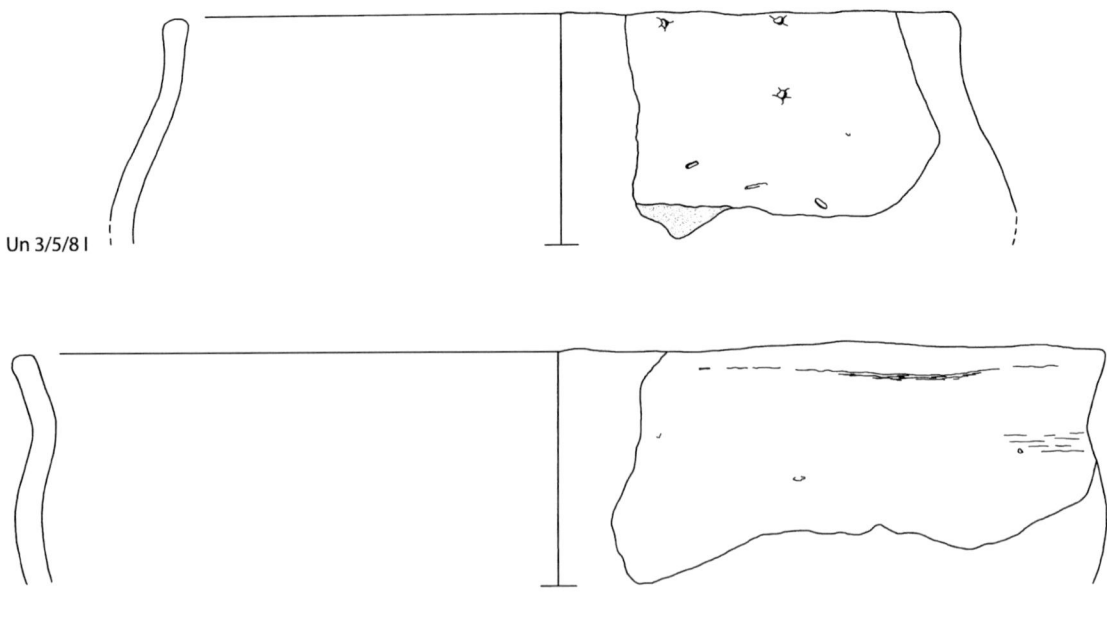

Un 3/5/8 I

Un 3/5/8 II

Undecorated vessels with such a faint S-shape are known from Wijk bij Duurstede, also in the province of Utrecht, where they are dated to the Roman Period (Taayke 2002, Fig. 9: 18) and from Utrecht-*castellum* (Van Tent 1989, Fig. 102: 543). Unfortunately, it is not quite clear whether the mentioned parallels were also potgrit-tempered. A date in the Late Iron Age should in our opinion certainly not be excluded. Hulst (1981) shows how undecorated vessels with small necks or neckless profiles are known from Late Iron Age context in the province of Gelderland north of the Rhine as well. We therefore opt for a date of both sherds in the Late Iron Age or Roman Period. It is possible that one of these finds is the native Roman pot (urn?) that was found in Unitas 3 according to Van Tent's documentation (1976). As he did neither describe nor depict this find, we cannot be sure of that.

Not much can be said on the remarkable long barrow Unitas 5 which is some 75 m to the south of Unitas 1. It is west-east oriented and is 45 m long, 10 wide wide, and between 1 to 2 m high (accounts on height vary). The *AWN* dug three small trenches through this mound. In trench C (southeastern end) they found a square "burnt spot with charcoal and cremation remains" (excavation find list and Van Tent 1976). Our investigation of the documentation makes clear that the remains, including charcoal, were not C14-dated, and unfortunately they could not be retrieved in the *Provinciaal Depot* anymore. Several pottery sherds were found in 1971, but these could also not be found in the *Depot* [55]. Two find nos (pottery sherds Un/Va/1 and Un/Va/2 seem to have been lying on the original surface, allowing us to provide a *terminus post quem*-dating. The original description of these finds informs us that they we are dealing with sherds that are respectively 9 and 6 mm thick and allegedly tempered with "fine stone grit". This suggests a dating in the (Early) Iron Age rather than Middle Bronze Age, but we cannot press the evidence too hard here. During our own excavation in 2006, the *RCE* investigated the barrow with one coring , which yielded the find of a potgrit tempered Iron Age/Roman Period pottery sherd from the mound (V105 in our excavation documentation).

Fig. 4.5 Pottery sherds found during the 1971 excavation in the nearby Unitas 3 mound. Scale 1:2. Drawing by A. Louwen.

---

55   Thanks are due to drs M. de Jong who helped us in the search for these lost finds.

4.8 Conclusion

Considering all finds described above, as well as their contexts, similarities between finds from several contexts, and the uncertainties involved, the following conclusions can be drawn.

The oldest material found are the Pot Beaker sherds (section 4.6), both within and beyond the mound, the Barbed Wire sherd complex (section 4.3) and probably four undatable flint flakes (4.1 and 4.2). One sherd found in the higher levels of the mound could not be identified, but might be older than the Iron Age (section 4.1.1).

The flint flakes are either intrusions in the mound, or were part of the material with which the mound was constructed. The latter interpretation is also an option for one or both Pot Beaker sherds found within the mound. It cannot be entirely ruled out, however, that at least one of them (the one found during the 1971 excavation) was already lying at the old surface before the barrow was constructed. These Pot Beaker sherds cannot be more precisely dated than Late Neolithic or Early Bronze Age, thus potentially being older than or contemporary with the mound. The 35 sherds of a Pot Beaker, found some 8 m of the mound are all from the same pot. It is a Neck Pot Beaker in Lehmann's typology, of a relatively complex decoration pattern. We do not see a possibility of dating it more precisely than Late Neolithic or Early Bronze Age, and it is therefore not possible to make clear whether it was buried before the construction of the mound or roughly contemporary with it. Our investigation of Pot Beakers does suggest, however, that they are a special category of vessel and there are several finds recording the deposition of largely complete specimen in relation to barrows and funerary practices. We are of the opinion that this special find bears a relationship to the signifance of the place, and to funerary rites – whether these precede the construction of the Unitas 1 barrow, or are contemporary with it.

The Barbed Wire sherds found by the 1971 excavation and by us, all must be part of the same pot, though they do not fit. They were deposited at the old surface of the mound, in relation with the funerary practices which finally resulted in the construction of the mound itself.

For the rest, there are hardly artefacts found in the mound which may date to the period of its construction. There are no finds of pottery from the Middle or Late Bronze Age. There is, however, a large number of material from the Iron Age or possibly Roman Period. The best find complex we have is the fill of the ditch S19 which was dug through the mound. A find concentration at a higher level can almost certainly be seen as part of this same fill (section 4.1.3), and probably the same applies to the sherds found in the backfill of the *AWN* trench. The sherds found in the ditch fill are too few in number to allow a systematic statistical analysis, but are consistent in nature: largely undecorated hand-made pottery, tempered with pot grit. The few rim fragments fit in shapes typical for – particularly – the Late Iron Age. The few finds of tephrite (including a quern fragment), loam and a burnt object do not contradict the proposed Late Iron Age dating.

Having compared all "Iron Age-Roman Period" finds discussed here, it is important to note a general similarity as to fabric (pot grit temper), incidental presence of smitten (*besmeten*) walls, faint S-shape pot profiles, and a general lack of wall decoration. This suggests that most Iron Age-Roman Period sherds more or less date to the same period, which is the period represented by the material in the ditch fill : the Late Iron Age (or possibly early Roman Period). A diffuse scatter of such sherds in the top of the mound (4.1.1) are to be interpreted as remains of activities, probably taking place at the time that the ditch was dug through the mound. The few small sherds found deeper in the mound (4.1.2) then, probably got there by bioturbation processes. The "footpath" finds are likely to represent an eroded part of these top-level finds (4.5.1). Comparable finds recovered outside the mound (4.5.3) indicate that such activities were not restricted to the Unitas 1 mound itself. In Chapter 5 we will see that a similar Iron Age/Roman Period complex is known from the Delfin 190 mound.

Chapter 5

FINDS FROM THE "DELFIN 190"-MOUND AND ITS SURROUNDINGS

*Q. Bourgeois, D. Fontijn, A. Louwen,
P. Valentijn, K. Wentink*

Following the approach set out in the previous chapter 4, this chapter will describe all finds recovered during the 2006 excavation of Unitas 1, according the relevant archaeological contexts as defined during the analysis of the features (Chapter 3). We will describe the finds starting from the highest and ending with the lowest levels of the mound, and also pay attention to the finds done during the mini-excavation of 1971, stray finds collected by members of the *WAR*, notably by Ms Ch. Delfin herself, as far as they could be retrieved from the *Provinciaal Depot Utrecht*[56]. Most of the finds lack inventory numbers. We will therefore refer to them with the text written on the attached labels.

Finds from our own excavation will be referred to with the administrative find number ("V"). As we worked with one find administration for the entire excavation of Delfin 190 and Unitas 1, find numbers 1 to 100 were reserved for Delfin 190, and numbers starting from V100 for Unitas 1. This was done as only a low number of finds was expected. However, the quantity of finds from Delfin 190 exceeded our expectations: over 100 find numbers were registered, which means that from the 100th onwards, we had to register the Delfin 190 in a different way, as find numbers between 100 and 200 were already reserved and used for finds from Unitas 1. Therefore, all Delfin 190 finds starting from the 100th find, are registered as no. V1000 and higher. Recorded finds that did not appear to be artefacts are not further discussed here. The material was studied by different people, and brought together and edited by D. Fontijn. Flint artefacts, Iron Age/Roman Period indigenous hand-made pottery and positively identified Pot Beaker and Bronze Age pottery are each described separately. Each author is mentioned in the section heading written by him. All sherds described are of hand-made pottery, unless stated otherwise.

5.1 Finds from the top layers of the mound *(by D. Fontijn, A. Louwen and K. Wentink)*

A few finds were done while removing the topsoil of the mound (20-30 cm; level 1). These artifacts were situated in the feature coded as S5040 in our administrative system (see section 3. 6 and 3.7.4). Most finds were situated in the A- and B horizon of the *holtpodsol* soil of in the top of the mound, a heavily bioturbated zone. None of the finds could be clearly related to an archaeological feature.

---

56 We are much obliged to drs Ton van Rooijen (*Landschap Erfgoed Utrecht*), drs Ruurd Kok (province of *Utrecht*) and drs Mirella de Jong (*Provinciaal Depot*).

5.1.1 Flint

Three flint artefacts were found. Two are unretouched flakes (V8 and V46), the other (V9) is V9 is a small thumbnail scraper (Fig. 5.1). High-power use wear analysis revealed a band of rough polish with a transverse directionality. This indicates that the scraper had been used for scraping hide. This analysis was carried out following the approach of Van Gijn (1990).

No precise dating can be given. All flint was made of material that is locally available (see remarks in section 4.1.2). Both the flakes and the thumb scraper cannot be dated on the basis of their form.

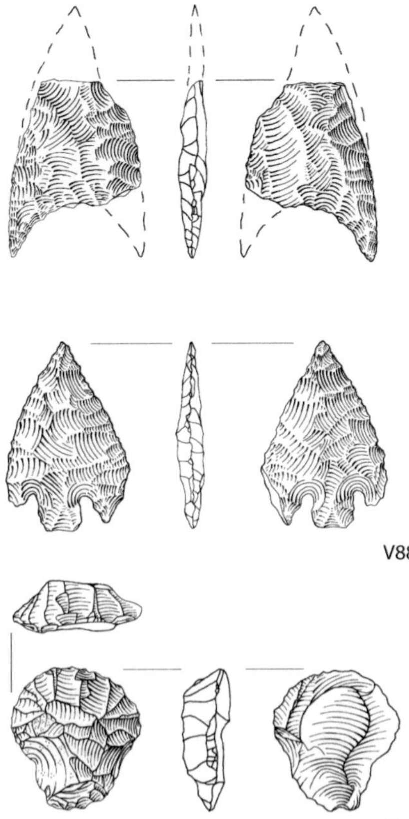

5.1.2 Pottery sherds from the Iron Age or Roman Period

Four wall sherds were found while removing the topsoil of the mound (V2, 6, 17 and 54). Two of them were secondarily burnt (V2 and 6) and one (V54) shows traces of gnawing by a mouse, indicating that these finds were displaced by animal activities. All are undecorated and tempered with potgrit. On the basis of these characteristics they can be broadly dated to the Iron Age or Roman Period (see the discussion in pottery typo-chronology in section 4. 2). V2 also has quartz temper (>2 mm), and this is something that is rarely seen on the pottery attributed to the Iron Age/Roman Period found in and around the Unitas 1 mound (see previous chapter). Mineral material was frequently used to temper Early Iron Age pottery in the Oss region, whereas potgrit is dominant in Late Bronze Age and Middle and Late Iron Age ceramics (Van den Broeke 1987, 101; Van den Broeke 1991, 206). However, recent research of Iron Age pottery from the vicinity of *Deventer* suggests that mineral temper is also added to pottery in the Middle and Late Iron Age and Roman Period of the central Netherlands, in contrast to contemporary pottery south of the river Rhine[57].

As finds present in the heavily bioturbated topsoil of the mound, at a steep slope that resulted from later digging activities, they only qualify as stray finds. However, it is conspicuous that similar Iron Age/Roman Period pottery was also found in the topsoil of Unitas 1 (section 4.1 and 4.5.2). It should be borne in mind that artefacts of more recent date (Medieval Period up until present-day) are lacking. So, even though the material might be disturbed by recent digging activities, bioturbation and trampling, it is likely that they represent the remains of Iron Age/Roman Period activities that took place on the top of both mounds. With regard to the flint finds: flint was rarely used during the Iron Age, and for that reason they must be older than the sherds. They can either represent inclusions in the mound construction material or later intrusions (which might have ended up there, for example, because of the disturbances in later period).

5.2 The urn of cremation grave S5 *(by Q. Bourgeois)*

At a depth of only 15 to 20 cm, ten undecorated sherds were found as well as cremated bone. They are concentrated in a zone, close to the place where in the profile a pit (S5) containing cremation remains and similar sherds were recognized (see section (3.7.2). They were registered as belonging to the S5030, which is the general heading for the homogenous mound material underneath the top fill

Fig. 5.1 Flint finds. Thumbnail scraper V9 (bottom); barbed-and-tanged arrowhead V88 (centre); triangular arrowhead found on the sand path west of the mound Delfin 190 (top). Scale 1:1. Drawing by R. Timmermans.

---

57 Louwen in druk; see also Van de Velde/Taayke 2000, 19 (*Winterswijk*); Scholte Lubberink 2006, 73 (*Borne*); Fontijn 1996b, 57 (*Zutphen*).

S5040 that contained the above described Iron Age/ Roman Pottery sherds (see section 3.6). When the concentration was recognized all the ground around it and underneath it has been sieved (with a sieve with measure width of 4 mm). At the end of the excavation, the small east-west section to its side has also been dug out and some more sherds of the same pot were found then.

We are dealing with relatively thick (13 to 15 mm) coarse undecorated wall sherds. All were tempered with coarse quartzite (c. 4-7 mm). Small patches of red-colored pot grit are sometimes visible as well[58]. Some of the sherds show gnawing traces of mice (V21, 100 and 1002), evidencing the rate of disturbance of this feature by bioturbation. As described before (3.7.2) Ch. Delfin also found sherds and cremation remains in the top of this mound long before our excavation. We were able to study the sherds she found as well[59]. There are eleven large wall sherds, two of which are fragments of the wall immediately on top of the bottom. Their characteristics are entirely comparable to those discussed above, though lacking gnawing traces. These sherds and cremation remains must be from the same burial. The coarse mineral tempering material used, as well as the thickness of the pot are characteristic for Middle Bronze Age pottery. The reconstructed pottery shape shows the lower part of a large vessel without further partitions (Fig. 5.2). This again is characteristic for Middle Bronze Age pottery (Theunissen 1999, 202-3). A more precise dating cannot be given, unfortunately.

We are thus dealing with a burial pit dug into the top of an existing mound, in which an urn with cremation remains was placed. This burial must already have been disturbed by bioturbation, and, to judge from the fact that Ch. Delfin was able to find stray finds of the urn on the surface, also eroded due to the sand extraction activities (see section 3.3). As rim sherds are lacking, we assume that the top of the grave was already lost before that time (perhaps by the cutting away of the flank of the mound in the course of the digging of the ditch in the west flank of the mound).

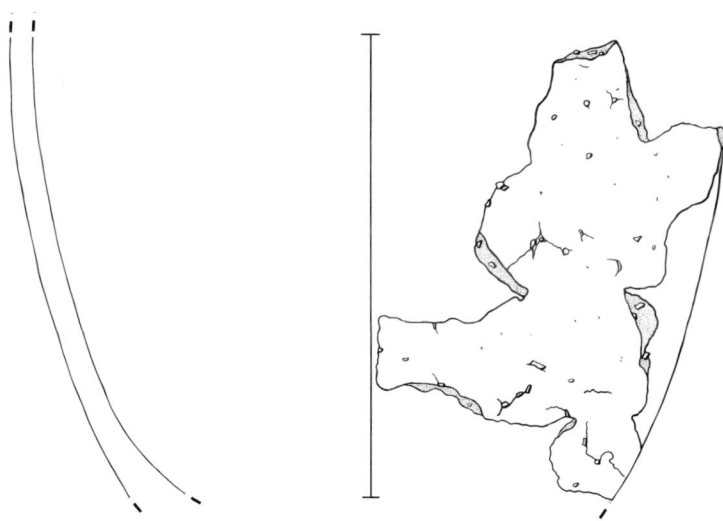

Fig. 5.2 Reconstructed shape of the Middle Bronze Age urn. Scale 1:4. Drawing by A. Louwen.

---

58   These finds are registered as V22, V31, V36, V38, V39, V50, V51, V1001, V1002.
59   Many thanks are due to drs Ton van Rooijen (*Landschap Erfgoed Utrecht*) for going through all the trouble of retrieving this find for us.

5.3 Finds recovered from the mound *(by Q. Bourgeois, D. Fontijn, A. Louwen and K. Wentink)*

The mound material below the topsoil and on top of the prehistoric surface is wholly homogeneous and cannot be further subdivided pedologically or litho-stratigraphically (section 3. 6 and 3.7.4). This zone, indicated in our administration as feature S5030 yields a number of finds from different positions and, confusingly, of different periods. The finds will first be described, and then it will be tried to interpret their presence in the mound material.

5.3.1 Flint and stone

Throughout this part of the mound, in all fifteen flint artefacts were found. These are five splinters, nine un-retouched flakes and one retouched specimen (V44). One of them was burnt (V55).All the flakes are made of material that is locally available (see remarks in 4.1.2) There was no particular concentration of flint, neither horizontal or vertical. Natural flint (frost-cracked pieces) and a fossile (belemnite) were also found. The finds cannot be dated.

5.3.2 Sherds dating to the Middle Bronze Age and one unidentified sherd

Several sherds were found throughout the mound. They stand out for the presence of coarse mineral tempering material.

A number of small sherds are of a highly similar fabric possessing potgrit, quartz (1 to 3 mm) and occasionally mica as tempering agent in a dense concentration (V14, V36, V41, V64, and V98). The sherds have a yellowish hue, and one is probably secondarily burnt (V14). Wall thickness is around 15 mm. All sherds are likely to be from the same pot and are small except for V64, which is clearly an undecorated wall sherd. The mineral temper is characteristic for Middle Bronze Age pottery, although it is not as coarse as in the Middle Bronze Age urn described in section 5.2. A small rim fragment has a similar fabric (V99; Fig. 5.3), including the quartz and mica as tempering agent. It is different for its relatively modest wall size (10 mm).

Another find that also should be dated to the Middle Bronze Age (V13; Fig. 5.6) is a rim sherd, tempered with coarse (broken) quartz (3 mm) and occasionally, with mica (thickness of the sherd is 16 mm). The rim form is the one defined as an A-type rim by Glasbergen (1954b, Fig. 56). Theunissen (1999, 205-6) established that these rims are associated exclusively to the *Hilversum*-period (early Middle Bronze Age A)[60].

Finally, we also found small undecorated wall sherd (V25) that has been tempered with relatively smaller quartz (c. 2 mm) and must come from a different vessel. Such a relatively small mineral temper is also known from Late Neolithic pottery and it might therefore be possible that this sherd does not date to the Middle Bronze Age, but to the Late Neolithic.

V99

Fig. 5.3 Rim sherd V99 found in the top soil of the mound. Scale 1:1. Drawing by A. Louwen.

60　V36 is also documented as being a mineral-tempered wall sherd with a decorated ridge, which is know from the Middle Bronze Age. Unfortunately, this sherd could not be retrieved anymore.

Fig. 5.4 Sherds found in the mound. V18 and the deviant V66; Scale 1:1. Drawn by A. Louwen.

V66

V18

5.3.3 Late Bronze Age, Iron Age/Roman Period sherds

A number of pottery sherds from the mound is datable to the (Late) Iron Age or early Roman Period on the basis of general characteristics as temper, and in two cases, decoration. They are of a comparable fabric as the Iron Age/Roman Period sherds found in the top soil (section 5.1) and also comparable to the Iron Age/Roman Period sherds found in Unitas 1 (previous chapter).

We are dealing with the following finds. A few very small sherds (< 10 by 10 mm) tempered with potgrit (V10, 12, 42 and 59), one of which is secondarily burnt (V10). There are four larger sherds (c. 25 by 15 mm), of which two are severely weathered (V19 and 49), the other one is an undecorated wall sherd (V22) and a rounded rim fragment with light fingertip impression on the outside of the rim(V18; Fig. 5.4). These are also tempered with pot grit. The latter is common for Late Iron Age pottery (Van Heeringen 1992 and see below).

A small potgrit tempered wall fragment has a different fabric (V66; Fig. 5.4). It shows a wall decoration of three horizontal grooves. This type of decoration is hard to match with finds from other sites, and may perhaps find its best parallels among thin-walled Late Bronze Age pottery.

More can be said of a small rim fragment (V53) with a faceted rim and nail or spatula decoration on the outside of the rim (Fig. 5.5). Both characteristics are typical for Late Iron Age or Roman Period pottery[61]. Both potgrit and mineral temper (1 mm) are visible. In the Central Netherlands, mineral temper is known to have been used more often than in the south (see section 5.1.2)[62]. A larger wall sherd (V15) is decorated with small "gullies" (Fig. 5.5). This is the so-called *Kalenderberg* decoration. This sort of decoration is known from native Roman pottery (*cf.* Taayke 2002, Fig. 16: 10, in combination with fingertip impressions). *Kalenderberg* decoration is known from the Late Iron Age in Van den Broeke's typo-chronology for handmade pottery from the Iron Age and Roman Period in the southern Netherlands (phases I to K; Van den Broeke 1987, 109-11, Fig. 9: 7). However, it is also known from Early Iron Age find complexes in the Oss region (Van den Broeke 1987, 109). The *Kalenderberg* sherd itself can therefore not be precisely dated.

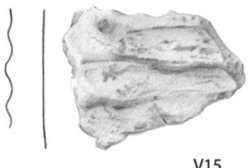

V15

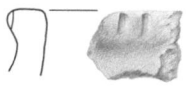

V53

Fig. 5.5 Sherds found in the mound. V15 and V53. Scale 1:2. Drawing by E. van Driel.

5.3.4 Interpretation of finds recovered "from the mound"

In all, a sizeable number of sherds has been found in the material construction material which date to different periods: Middle Bronze Age A (*Hilversum* pottery phase), Middle Bronze Age unspecified, possibly Late Bronze Age and (Late) Iron Age or Roman Period. As shown in section 5.1 and 5.2, both in the Middle Bronze Age and Iron Age, activities were carried out on top of the mound. The presence of sherds from both periods may therefore be explained by processes of intrusion in the mound following erosion (the digging away of part of the mound's flank for the construction of a large ditch through the mound in the 19th century) and subsequent bioturbation (roots, mice). Several sherds are rather small – which might

---

61   Bloemers 1978, 344-5; Fig. 154; Taayke 2002, Fig. 7: 16 for an example from Wijk bij Duurstede; Van Heeringen 1992, Fig. 43.

62   Based on pottery finds from Deventer studied by A. Louwen, as yet unpublished.

be expected for artefacts that are transported vertically by bioturbation; the same applies to the flint finds, of which several examples are no more than splinters. Also, in the highest parts of the mound (S5040, see section 5.1 and 5.2), gnawing traces of mice have indeed been observed on a number of sherds. However, several artefacts are also likely to have become engrained in the mound material due to the fact that sods or earth was collected from older settlement sites. Such finds then provide a *terminus post quem*-dating for the construction of this part of the mound. The oldest material with a secure dating, dates to the Middle Bronze Age A (V13 and V36)[63].

5.4 Finds from the peripheral ditch fill S9 *(by D. Fontijn and K. Wentink)*

Three small pottery fragments were found in the ditch fill (V87). They are tempered with quartz (< 3 mm) and are for this reason likely to be dated to the Middle Bronze Age. In addition, three flint flakes were found, two of which are burnt (V74).

5.5 Middle Bronze Age-A finds from features underneath the mound *(by Q. Bourgeois, D. Fontijn and K. Wentink)*

No finds could be positively associated with the prehistoric surface buried underneath the mound (S5550), but many finds were done in the fill of several pits underneath the mound, pre-dating the barrow, which we interpreted as remains of a settlement (3.7.6). We are dealing with several pits/postholes, some of which contain quite some finds.

5.5.1 A flint barbed-and-tanged arrowhead from S16

Just some 5 cm above the level where posthole S6 and the pit fills S7, 11, and S15 would be observed (see section 3.7.6), a soil discoloration was visible of which the interpretation was not entirely clear. When deepening to level 4, the pit features S11 and 15 became recognizable. In retrospect, we thought it useful to give the higher discoloration a separate feature number: S16. It was interpreted as a local dip in the surface caused by compaction of pit fills (the fills of S6, 11 and 15). In this feature, one flint artefact was found (V88; Fig. 5.1). This is a well-preserved barbed-and-tanged arrowhead (l. 2,3 cm; w. 1,6 cm; thick 0,3 cm). The arrowhead itself was in mint condition. High power use-wear analysis did not show any indications of use: wear traces nor characteristic impact fractures could be observed. However, this does not exclude that the arrowhead was used: experiments show that wear traces or impact fractures do not always occur after shooting (Van Gijn 1990). This type of arrowhead can best be attributed to the Bell Beaker culture (Butler/Fokkens 2005, Fig. 17.19); Drenth 2005, 338).

5.5.2 Middle Bronze Age-Hilversum pottery, flint and stones from posthole S6

A remarkable large number of objects was found in the fill of feature S6 (Fig. 5.6). In 3.7.6, it was already remarked that this is particularly strange as this feature must be interpreted as the traces of a posthole, a type of feature in which normally

---

63 The only find for which an older dating might be an option is V25, found relatively high in the mound (S5030). For this small wall fragment a Late Neolithic dating cannot be excluded, but is far from certain. See 5.3.2.

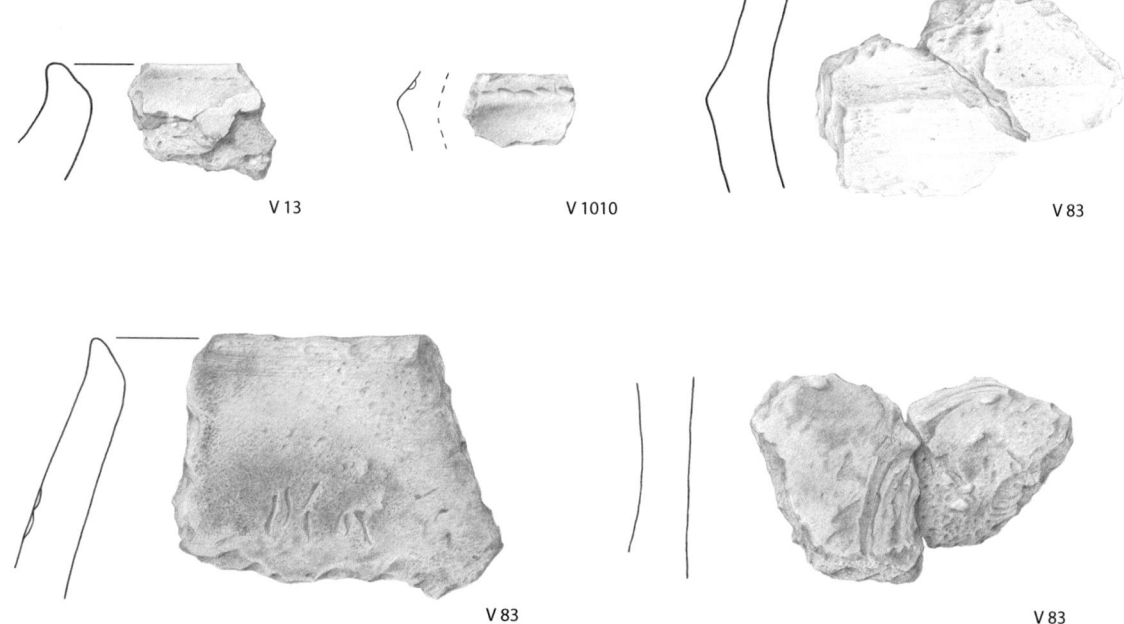

V 13   V 1010   V 83

V 83   V 83

Fig. 5.6 Middle Bronze Age pottery sherds. One was found in the mound (V13). The other sherds are from features that pre-date the mound. Three are from the fill of S6 (V83), one from the fill of S11 (V1010). Scale 1:2. Drawing by E. van Driel.

hardly anything is found. Practically all finds described below were found in the fill of the posthole itself – implying that the post had been removed at an earlier stage.

Flint and stone

A large number of stones was found in the fill of this post pit (1.4 kg; V63, 80, 84). Their sharp breaks indicate that they cracked because of abrupt temperature change. In the Bronze Age of the Netherlands, such conditions only rarely have natural causes, and mainly reflect the use of stone for cooking activities. The stones themselves are un-worked. Seven flint artefacts were identified (collected as V82 and V85). These were all found in the second fill of the pit (from the top down there are five un-retouched flakes, one flint block and one hide thumb scraper (in V82). The latter was subjected to high-power use-wear analysis, where traces could be identified that are characteristic for scraping hide (*cf.* Van Gijn 1990). It is noteworthy that although the pebbles all were modified by intense heat, this does not apply to the flint artefacts. The associated pottery finds (below) show that we are dealing here with Middle Bronze Age A flint artefacts.

Pottery and a lump of burnt loam

In total 470 g of sherds were found, all in the top fill (fill 1) of the pit. Half of the sherds were secondarily burnt. Their fabric is characterized by the presence of coarse quartz tempering material (between 4 to 7 mm thick), and often potgrit is visible as well. Small glimmering material is visible as well, possibly mica. The sherds are relatively thick (on average 14 mm). Such a fabric is characteristic for Middle Bronze Age pottery; the presence of some decorated wall sherds underlines this and provides us with an argument to date the find complex to the Middle Bronze Age-A *Hilversum* period. Decorated examples of the coarse ware sherds are depicted on Fig. 5.6.

Three sherds with a cordon were found (V72 and 83). Cordons are typical for the Middle Bronze Age (Theunissen 1999, 205). Two weathered sherds had a furrow, which was cut into the wet clay (V83). This furrow was probably used as the basis for an applique. The applique would then have had the shape of a horseshoe-shaped handle, a decoration technique seen exclusively on Hilversum-type pottery (Glasbergen 1969, 18). Parallels are the decoration at the urn of *Budel-Weert* (Glasbergen 1962), several sherds at *Den Haag-Bronovo* (Bulten *et.al.* 2008, 8) or at *Schagen* (Bloo 2003). The sherd from *Schagen* was radiocarbon dated on carbonized material still attached to the sherd to the period between 1880-1690 cal. BC (KiA-19642: 3458±34 BP). Two other fitting sherds have an undecorated ridge on the outside and might have been part of a pot where such a ridge was decorated with horseshoe handles in places. In the same feature a large sherd from the rim of a vessel had two paired nail impressions on its shoulder (V83) The rim itself was beveled inwards. The paired nail impressions are also exclusively found on the *Hilversum*-type pottery, while the beveled rim is, according to Glasbergen (1954, 90) typical for *Hilversum*-style pottery (Theunissen 1999, 205-206). Paired nail-impressions is also known from some late Barbed Wire Beakers (*cf.* a small beaker found underneath a barrow at *Garderen* (Bursch 1933, 76) or early *Hilversum*-urns, as for example the urn at *Vorstenbosch* (Modderman 1959).

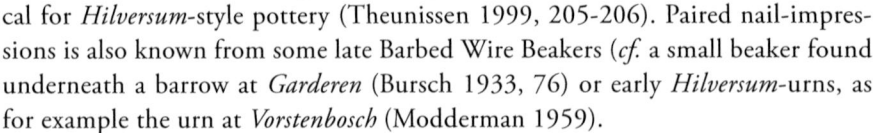

V68

V85

Fig. 5.7 Sherds of deviant fabric and decoration from S6. V68 and V85. Scale 1:1. Drawn by A. Louwen.

Two sherds are somewhat different (Fig. 5.7). They are the only thin-walled sherds and at first sight do not easily fit in what is known on Middle Bronze Age A pottery. One sherd (V68) had small nail impressions on the top of its smoothened out rim. Mineral temper was used (4 mm thick), not unlike that found in the pottery described above, but it was less thick (9 mm). According to Stijn Arnoldussen[64] (personal communication) nail impression at the outside of the rim is known from the *Den Haag-Bronovo* site (V4102) and from the Barbed-Wire-*Hilversum* vessel from *Vorstenbosch* (Modderman 1959). The other sherd is somewhat thinner and is decorated with a ridge with impression of fingertips or a spatula. Something like this is not unkown from Middle Bronze Age A ceramics (so-called *Drakestein* pottery) but such vessels are often thick coarse ware. However, according to Arnoldussen (personal communication), some thin-walled specimens are known as well (*Betuweroute*-site 28, 8 mm thick and see also Glasbergen 1954, 125 no. 3). In view of the homogeneity of the *Hilversum* coarse ware complex found in the fill of S6 described above, the presence of these two somewhat deviant types of pots is noteworthy, but so far everything indicates that we are dealing with one closed find complex.

In addition, a hump of burnt loam was found (V63, 340 g). L. Jacobs of the Leiden Pottery Institute put a fragment of it in a heated kiln, and showed that it was originally made at temperatures around 550 ° C.

5.5.3 Middle Bronze Age pottery and stones from pit S7

The fill of this pit contained a number of fire-cracked stones (*cf.* supra, 0.5 kg) and one undecorated wall sherd of a fabric wholly comparable to the sherds from S6, S11 and S15: it was tempered with coarse broken quartz (c. 5 mm thick) and potgrit. Nothing can be said on the precise relation between this sherd and a possible pit fill layer.

---

64 Many thanks are due to dr. Stijn Arnoldussen (*RCE* and Groningen Institute for Archaeology) for informing us on this.

5.5.4 Middle Bronze Age pottery, flint and stones from pit S11

Five fill layers could be recognized in this pit (with 1 at the top). The majority of the finds was concentrated in fill 2 and 3, whereas hardly anything was found in the lowest layers 4 and 5. The following finds were done: a large number of burnt and cracked stones were found (1.25 kg, V1007, V91, V96, V97), one un-burnt flint flake (V90) as well as a number of wall sherds, just like in the case of S6 (266 g). They are wall sherds that were all secondarily burnt and weathered (V89, 92, 93, 1008, 1009, 1010) and they are all of a fabric that is very comparable to that of the sherds in S6 and S7. They were tempered with coarse quartz (4-7 mm thick), and often also potgrit and a glimmering mineral material (mica?) is visible. One sherd has a horizontal applique (Dutch: *stafband*) with rope decoration on it (V1010; Fig. 5.6). The horizontal appliqué with rope-decoration is characteristic for *Hilversum*-period pottery (see Theunissen 1999, 205).

5.5.5 Middle Bronze Age pottery from pit S15

In the fill of pit S15, we distinguished between four different fills. Unlike the other pits discussed here, only one sherd and no stones or flint were found. The sherd is a not secondarily burnt wall sherd (V1011) that has a fabric similar to that of the sherds found in S6, 7 and 11.

5.5.6 Discussion

We reached the conclusion that all of the discussed sherds in this section are part of one and the same complex which can be dated to the *Hilversum*-pottery phase of the Middle Bronze Age-A. With the exception of S16, the finds from the above described features all contain relatively thick pottery sherds that have been tempered with coarse mineral material. In all cases, the fabric displays tiny elements of a glimmering mineral, presumably mica. We assume that this was an inclusion in the original clay, and not an addition. Most sherds are undecorated. These are all characteristics of Middle Bronze Age pottery (*cf.* Theunissen 1999, 205-6). In the fill of S6, decorated wall and rim fragments were found as well. The various decoration types recognized all are characteristic of *Hilversum* pottery (Theunissen 1999, 206: the paired-nail impressions, the cordons, the beveled rims, the horseshoe-handles and the occasional rope-decoration. This is dated to the early Middle Bronze Age-A (*c.* 1800-1600 BC, *cf.* Arnoldussen 2008, 178, note 40). Even though the other features only contain undecorated sherds, the similarity in fabric is so striking that the sherds must all have been contemporary. In other words: the *Hilversum*-period dating can be applied to the other features as well.

Most of the pits have different fills, evidencing a gradual silting up after their primary function was fulfilled: the deepest pit fills hardly contain finds: artefacts are concentrated in the top fill layers (S6) or in the middle (S11), suggesting that the pits were open for a while, to be finally filled in. We assume that this was done with settlement debris. The dominant presence of fire-cracked stones in several fills – probably cooking stones – is conspicuous. It suggests that the pits were dumped with material from domestic activities (food preparation). It is not likely that the pits themselves were used for these activities: they did not show traces of burning themselves. Most sherds were burnt, and several were severely weathered. The flint was not burnt. Also, the sherds rarely fit together. This rather gives the impression of material scattered in a corner of a settlement, which was later dumped into pits that were originally used for some other purpose (for a further discussion on pit use and pit clusters from other sites, see 3.7.6).

5.6 Pot Beaker sherds found during the AWN excavation *(P. Valentijn)*

Among the finds recovered during the *AWN* excavation of 1971, there are two Pot Beaker sherds.

One is a rim fragment (Fig. 5.8). The rim is slightly bevelled. Directly beneath the rim there are two rows of paired nail impressions. At about two centimetres beneath the rim the remains of two holes (diameter ± 3 mm) can be seen at the edges of the sherd, about two centimetres apart. The holes pierce through the wall and have a double-conical cross-section.

The other sherd from Delfin 190 is a slightly concave fragment (Fig. 5.8). The sherd is decorated with a row of paired nail impressions. Beneath this row of impressions there are three shallow, but rather broad grooves (3 mm wide and 1 mm deep). The grooves are separated by three broad, undecorated zones (6 mm wide). Beneath the grooves a possible nail impression can be seen, perhaps being part of a row of nail impressions. Both sherds from Delfin 190 probably belong to the same vessel, since their colour and tempering are similar. Also the wall-fragment tapers towards the top and the entire fabric of the top of the sherd is pink, indicating full oxidization during firing, which makes it likely that the fragment was originally positioned just beneath the rim. The two rows of nail impressions on the top of the wall-fragment are therefore probably the same ones as on the top of the rim-fragment. It is most likely that the sherds are part of a Pot Beaker with an s-shaped profile, a so-called Trumpet Pot Beaker or a Belted Pot Beaker, since most of these have holes beneath the rim (Lehmann 1965, 5 and see the discussion on typology in 4.6). However, the profile of the sherds indicate that it was positioned almost vertically, which is only seen on Neck Pot Beakers. The sherd may therefore be of a rather unique pot, namely a Neck Pot Beaker with holes beneath the rim (Lanting 1973, 253). Another possibility is that the sherds are from an s-shaped pot with an almost cylindrical neck.

As remarked in section 3.4, it was on the basis of these Pot Beaker sherds that the dating of the Delfin 190 mound to the Late Neolithic Bell Beaker Period was based. This is doubtful for two reasons. The first is the problem with assessing their precise stratigraphical position in the mound (discussed in section 3.4). The second is that in our opinion, there are no firm grounds to make distinctions between Late Neolithic-Bell Beaker and Early Bronze Age Pot Beakers (*cf.* the discussion in section 4.6 on typo-chronology).

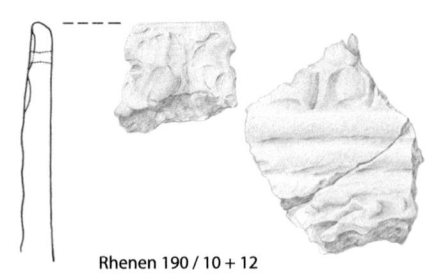

Rhenen 190 / 10 + 12

Fig. 5.8 Two Pot Beaker sherds from Delfin 190 found during the 1971 excavations. Scale 1:2. Drawn by E. van Driel.

5.7 Stray finds around the mound *(by D. Fontijn, A. Louwen, P. Valentijn and K. Wentink)*

Several finds have been done around the Delfin 190 mound in the course of time by amateur archaeologists. In all cases, exact provenances or contexts could not be recorded.

5.7.1 Flint artefacts from the sand path to the west of the barrow

We retrieved four flint artefacts that are reported to have been found on the sand path close to the mound "190" (meant is: Delfin 190). They are coded "*AWN*-190". This must be the *Westerlaan* in between the mounds Unitas 1 and Delfin 190 (chapter 1, Fig. 5.1).

These are three flint flakes, of which one is retouched, and a fragment of a barbed arrowhead. The flakes cannot be dated, but more can be said of the arrowhead. The arrowhead is triangular in shape, has sharp pointed barbs and a concave base. In shape, the arrowhead is similar to those of the Middle Bronze Age-A *Sögel/Wohlde* phase, although an earlier date in the Late Neolithic B is also possible (*cf.* Butler/Fokkens 2005, Fig. 17.19: 2 and 4; Drenth 2005, 338). Both the tip and one of the barbes was broken off. Although such fractures could be attributed to impact after shooting, the context of the find (on a road) makes it impossible to come to any definitive conclusions. High-power use-wear analysis was carried out, but no distinctive wear traces could be detected. The finds are without context, but it is probable that they came to light as a result of the sand extraction carried out on the Delfin 190-mound, by which sand of the mound was used to pave the sand path.

5.7.2 A Pot Beaker sherd

In the *Provincial Depot*, we retrieved one more Pot Beaker sherd (Fig. 5.9). All information on find context is lacking. It was stored with the other finds that were reported to have been found close to Delfin 190, but unfortunately, this is as far as we could get.

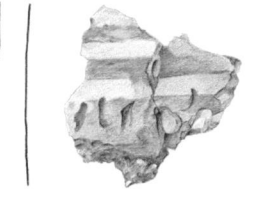

Fig. 5.9 Sherd of a Pot Beaker, presumably found in or near the Delfin 190 mound. Scale 1:2. Drawing by E. van Driel.

The sherd is decorated with two shallow, but broad grooves (± 1 mm deep, 4 and 8 mm wide) separated by a smooth surface. Beneath the grooves there is a row of paired nail impressions. In some of the nail impressions a small amount of a glimmering, black substance is present. It is not known what this substance is and if it was originally present or if it is a post-depositional concretion. A possible fourth shallow groove can be seen on the bottom of the sherd. The sherd cannot be assigned to one of the Pot Beaker types.

5.7.3 Middle Bronze Age, Iron Age/Roman Period sherds found during the sand extraction in 1983

Another small find complex stored in the provincial depot is labeled: "*Prattenburg grafheuvel 190, 163/445, uit opengebulderde grafheuvel 163/445, dec. ' 83*"[65]. These finds must have been done by amateurs after the mound was partly dug by a bulldozer for sand extraction in 1983. The bag contains one rim sherd stored separately from the rest. On this bag is written "*buldozerstrt*" (spoil heap from bulldozer). This is an undecorated rim sherd of which both the inner and outer wall are yellow to light orange in color (Fig. 5.10). The sherd is tempered with (red-colored) pot grit and its surface has been smoothened. The rim is not faceted and undecorated as well. Its sharp S-curve is characteristic for Late Iron Age pottery or native Roman Period pottery as found in *Jutphaas* (Van Tent 1978: 23: 2, but this sherd has been tempered with organic material).

Six undecorated wall sherds are stored in this bag as well. Three of them are undecorated and potgrit tempered (suggesting a dating in the Iron Age or Roman Period). Two others are rather thick (17 and 13 mm) have an oxidized surface

Fig. 5.10 Rim sherd, found at the spoil heaps after the mound was damaged by sand extraction. Scale 1:2. Drawing by E. van Driel.

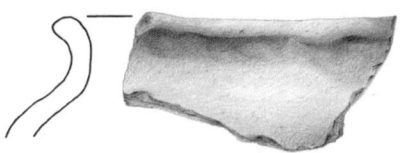

---

65   Translated: Prattenburg barrow 190, 163/445 (i.e. approximate coordinate (ed.)), from dug-out barrow 163/445 (ed.), December 1983.

and are tempered with (broken) quartz (up to 3 mm) which is characteristic for Middle Bronze Age pottery. A third small fragment has the same temper and must be dated to the Middle Bronze Age as well.

Similar to the flint finds found on the sand path, these sherds may have been from the Delfin 190 mound when it was disturbed by sand extraction. As described in this chapter, late Iron Age/Roman Period pottery and Middle Bronze Age pottery are present in the mound material in considerable numbers.

5.7.4 Iron Age or Roman Period finds labeled "Grafheuvel 190"

A further bag only has the label "*Grafheuvel 190 Rhenen*"[66]. As it was stored together with Ms Delfin's finds, it must have been found at or close to the mound Delfin 190. We do not known on which occasion they were found, nor is the exact position known. The bag contains charcoal, a stone, and eight wall sherds and a few tiny pottery fragments. All sherds are tempered with potgrit and have an oxidized surface. One has a smitten (*besmeten*) surface, the other fragment has a groove decoration (Fig. 5.11). As far as can be judged from a 19 by 26 mm sherd, the grooves seem to lack a clear pattern. Groove decoration is known from native Roman Period sites in the province of *Utrecht: Jutphaas* (Van Tent 1978, Fig. 19: 8) and *Wijk bij Duurstede* (Taayke 2002, Fig. 14: 11[67]). According to Van den Broeke's typo-chronology for Iron Age and Roman Period pottery from the Oss region, groove decoration is among the frequently used wall decoration types in the Late Iron Age, but we cannot automatically assume that this applies to pottery traditions from north of the Rhine as well (Van den Broeke 1987, Fig. 5).

Fig. 5.11 Sherd found at or close to the Delfin 190 mound. Scale 1:1. Drawing by A. Louwen.

5.7.5 Iron Age or Roman Period finds "39E-132"

Six undecorated wall sherds and a few tiny pottery fragments are stored in a bag labeled "*Rhenen 39E-132-IJz scherven gevonden na restauratie heuvel (1987)*". 39E-132 is assumed to refer to Delfin 190 find no. 132. However, the number "132" might also mean "mound Delfin 132", which is the other name for the barrow conventionally called "Unitas 3" (see section 4.7). The latter is also known to have been damaged by digging activities and was also restored in 1987. The confusion is caused by the fact that the numbers after the site name sometimes refer to the number of a burial mound, but sometimes only to a number in the find administration. For an example of the latter, see the following section: "39 E *vondstnr* (=find no) 31"! In the case of this "39E-132" find we simply do not have a clue. For pragmatic reasons, the finds are described here. They are all undecorated wall sherds , probably all tempered with potgrit. For that reason it is most likely that they date to the Iron Age or Roman Period.

5.7.6 Middle Bronze Age sherds labeled "39 E vondstnr 031-kapotte grafheuvel"

Two fitting sherds labeled "*39 E vondstnr 031-kapotte grafheuvel* [68]" were probably also done after the mound was partially destroyed by sand extraction. The label indicates the following coordinates for the find: 16360/44512. If these coordinates are correct then the find spot would be at or a few meters to the north of the mound. We are dealing here with sherds with an oxidized outer surface that

---

66   Grafheuvel= barrow
67   In the latter site, one gets the impression that this decoration type is not found very frequently. Among the *Jutphaas* pottery sherds, only 2.5 % has decorated walls (out of a total of some 3300 sherds). Just three sherds (0.1 %) have groove decoration (Van Tent 1978, 219).
68   Translated: 39 E Find no. 31 damaged barrow.

Fig. 5.12 Sherds found at a location c. 1 km to the north of Delfin 190. Scale 1:1. Drawing by A. Louwen.

are tempered with gravel and broken quartz (sizes c. 3 mm by 3 mm). The sherds are 16 mm thick. Their fabric is characteristic for Middle Bronze Age pottery, but different from the fabric of the Middle Bronze Age urn found in top of the mound (section 5.2)

5.7.7 Iron Age and Middle Bronze Age sherds from a northern location

Five sherds, a few tiny pottery fragments and fragments of a (modern) shell of a type often used in footpath pavements are recorded to have been found around the coordinates 16371/44620. This is approximately in the forest one kilometer to the north of the Delfin 190 mound, in the *Prattenburgsche Bosch,* probably around the present-day *Westerlaan* sand path. There are three dark-colored sherds where tempering material is hard to detect. It seems to contain tiny pieces of sand. Two are decorated with fingertip impressions (Fig. 5.12), which indicates a dating to the Iron Age. In temper and decoration they are different from the other sherds described in this section. Another sherd has a brownish color and is decorated with nail impressions. It is tempered with coarse broken quartz (5 mm) which is characteristic for Middle Bronze Age pottery rather than Iron Age pottery. It is is 12 mm thick. Its fabric suggests a date in the Middle Bronze Age, but nail impression decoration is rather rare in this period, although it is occasionally present on *Hilversum* pottery (Middle Bronze Age A, see section 5.5) and on late Middle Bronze Age pottery (Arnoldussen/Ball 2008). Further there is a remarkable sherd that is very thin (4 mm), fully oxidized and tempered with quartz and a glimmering, unidentified mineral. This sherd cannot be further determined.

5.7.8 An Iron Age/Roman Period sherd and a fragment of a La Tène glass bracelet from the Westerlaan

To the west of the mound, on the *Westerlaan* sandpath a small pottery fragment and a glass fragment were found. Find coordinates are 16350/44510. The sherd can be determined as a rim fragment. No tempering material can be observed. It can be dated to Iron Age or Roman Period. The glass fragment is 18 mm long and has a D-shaped section. It has a dark blue color and is slightly curved. It can be determined as a fragment of a *La Tène* bracelet, of the single, D-sectioned type (Van den Broeke 1987, 39). It is datable to the Late Iron Age or early Roman Period (Van den Broeke 1987, 39-40; Fig. 11). Its precise location is unknown but they were stored together with the finds of the Delfin 190 mound. At this sand path, also some flint finds were done (5.7.1). It might well be that we are dealing here with material dug from the Delfin 190 mound itself that was used to pave the sand path.

5.8 Conclusion

The following conclusions can be drawn on the basis of our study of the finds.

The oldest finds are a flint tanged-and-barbed arrowhead that dates to the Late Neolithic Bell Beaker Period and Pot Beaker sherds. The arrowhead was found in secondary position on top of a *Hilversum*-phase Middle Bronze Age pit. The Pot Beaker sherds were found in the mound. Although there is some confusion on their find stratigraphical position, it is most likely that they are in a secondary position as well (as inclusions in the material with which the mound was built). Undisputable evidence that the area was used during the Late Neolithic period or Early Bronze Age has not been found.

The area was probably the location of a settlement during the *Hilversum*-phase of the Middle Bronze Age-A (c. 18th to 16th century BC). This is based on the pottery found in the fills of a complex of feature (pits and posts) underneath the mound. A study of the pottery from these sealed-off features shows that they are all of the same fabric, and must all be dated to this same phase. Pottery with characteristic *Hilversum* decoration was also found inside the mound, though with a slightly different fabric. Such sherds can be interpreted as inclusions in the mound material. On the basis of lithology of the mound construction material, we have reason to believe that the mound was constructed with material from its near surroundings. Since we might expect that a settlement area extends beyond the location of the mound, it is likely that settlement debris will have been included as well. The presence of flint flakes can be interpreted in the same way. With regard to the spatial extension of Middle Bronze Age activities: it is interesting to note that a stray find of Middle Bronze Age pottery has also been found at around one km to the north of Delfin 190 (5.7.7)

The complex of Middle Bronze Age features underneath the mound often consist of non-fitting sherds, flint artefacts and cooking stones, which must have been deposited in the pits after these were dug for some other purpose.

Once the mound was constructed, at some point in the Middle Bronze Age, it was again used for burial. A Middle Bronze Age urn was dug into its surface. The sherds found by Ms Ch. Delfin in 1970, and those found by us appear to belong to one and the same urn. Perhaps it was during such activities that flint artifacts as the thumb scraper (section 5.1.1) became included in the top layers of the burial mound.

Just like at the Unitas 1 mound, Iron Age/Roman Period pottery sherds are included in the highest levels of the mound. Two old pits dug evidence activities, and a concentration of Iron Age sherds close to one of them, may suggest a relation (see section 3. 7.3 on the pits). As in the case of Unitas 1, the majority of the Iron Age/Roman Period pottery[69] from different contexts have the same characteristics. They all are tempered with pot grit, they lack wall decoration, and there are pot forms characteristic for late Iron Age/native (early) Roman pottery. As a whole, the pottery is also similar to the Iron Age/Roman Period pottery from Unitas 1. Severe bioturbation from roots and animals have clearly displaced sherds to deeper levels. Soil process have made it very hard to read the top soil of the mound for the presence of any features. The consistency of the characteristics of the Iron Age/Roman Period finds, however, and the complete lack of later material (wheel-thrown pottery from Roman and later periods) are arguments to interpret these scatter of Iron Age/Roman Period finds as remnants of activities at and around the mounds. In view of the similarities to the Iron Age/Roman Period pottery from Unitas 1, a dating in the Late Iron Age seems the most likely.

---

69 Exception are two sherds that contain mineral tempering material in addition to potgrit: V2 (section 5.1.),V53 (section 5.3.3).

The Delfin 190 mound has been severely disturbed. First by the digging of the large ditch in its west flank , and later because it was used for sand extraction. Fortunately, amateur archaeologists have been following the destructive activities. Many of their finds represent displaced material from the mound or its immediate environment. These finds are similar to the artefacts found by us: Middle Bronze Age and (late) Iron Age/Roman Period sherds, including a fragment of a late Iron Age glass *La Tène* bracelet, and some flint.

Chapter 6

POLLEN ANALYSIS

C. Bakels

6.1 Introduction

One of the aims of the excavation was the reconstruction of the landscape in which the barrows were raised. Vegetation is a significant element in a landscape and a study of the former vegetation by means of pollen analysis was therefore part of the *Rhenen-Elst* barrow research.

6.2 Materials and methods

The aim was to sample the old surface beneath both barrows and the surfaces of their construction material *i.e.* sods. If all is well this material provides pollen deposited during the time of construction (Waterbolk 1954; Casparie/ Groenman-Van Waateringe 1980). Moreover, the ancient soil under the barrows was sampled (Fig. 6.1 and 6.2), because the pollen content of its several horizons reflects the history of the vegetation preceding the construction of the barrows (De Kort 2002). In practice two problems were encountered. Sods were not visible at all and the position of the old surface was open to debate (particular in the case of Unitas 1, see Chapter 2 and 3). As a result, sampling the ancient surface of sods was impossible. The original surface was sampled at the most likely places and the ancient soils under the barrows were sampled by driving boxes into the sections provided by the excavation.

In the end ten samples have been analysed. Seven samples were taken from the 50 cm long box driven into a section of the Unitas 1 barrow. Because the old surface was invisible samples were taken at the levels 5, 10, 15, 20, 26, 30 and 40

Fig. 6.1 (top) Location of box in the profile of the Unitas 1 mound.

Fig. 6.2 (bottom) Location of box in the profile of the Delfin 190 mound.

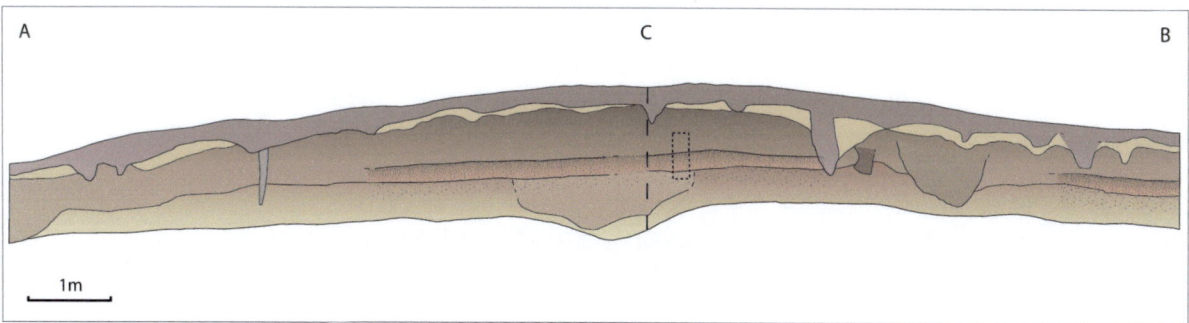

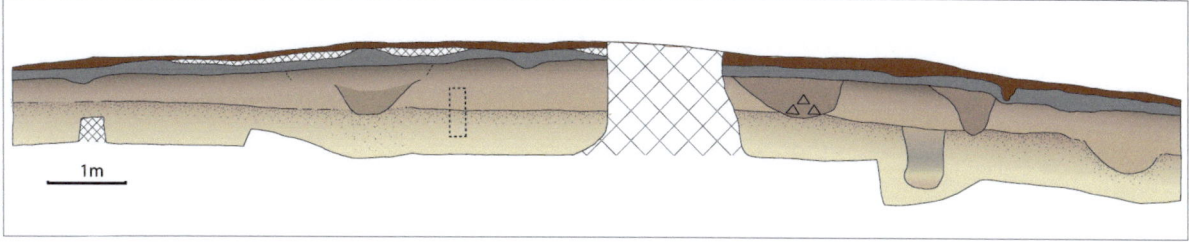

cm of its fill (5 being situated near the top end) in the hope of detecting the old surface somewhere during the laboratory work. Three came from the Delfin 190 barrow (findnumber 70, 71 and the old surface as seen in the box). The sandy sediments were treated in the classic way with KOH, HCl, specific gravity separation and acetolysis.

6.3 Result

The result was disappointing. The Unitas 1 samples revealed no pollen at all. Initially one of the surface samples obtained from the Delfin 190 barrow, 71, looked more promising, although the preservation of the pollen grains was far from optimal. *Calluna* pollen was the type most frequently encountered, suggesting that the space occupied by the barrow was originally a patch of heath, a circumstance that is frequently encountered connected with barrows. A pollen grain of *Juniperus* (juniper) indicates that the heath was disturbed, possibly by the frequent grazing of animals. But the slide showed also several pollen grains of Cerealia (cereals, but not of the rye type), *Plantago lanceolata* and a *Rumex*, presumably *Rumex acetosella*. This kind of plants is not commonly found from soils covered by barrows. They are witnesses of crop cultivation and more precisely, the processing of crops in a settlement. The result would match the conclusion reached by the analysis of the archaeological finds i.e. that the barrow Delfin 190 was constructed on a place of human activity, perhaps a former settlement. Nevertheless, the combination of a relatively large number of *Calluna* pollen and indicators of cereal crops asked for confirmation by the analysis of other samples, because the barrow showed a considerable amount of traces left by roots and burrowing animals and the pollen grains might have their source in contamination by younger material (*cf.* Chapter 3). Therefore two other old surface samples were subjected to analysis. As these two did contain hardly any pollen, the conclusion must be that the pollen content from the sample mentioned above has to be regarded as contamination indeed.

6.4 Conclusion

A reconstruction of the former vegetation is not possible. The reasons for this are not entirely clear yet. In the case of the Unitas 1 barrow, the absence of a visible a-horizont (see Chapter 2) may eventually be attributed to a levelling of the surface before the construction of the barrow, which would have erased pollen present on the original surface. However, pollen were also absent from all other levels in the mound samples. In the case of the Delfin 190 mound, prehistoric pollen are also largely absent, but here there is no evidence for any prehistoric leveling of the original surface. The absence of pollen, therefore, should be explained by other factors. Hopefully, the research that is currently carried out by Marieke Doorenbosch of the *Ancestral Mound* research group will shed more light on explaining and predicting the presence or absence of prehistoric pollen underneath barrows.

Chapter 7

BARROW PROSPECTION BY HAND SOIL AUGER AND DIGITAL PENETROLOGGER – AN EXPERIMENT

E.M. Theunissen, A. Müller

7.1 Introduction

Within the framework of an assessment project of the *RCE* (Cultural Heritage Agency), the two barrows of the *Elsterberg*, 'Unitas 1' and 'Delfin 190' were investigated with a penetrologger and hand auger. The excavation of the two mounds was seized as a good opportunity to perform a blind test. This was done to evaluate the use of a penetrologger. The test was carried out in the field on Monday 21 and Thursday 24 August 2006.

7.2 Using the penetrologger and corings as method of prospection

7.2.1 Penetrologger prospection

Since April 2006 the *RCE* is testing the use of a so-called digital penetrologger on barrows. A penetrologger is a versatile instrument for *in situ* measurement of the resistance to penetration of the soil. Normally, the penetrologger is applied in the agricultural sector as well as in the civil engineering division. It can be used to check whether or not the soil is suitable for specific agricultural purposes, to check for artificially-made compactions or for foundation technology. With a penetrologger, it is possible to determine the ground load-bearing capacity. The resistance to penetration is a mechanical characteristic that, given a certain texture, depends on changing parameters such as degree of humidity, density and the strength of the connection between the mineral particles.

The application of the penetrologger on archaeological objects is as yet new. The Agency expects that this instrument can be useful in the identification and assessment of archaeological heritage, for example, in tracing linear elements as wooden track ways hidden in peaty soils. But also in sandy soils the penetrologger can detect transitions, differences in materials. Subtle changes in the subsoil can be recorded. Due to this quality the application is tested on barrows. The basic assumption is that difference of the resistance to penetration can be used to distinguish prehistoric grave monuments, erected in the past and made of stacked sods, from recent natural phenomena, like sand dunes. On top of that, it may even be possible to trace old surfaces and other subtle transitions in the subsoil.

If the penetrologger can be successfully applied in the field, a very useful device for assessment of the archaeological heritage management would be available, which allows quick and non-disturbing investigations. As barrows still account for the majority of scheduled monuments in the Netherlands, the Heritage Agency has to deal with many questions about these mounds, and it seemed worthwile the seize the rare opportunity of a barrow excavation to further test the device. In view of its promising features the digital penetrologger has been tested on mounds on several occasions. As part of an assessment project in which all listed sites were valued (project 'Evaluation of the scheduled monuments') the instrument was used on anthropogenic built mounds as well as drift sand dunes (Theunissen/Van den Dries 2006). The barrow research of the *Elsterberg* cluster provided an excellent occasion for a new trail of the penetrologger because of the (temporary) availability of vertical sections. The detected differences in resistance to penetration can be related to the recorded profiles and the constitution of the barrow.

7.2.2 Coring

In addition to this, we also used the more traditional hand soil coring method. The coring information about the constitution of a mound is still a necessary condition for a well-founded assessment on the nature of the mound (natural or artificial?). In the difficult circumstances of mounds built on soils without outspoken discolorations as is the case here, we thought it useful to independently prospect the mound-build up with hand coring samples to compare our results later on with the information from the complete barrow profiles of the excavation.

7.3 The fieldwork: method, used equipment and criteria

In the approach of the assessment of barrows a number of criteria were defined (Theunissen *et al.* in prep.). The form and position of the mound in the landscape and the soil features in and outside the mound are the most important parameters. The characteristic of the subsoil outside the mound is important background information; it can be used as points of references.

As a rule, four to five corings were set in a row across the mound; two to three corings in the mound (Fig. 7.1 and Fig. 7.2). These were set mostly on the side, because the centre is often disturbed (in the recent past) by treasure hunters. One to two corings are set outside the mound to obtain information about the natural soil. Parallel to the hand auguring the penetrologger is pushed in the subsoil (Fig. 7.3 and 7.4). By pushing it four to five times in a restricted area of 50 by 50 cm an average value is obtained. This repetition is essential to obtain well-founded data. Peaks in resistances – caused by roots, gravel or animal disturbance – are averaged in this way.

The hand coring equipment consists of a gouge (3 cm width) and an *Edelman* auger (7 cm width). Depending on the type of soil (the degree of fine or coarse sand, the amount of gravel or pebbles) the researcher decides which type of auger is to be used.

The digital penetrologger (type 06.15) is on loan from the Ministry of Defence. The device consists of a small computer with handles (internal logger) with a force sensor, a bi-partite rod, a cone and a depth reference plate. By pushing the cone slowly and regularly in the soil the resistance of penetration is measured. The depth reference plate, which is placed on the soil surface, reflects the signals which are used to control the penetration speed. The measured resistances to penetration are stored in the internal logger, to a maximum of 500 measurements. As the probing rod has a length of 80 cm the penetration depth is limited. The resistance of penetration is expressed in Mpascal or Newton and visualised on a graphic display on a monitor. After the work in the field the internal logger can be connected to a PC for data output.

Fig. 7.1 A gouge of 3 cm width can be used in barrows consisting of sandy sods. Photograph by L. Theunissen.

Fig. 7.2 When the barrow is erected in a soil environment of gravel and coarse sand an Edelman auger is more useful. Photograph by L. Theunissen.

Parallel to the vertical sections of barrow Unitas 1 and Delfin 190 eleven times a coring gouge (3 cm) and the penetrologger were set. The mound of barrow Unitas 1 is penetrated at four locations; on the central north axis (measurement 2 and 3) and the central east axis (measurement 4 and 5). Measurement 1 was situated outside the barrow.

The mound of barrow Delfin 190 is penetrated at five locations (measurements 6, 7, 8, 9 en 10). The reference measurement outside the barrow is location 12, just at the north. The use of the penetrologger in practice is hard work (in a physical sense). Pushing the cone in soils which consist of gravel and coarse sand (ice pushed ridges) requires considerable strength.

7.4 The results

7.4.1 Barrow Unitas 1

Corings

In general the soil environment consists of sedimentary, glacial deposits: an ice-pushed mixture of silty sand, coarse sand and gravel. The reference coring indicates that several distinctive layers occur, five in number (Fig. 7.5). The first horizon, at the surface, is the O-horizon. It consists of organic matter; a litter layer of plant residues in relatively undecomposed form. Below this organic layer lies the Ah horizon. It can be described as a layer of dark grey, moderately fine sand. In this layer of mineral soil the accumulation of organic matter has occurred. Also, the process of bioturbation (biological activity) is strong. This layer is approx. 30 cm thick. Below this Ah horizon a much darker layer of coarse sand is noticed, the Bh-horizon. In this layer all the minerals (such as iron) and organic matter is accumulated. At the depth of approx. 45 cm the colour changed to yellow-brown, which indicates that the content of organic matter is much lower. This is called the BC horizon, a layer with very little humus. Below this horizon the C horizon is present. This parent material is yellow coarse sand. The soil is hardly affected by soil forming processes. No pedological development took place.

The corings in the barrow of Unitas I show a clearly different structure of the soil. Below the O and Ah horizon lies a dark gray spotted layer of approx. 20 cm thick. This layer, called A*an*, is man-made, and is interpreted as the mound. The A*an* horizon is situated on the BC and C horizon, the natural sequence of a sand soil. In coring 4, located at the centre of the mound, it was noted that the first 55 cm of the section was disturbed.

Resistance measurements

Measurements 2, 3, 4 and 5 display more or less the same graph; section 0 to 10 to a quick increase of the resistance around 1 Mpa, followed by a slow decline below 1 Mpa (Fig. 7.6a). In two graphs a slight increase of the resistance can be noticed, on 60 cm below surface (measurement 2) and 70 cm below surface (measurement 3). The back ground measurement 1 gives a graph with a strong resemblance of the mound penetrations. This indicates that may be a thin mound layer is present, but as this part was not excavated, this assumption cannot be tested. The reference measurement 12 shows a complex image of alternating resistances, strongly fluctuating around 1.5 Mpa (Fig. 7.6b).

Fig. 7.3 The digital penetrologger in action. By pushing the cone slowly and regularly in the soil the resistance of penetration is measured. Photograph by L. Theunissen.

Fig. 7.4 The digital penetrologger in action 2. The cone has reached maximum depth. Photograph by L. Theunissen).

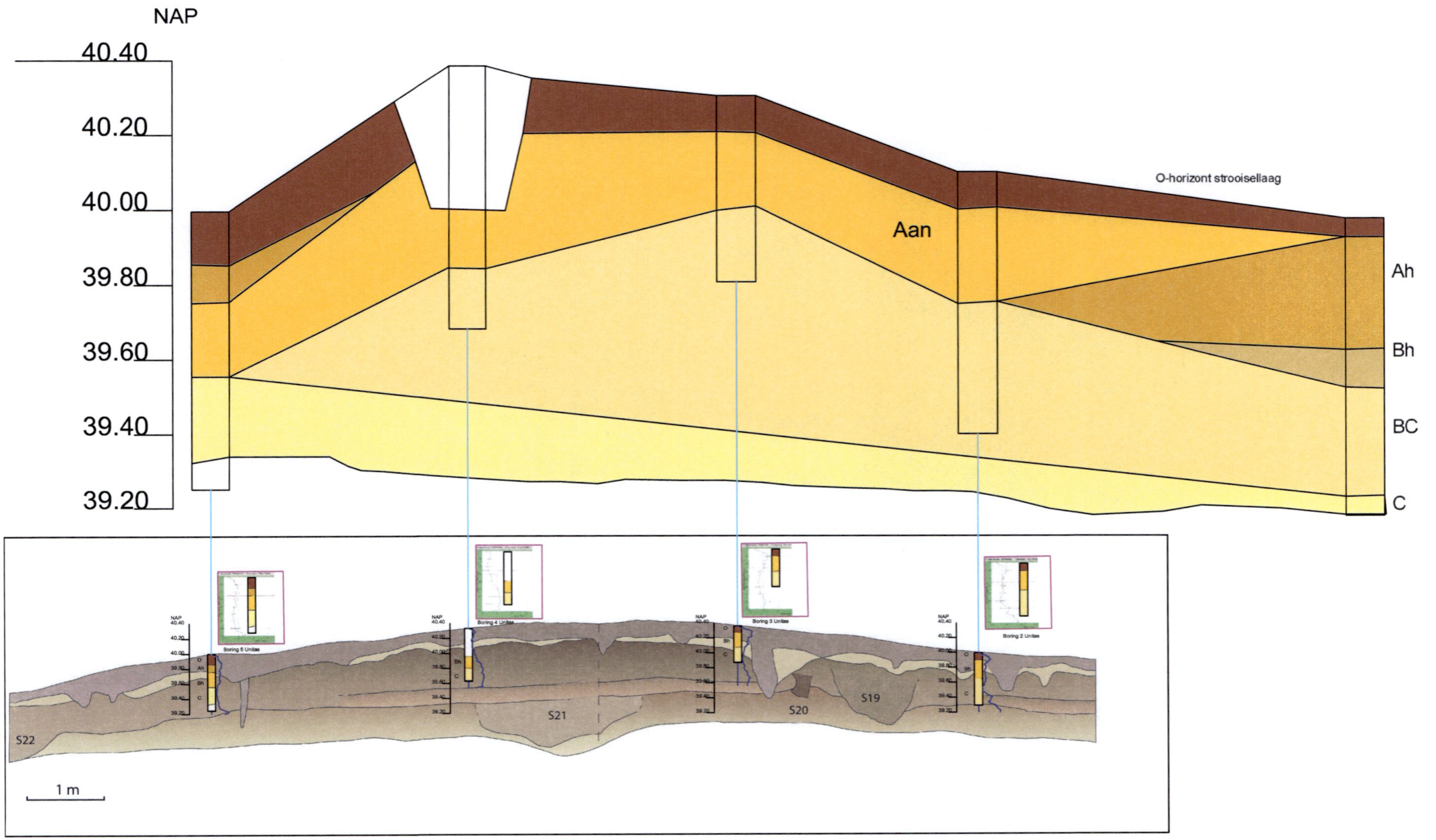

Fig. 7.5 The vertical section of barrow Unitas 1 in which point information (corings and penetrologger measurements) is combined with the more detailed excavated profile. Drawing RCE.

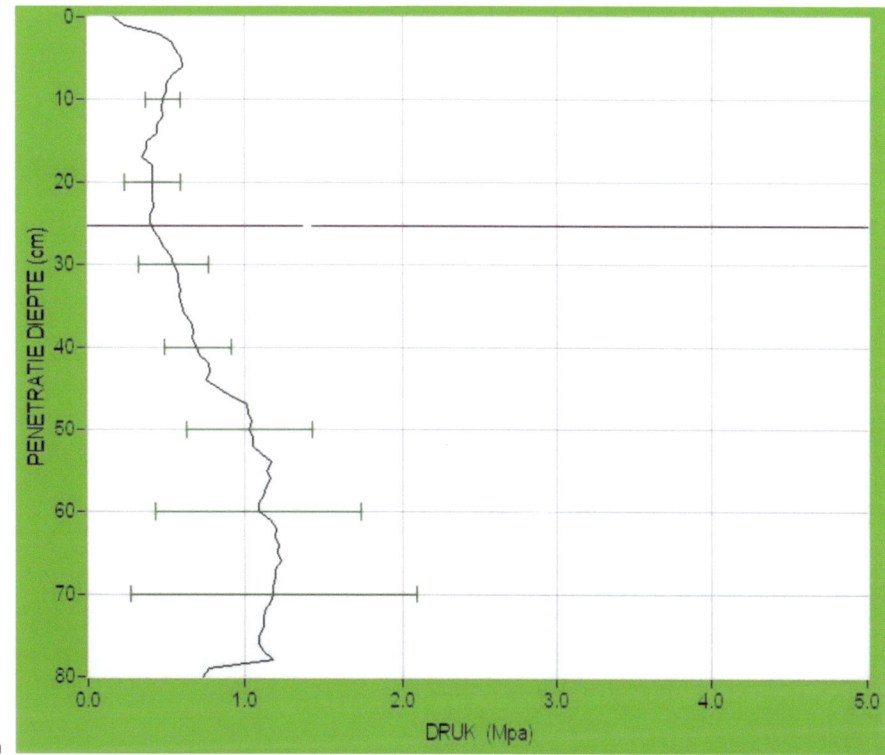

a

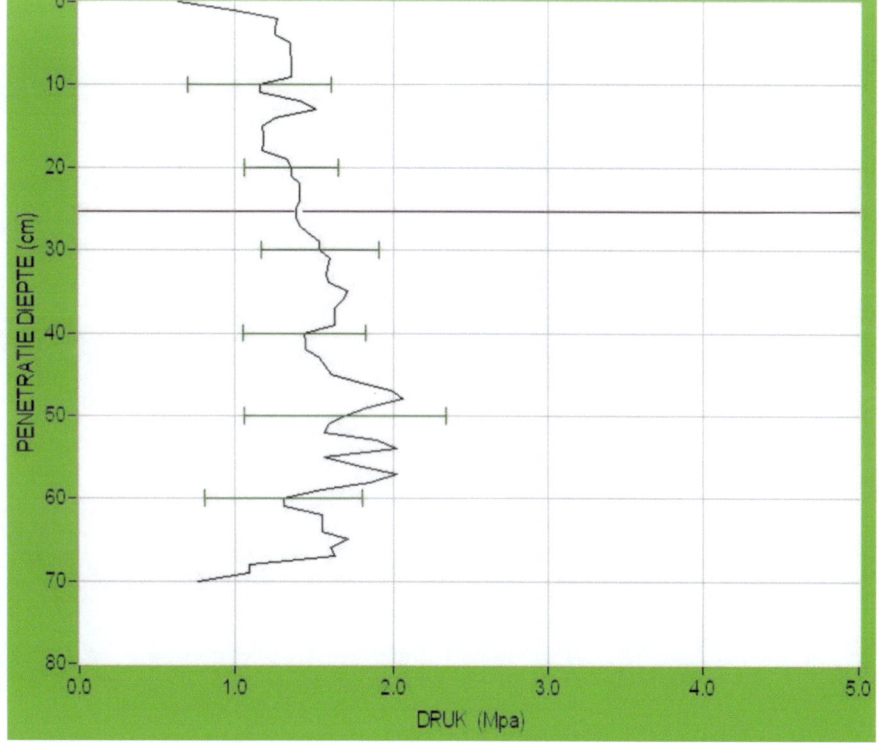

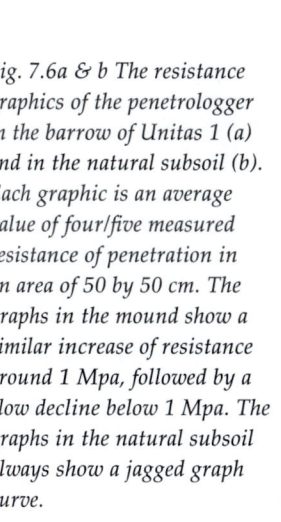

Fig. 7.6a & b The resistance graphics of the penetrologger in the barrow of Unitas 1 (a) and in the natural subsoil (b). Each graphic is an average value of four/five measured resistance of penetration in an area of 50 by 50 cm. The graphs in the mound show a similar increase of resistance around 1 Mpa, followed by a slow decline below 1 Mpa. The graphs in the natural subsoil always show a jagged graph curve.

b

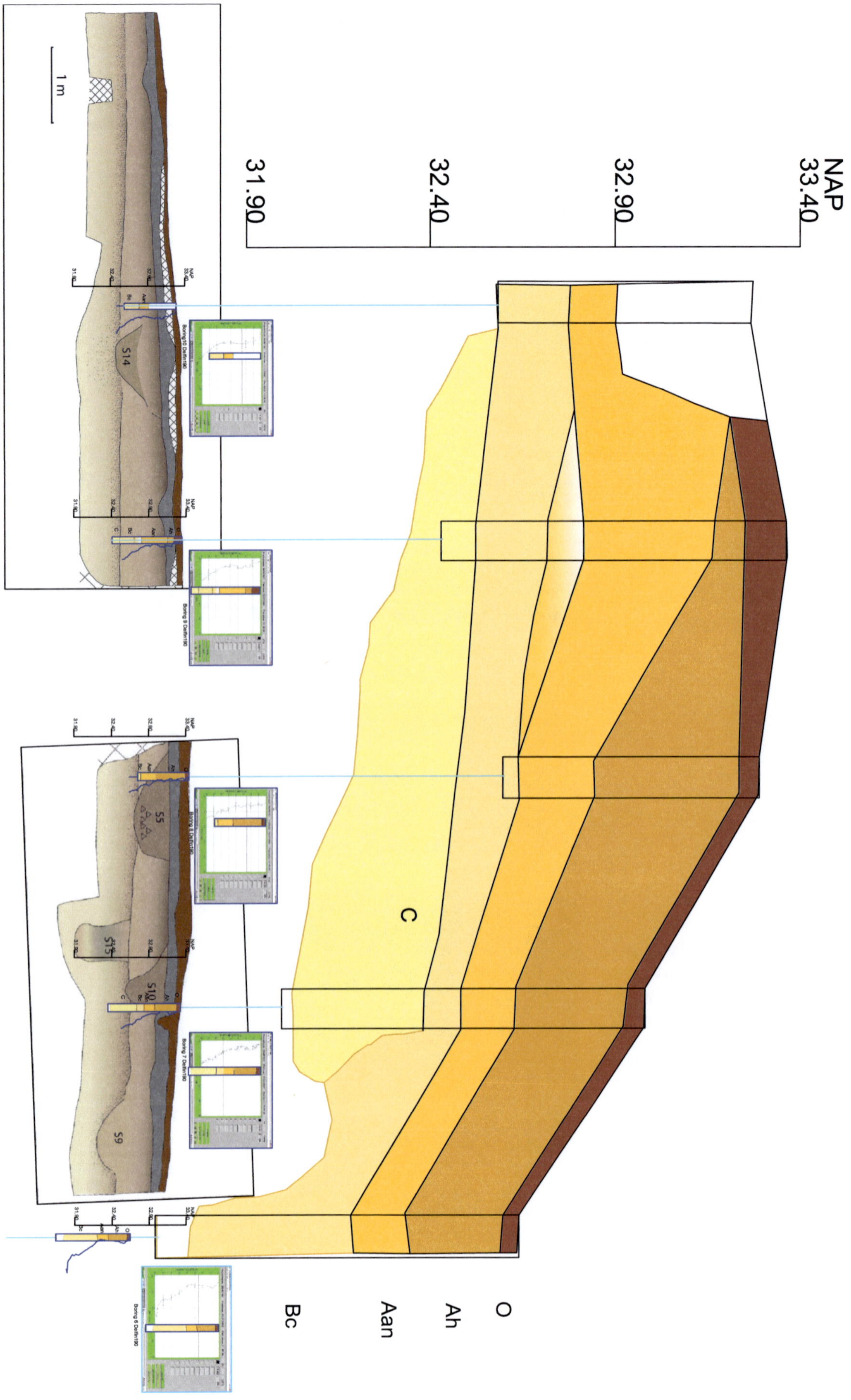

Fig. 7.7 The vertical section of barrow Delfin 190 in which point information (corings and penetrologger measurements) is combined with the more detailed excavated profile. Drawing RCE.

7.4.2 Barrow Delfin 190

Corings

The subsoil of the environment of the barrow Delfin 190 consists also of sedimentary, glacial deposits: a mixture of silty sand, coarse sand and gravel yet not as coarse as in the case of Unitas 1. The reference coring indicates that four distinctive layers occur (Fig. 7.6). The first horizon is the O-horizon, a layer of organic matter, followed by a dark gray sand layer, the Ah horizon, in which accumulation of organic matter has occurred. The Bh horizon, the much darker layer of coarse sand, is not present, but a much lighter coloured version, brown gray. This layer is interpreted as a B*w* horizon with features of weathering. These kinds of horizons occur in loamy soils where minerals and humus does not erode rapidly. Below the B*w* horizon the colour of the sand changes to yellow brown, the transition horizon to the parent material, called BC.

In the corings in the barrow of Delfin 190 a dark brown gray spotted layer was recognized below the Ah horizon. This layer was added by man, and called the A*an* horizon. The height of the mound layer is approx. 35 to 65 cm thick. Below this anthropogenic sediment, the sand is light brown, which is interpreted as a natural BC horizon. In coring 10 the soil profile seems to be disturbed until 50 cm below surface, probably caused by a tree fall.

Resistance measurements

The general view of the measurements in and around this barrow is more or less the same as barrow Unitas 1: the measurements in the mound (6, 7, 8, 9 en 10) display more or less the same graph and the back ground measurement shows a complex image of alternating resistances, mostly above 2 Mpa. In the barrow the resistance to penetration is constant, with a slight incline around 10-15 cm and a more even incline to 1 Mpa below 60 cm. Some graphs display a slight increase at 70 cm below surface.

7.5 Comparison of the results

General

When comparing the three information sources on the vertical section of the mound, the corings, the resistance measurements and the excavation sections several remarks can be made (Fig. 7.5 and 7.7). We have to keep in mind that the location of the corings and resistance measurements differ approx. 50 cm from the position of the vertical section; in other words they show a slightly more backward cross section, which is also based on point observations.

- in both cases the natural soil profile and the anthropogenic built-up of the barrow were recognized as well as in the corings as in the differences in soil resistance by the digital penetrologger;

- also the resistance measurements in the mounds show a consistent pattern, very different from the reference measurements. The slight increases at resp. 60 and 70 cm below surface correspond fairly well with the location of the old surface. Also the reference measurements look alike – complex images of alternating resistances – and clearly deviate from the barrow measurements. The man made mounds clearly differs from the heterogenic mixture of the natural soil composition.

Specific

Unitas I
- it can be stated that the mound is recognized in the corings as an anthropogenic layer. But surprisingly, in the barrow of Unitas 1 this layer was much thinner than the mound as seen in the excavation section. The difference is approximately 50 cm. Maybe this discrepancy can be explained by the fact that the transition to the natural soil (BC) is hard to see in a narrow core view. Resistance measurement 2 and 5 show a good match with the vertical section: in both cases a slight increase was detected at the level of the old surface.

Delfin 190
- also the mound of Delfin 190 was recognized in the corings as an anthropogenic layer. In the barrow of Delfin 190 this difference was less outspoken: in these corings the old surface (the transition to the BC horizon) was well visible. The resistance measurements show less fluctuations: the increases in resistance are more subtle.

Chapter 8

A DISTURBED IRON AGE BARROW AT RHENEN – ELSTERBERG (UNITAS 4)[70]

S. Arnoldussen, J.-W. de Kort

8.1 Introduction

During a stroll through the forest on the 14th of September 2008, an observant hiker noticed that a large pit was dug in the top of the barrow known as 'Unitas 4', which is inaccessible by normal hiker trails and a few tens of metres from the nearest road. This disturbance was reported to the estate forester (Mr. J. de Groot) two days later, who informed Ms. J. Schreurs of the National Heritage Agency (*RACM,* now *RCE*). On the following day Mr. J. de Groot – together with a consolidation specialist (Mr. R. Datema) from the *Archeologische Monumentenwacht* – inspected the barrow, that turned out to be significantly disturbed. A police report was filed for the disturbance of this scheduled monument. On the 20th of September, Ms. J. Schreurs, Mr. J Deeben (both *RCE*) and Ms. I. de Vriendt (GIA, Groningen University) inspected the pit sides, where a darker patch of sand with charcoal and specks of burned bone was observed in the profile section. In the dug-out soil, c. 15 sherds of presumed Iron Age fabric were discovered. These sherds mostly originated from the topmost part of the spoil-heap, suggesting they originated from the lowermost fill op the pit and – judging by the darker colour due to charcoal particles in the surrounding sand – presumably from the observed feature in the section. It was decided that the *RCE* would further document the archaeological remains still present at the site. To this end, fieldwork by the two authors and Axel Müller (all *RCE*) and Marieke Doorenbosch (Leiden University, Faculty of Archeology, Ancestral mounds project) took place on September 23rd 2008.

8.2 Description of the mound and its disturbances

The disturbed barrow is known as Unitas 4 or Delfin 133 (as well as by monument code 39E-008 / no 7143 and Archis no 26537). It is situated at c. 210 m to the northwest of Unitas 1. During the 1971 *AWN* fieldwork campaign, no test-trench was dug into Unitas 4, but its size was recorded and a description of its preservation condition was made. This description tells of a surface area disturbed by 'grooves and a pathway'. Presumably, this tallies with Delfin's original description of the top of the barrow having been affected by wagon-tracks.

Remarkable is the fact that the size of the barrow differs between the various descriptions. In the documentation of the 1970 *AWN* fieldwork campaign, the diameter of the barrow is described as measuring 18.7 m (height 1.15 m), while the documentation at the *RCE* archives (*Loeb-* and *CMA* sheet) list 12-13 m diameter and 0.9-1.2 m height for this barrow. Judging by the observations during the most

---

70 An earlier, slightly different version of this text was published as Arnoldussen *et al.* 2009.

recent fieldwork (diameter *c.* 6.5-8.5 m, height *c.* 0.7-0.8 m; Fig. 8 2, b; Fig. 8.4), either the latter dimensions seem more probable or the barrow has a very minimal to undistinguishable slope near its outer margins.

When we set out to inspect the mound, it was heavily disturbed. Roughly at the location of the presumed centre of the barrow, a 2.7 m wide and 4.4 m long pit was dug (Fig. 8.2). In the north, a 1.2 m long and 0.4 m wide funnel-shaped entrance connected to the main pit, and this connected the surface level (at 50.3 m above *NAP* or Dutch Ordnance Datum to the deepest part of the pit (at 49.46 m above *NAP*). In the southernmost part of the pit, a small area of 0.7 by 0.5 m was dug even deeper to 49.16 m above *NAP*. The sides of the pit slanted inwards, which means that generally the bottom edge of the pit was 0.4 m from the pit's edge at surface level. The dug-away soil was placed all around on top of the pit's edges, presumably to intentionally form low banks (Fig. 8.1). On the western side of the barrow, a small area of 0.8 by 1.5 m of the dug-away soil was covered by small patches of moss and plant material (Fig. 8.1). On top of the low banks of spoil, nine small stems of trees (mostly birch) that had been stripped of side branches, had been placed in an east-west pattern (Fig. 8. 1). At some meters to the south of the pit, a collection of *c.* 30 large stones (mainly white quartz and quartzite cobbles) was placed a in small depression (*c.* 30-40 cm across) on the southern slope of the barrow.

Fig. 8.1 a&b (left page) Photographs of the situation at the destroyed barrow on September the 19th 2008. Photograph by RCE.

Fig. 8.2 (below) Extent of the woodland cover (a), certain extent of the mound body (b), assumed maximum extent of the mound body (c), recently dug pit (d) and cluster of handpicked stones (e, see fig. 1, bottom-left).

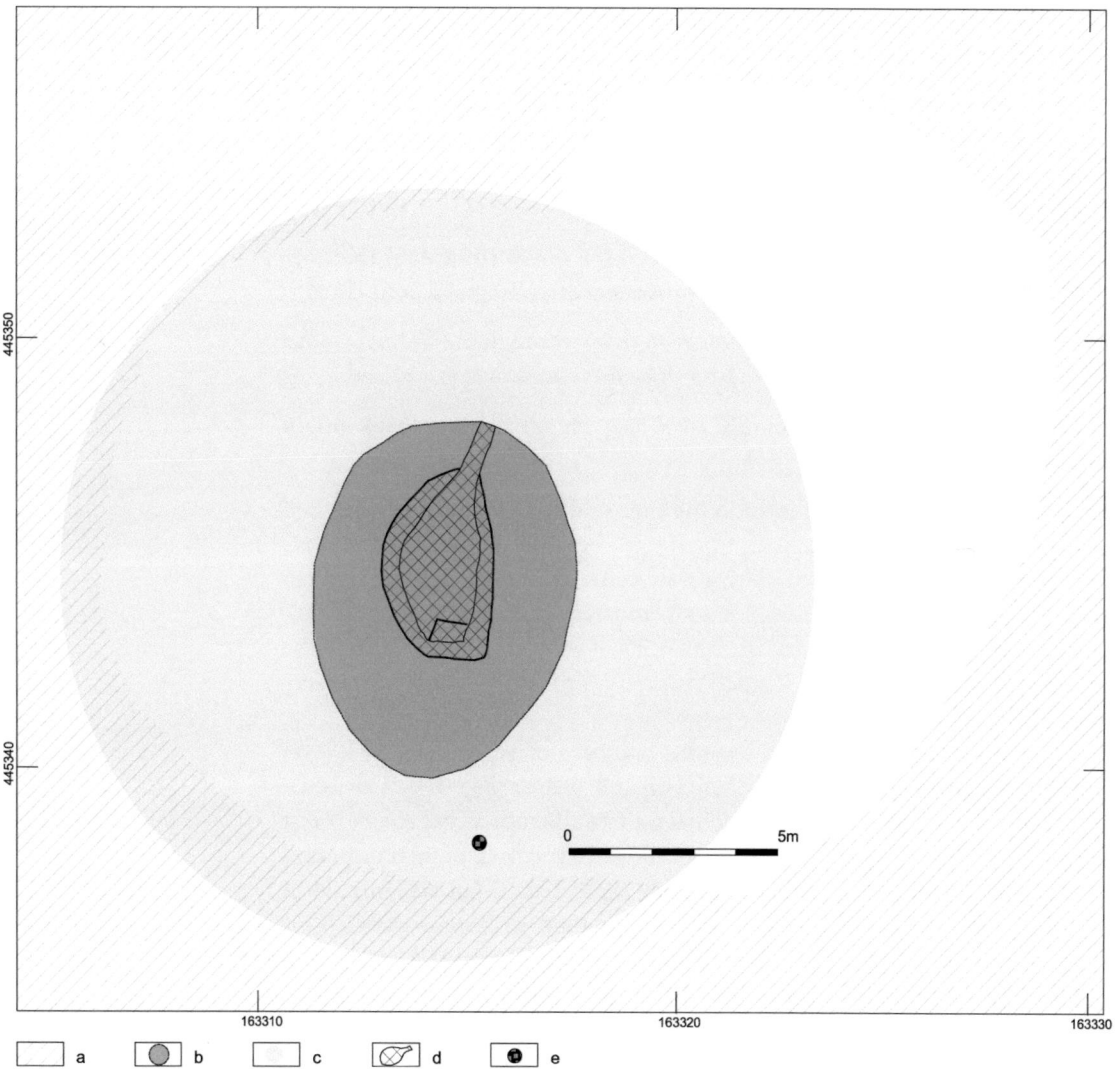

| | a | | b | | c | | d | | e |

From the size, shape and initial roofing construction of the pit, it seems most plausible that it was intended as a temporary shelter for one or more individuals that intended to stay in the woods for some time. The constructional details, such as the oblique sides (to counter collapse), the lowered section (for an overnight fireplace?), the possible use of the stone-concentration as an outside fireplace, and the effort put into the pruning of the roof-beams all suggest a well thought-through plan and adult culprit(s). The fact that the yellowish sand of the spoil-heaps was partly camouflaged by moss and that the most remotely positioned barrow of a larger barrow group (see below) was used, suggest that those digging this pit were aware of the illegal nature of digging there, or of the activities to be deployed from within the intended shelter. Most likely, the pit was intended as a poachers' stake-out and/or overnight shelter.

Unfortunately, this was not the first disturbance. Already some time between late February and December 1997, a *c.* 1.6 by 1 wide and 0.7 m deep rectangular pit was dug. Its outline could be identified roughly halfway north-south of the eastern pit side (Fig. 8.3, section 'A'). The pit was interpreted as having been dug by treasure hunters (letter R.R. Datema, d.d. 19-3-1998) and was refilled by the *Staatsbosbeheer* forester and covered-up with sods again. Possibly, the fact that this barrow and others in its vicinity had been consolidated and cleared of trees (Douglas firs, planted only 6 to 7 years earlier) in 1987, has contributed to its appeal to treasure hunters.

8.3 The fieldwork

During the fieldwork by the *RCE* in September 2008, the side walls of the pit were cleaned with a shovel, photographed and drawn. In addition, a large part of the dug-out soil was sieved by hand with a 4 mm mesh sieve. Finds were collected from three different contexts:

a.   those recovered from the profile section, and for which contextual information was precise (all originated from a possible cremation grave, see below),

b.   those sieved from the parts of the spoil heap that – through the distinct colour of the soil – *presumably* originated from the aforementioned grave, and

c.   those sieved or hand-picked from the spoil heap for which no probable origin could be argued.

After the fieldwork, the finds collected at the time of discovery and field-check of the new disturbance were also studied. In order to check on the dating of the barrow construction, samples for OSL-dating were collected, as well as several pollen samples. The initially processed samples, unfortunately, no longer contained pollen (pers. comm. M. Doorenbosch). In total, 4.2 g of charcoal, 26 g of burnt bone (presumable cremation remains), 2 small stones (1.5 g) and *c.* 1.3 kg of pottery (81 sherds) were collected.

The topmost layer of the sections recorded consisted of a 5 to 7 cm thick layer of recent plant remains and half decomposed organic matter (Fig. 8.3). This is the A horizon of the podzolic soil that developed under influence of the recent forest vegetation. Minerals and humus particles from this layer have been transported into the topmost 7 to 20 cm of the underlying layer. This B horizon formed in a 50-60 cm thick layer of light brown, slightly silty sand with some gravel. This layer is interpreted as a humanly reworked layer of soil. No evident sods could be identified in the profile. The situation here is very similar to that encountered in Unitas 1 and Delfin 190 (Chapters 2 and 3). This layer appears to have been deposited in a single episode, as the main barrow body for a – not discovered

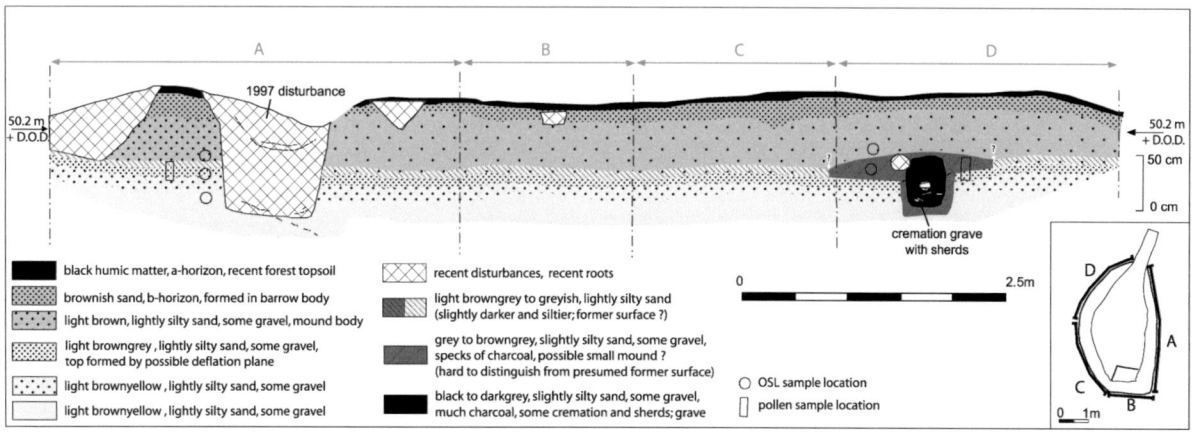

Fig. 8.3 Schematized sections of the pit walls, showing the location of the Iron Age cremation grave and its most plausible stratigraphic position.

– primary interment. The boundary between this layer and the underlying natural sediment is formed by a very faint somewhat more darker grayish-brown and seemingly siltier layer of *c.* 7-10 cm thick light brown-grey sand. Possibly, this represents (or reflects) the (limited) soil formation that took place in the natural ice-pushed sediment. Near the lowermost limit of this darker band, significantly more coarse sand and small pebbles could be observed. This band of pebbles may represent a phase of cryogenic sorting, in which coarser components sink in liquefied thawing sediments, or – albeit less likely – a deflation plane where (prior to the later soil formation) the smaller silty and sandy fraction of the sediment has been blown away. The somewhat darker, siltier, layer on top of the deflation plane presumably indicates the location of the former, prehistoric surface. Both the gravely subsoil and the hardly distinguishable prehistoric surface recall the situation encountered underneath the Unitas 1 barrow to the south (see Chapter 2). We were under the impression that this represents a decapitated soil (e.g. when sods were taken for barrow construction) but conclusive evidence is lacking. It is therefore also possible that the top of the more darker, siltier, layer is in fact the original topmost surface at the time the grave was dug. The topmost 20-25 cm of the natural sediment underneath the presumed former surface is somewhat light brown-grayish of colour and consists of lightly silty sand with some gravel. This sediment comprises ice-pushed layers that dip towards the south, unlike at other parts of the ice-pushed hills in the Netherlands. At greater depths, the sediment is lithologically identical, but of light brown-yellowish colour. Presumably, this difference in colour indicates the limited depth of former soil formation, with the upper (light brown-grayish) layer being interpreted as the B horizon and the lowermost (brown-yellowish) layer as the C horizon.

The sequence of deposits described above applies to all sides of the recently dug pit, but is in several locations disturbed at the top by recent pits of unknown origin, roots and disturbances such as the 1997 disturbance. In the northwest part of the section, at the position of the assumed former surface, a darker patch of soil is visible (Fig. 8.3-8.4). The darker colour is caused by the distribution of small charcoal particles. This darker patch appears to be asymmetrical in shape: its lower boundary is more or less level around the main pit, while its upper limit is concave in shape, with a maximum thickness of *c.* 10-15 cm. Establishing its exact shape and extent however proved difficult. Tentatively, an a-symmetrical (mushroom) shape of the charcoal dispersion pattern is suggested (Fig. 8.4). This could indicate that originally a low body of sediment must have been present on top of the former surface, in which charcoal particles could be dispersed (presumably through bioturbation) *prior* to the construction of the main mound body. This suggests that for quite some time, a charcoal rich pit that had been covered by a very small (1.3 m diameter, 5-15 cm height) mound, was subject to bioturbation *prior* to later mound construction. However, it is also possible that only

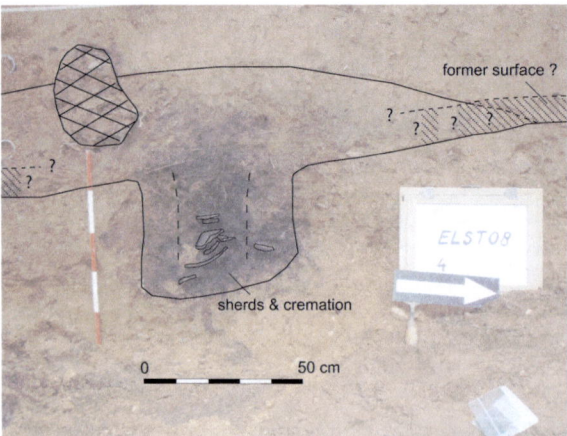

a very low body of soil covered the cremation grave, and that charcoal from its centre was transported laterally (creating the width of the mushroom) within the darker, siltier layer (presumed old surface level). In that case, the body of soil that was situated above surface level in prehistoric times was much smaller (*i.e.* 5 to 10 cm max; pers. comm. Q. Bourgeois, Jan. 2009). In any case, determining the horizontal limits of the charcoal dispersion was difficult, as it indeed appeared to blend in with the thin, more grayish and silty layer that has been described above as (a possible remnant of) the original soil formation. In fact, the discussion whether or not a small ('mushroom-shaped') mound was present on top of the cremation pit is irrelevant to the main observation that it evidently represents a feature that was created *prior* to construction of the later mound body, as it has not been dug into the latter. Within the darkest and most charcoal-rich centre of the pit underneath the charcoal distribution, specks of burned bone were observed and collected, as well as several sherds (Fig. 8.5). The position of the sherds was documented in drawing and photography, and the sherds were assigned individual numbers and documented separately in order to reconstruct any special sequence of depositing after recovery.

Fig. 8.4 Photograph of the cremation grave with sherds in situ. Around the sherds, specks of burned bone could be observed, but these are not visible on the photographs. To the right an interpretation of the stratigraphy with the position of the sherds indicated. The height of the covering sediment (the 'mushroom cap') may in reality have been lower. Photograph by RCE.

8.4 Finds: description of the pottery

In addition to two small natural stones (1.5 g) that have been misinterpreted as ceramics during finds processing, the majority of the finds recovered comprised burnt bone (115 fragments, total 26 g) and pottery (81 fragments, 1316.8 g). The fragments of burnt bones have been analysed by L. Smits, who confirmed the presence of both human and animal remains amongst the burnt bone fragments (of these, 1 g of human and 1 g of animal bone were recovered from the (cremation)pit in the profile; Smits 2009). A fragment recovered from the sieved darker soil (presumably originating from the cremation grave), indicated a person older than 6 years based on bone robustness (Smits 2009, 4) The pottery fragments recovered will be described in more detail below, starting first with a description of the 13 contextualized sherd from the cremation pit and thereafter for the assemblage as a whole (including the previous 13 sherds).

A total of 13 sherds (413 g) was recovered from the cremation grave in the section, and for nine sherds (380.9 g) their exact position in the profile section could be documented (Fig. 8.4). These were collected individually. All 13 sherds are (based on their wall thickness (7.2-12.6 mm), tempering (sand and pot grit; combined, with no dominance of either) part of one pot, which is not (archaeologically) complete and secondarily burnt. Diagnostic sherds are drawn here as Fig. 8.5 nos. 1-3 (row A). This vessel was fired in an incompletely oxidizing en-

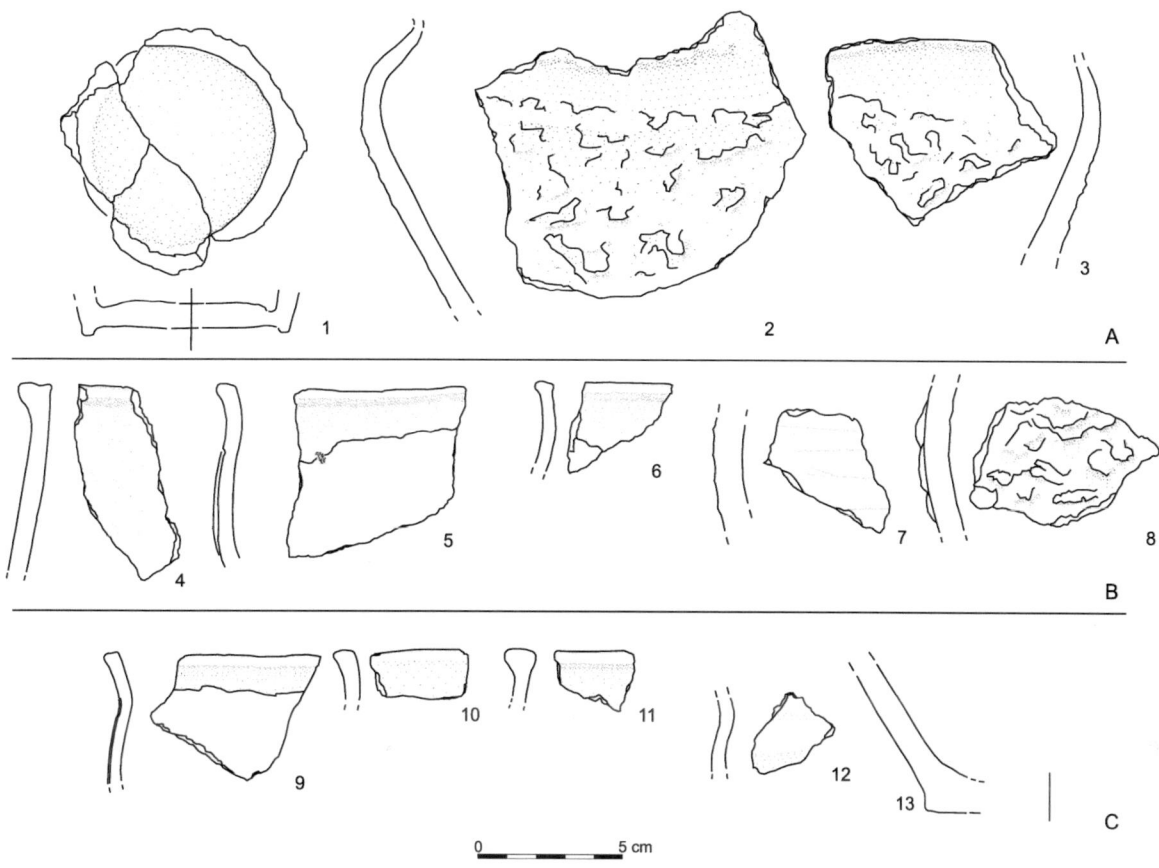

Fig. 8.5 Selection of sherds recovered by hand from the assumed cremation grave (A), the black soil on the spoil-heaps presumably originating from the same feature, recovered by sieving (B) and sherds sieved from the spoil-heaps for which no inferences on their original context(s) may be made (C). Drawing by S. Arnoldussen.

vironment (or could oxidize after being taken from the furnace), and its inner core remained grey in colour. The outer colour was presumably reddish, but has been affected by the secondary firing (on the cremation pyre?) to such an extent that the original outer color must remain speculative. Based on the largest wall fragment, the pot's width approximated 26 cm in diameter. Remarkable is that the pot's foot-ring was found above wall-sherds positioned with their inner side down. This indicates that the pot had not collapsed *in situ*, but that the several sherds were placed into the feature after fragmentation. The fact that breaks of the sherds are secondarily burned as well suggests that breakage could have preceded the re-firing (although breakage due to differential heating during cremation may also have resulted in re-fired sherd sides). One sherd presumably also belonging to this pot was found while sieving the dug-out soil (Fig. 8.5, no. 8).

Amongst the other sherds found while sieving (and for which consequently their original context is unclear) at least eight other vessels are represented (by different rim shapes, wall finish, or pot morphology; see Fig. 8.5, nos. 4-13 for examples). In the sections below, general characteristics of the pottery (including the sherds collected with certainty from the grave) are discussed as a single assemblage.

Of the 81 fragments, 12 pieces (5.4 g) are too small for meaningful analyses and have been recorded as 'hand-made pottery, presumably prehistoric' and are omitted below. The remaining 69 sherds have a mean weight of *c.* 19 g each, indicating that they have not been severely fragmented (see also Fig. 8.5). In various aspects (such as method of production, tempering material and post-manufacturing traces), the sherds appear to be a rather homogenous group, save for incidental outliers.

All sherds originated from vessels that were hand-made. From the breakage pattern of one sherd (showing a N-joint), is was clear that coils or strips of clay had been kneaded together to form the pots. Several sherds indicated that pots of bipartite form (Dutch *twee-ledige vormen*, e.g. Fig. 8.5, nos. 4; 6; 11) as well as pots of tripartite form (Dutch *drie-ledige vormen*, e.g. Fig. 8.5, nos. 2; 5; 9; 12) are represented. Both flat (Fig. 6, no 13) as well as raised (Fig. 8.5, no 1) bottom sections were recognized. Rim sherds either showed rounded-rectangular rim–shapes (e.g. Fig. 8.5, nos. 5; 9; 10) or slightly outward extruded rims (e.g. Fig. 6, no. 4; 6) that most probably both were positioned at slight (*c.* 0 -15 degree) angles outward. The two partly present vessel bases suggest base diameters exceeding 8.6-10 cm in size, while only two rim sherds were of sufficient size to estimate a pot diameter (> *c.* 15 and 20 cm respectively). Documented wall thickness ranges from 5.6 to 14.6 mm, but 80 % measures between 7-12.2 mm).

The pot surfaces were often smoothed on the inside, which incidentally (four sherds) left finger-wide shallow grooves. Such grooves were also observed four times on the outsides of pots (e.g. Fig. 6, no 7) but various sherds were presumably smoothed with the help of a cloth, or stone or bone smoother (Dutch *lomer*) although only one sherd showed the distinct small smoothening traces left by such an item. Possibly, a thin clay slib cover was applied to some sherds prior to smoothening, as with some sherds the uppermost layer has detached from the sherd's outer surface (e.g. Fig. 8.5, nos. 5; 9). Seven sherds had a (still) rough or intentionally roughened outer surface, while the outer surface of 11 sherds (*c.* 16 % in number) was clearly smitten (implying the deliberate application of moist clay (Dutch: *besmeten*)). No decoration of rims or pot walls was observed, although a single (unintentional) impression of a finger-tip was observed on the inside of a sherd from the assumed cremation grave.

For 57 sherds the circumstances in which the pots were fired could be observed. The majority show reddish coloration of the outer- and inner surfaces of the pot walls, while the core displayed a grey to dark-grey colour. This suggests that the pots were fired in a not-fully oxidizing atmosphere. Alternatively, oxidation of the surfaces may have occurred during cooling after initial firing, but the oxidized sherds of pot bottoms recovered and the thickness of particularly the oxidation of the outer pot surface argues in favor of a principally not-fully oxidizing atmosphere during firing. Only four sherds showed a cross-section that indicated that the sherd's core as well as the pot's inside wall were baked in a oxygen-deprived atmosphere. Presumably, these vessels were baked while standing on their rims. For 65 sherds the tempering materials could be identified (table 1).

With the majority of sherds (*c.* 77%), pot grit was the sole (12 sherds) or dominant tempering material used. Sand frequently was observed in addition to other tempering agents but it remains unclear whether it was intentionally added to the clay, or whether the sand admixture to the clay was natural. The presence of 13 sherds in which no sand was observed as well as sherds with solely sand suggests that either sand was added intentionally or that different clay sources are represented in the material. Organic matter might have been added to 13 sherds, but identification was generally uncertain (the voids may alternatively represent poorly kneaded clay) and of these only a single sherd was tempered with organic matter exclusively. Considering the small size of this latter sherd, non-exclusive use of organic tempering seems most realistic. Frequently, there was much uncertainty on whether the small pores (generally < 1 mm) represented burned-out organic matter, and poor kneading of the clay may have been responsible for part (but not all) of the cavities observed.

Besides a possible small fragment of charred contents on the outside of a single sherd (Fig. 8.5, no 5), clues to the former functions of the pots are absent. It can therefore only be assumed that most vessels were used for food-preparation and/or food-storage, which in any case tallies with the few assumed pot sizes that could be reconstructed (15 to 20 cm). It is very remarkable that nearly all sherds have been secondarily re-fired. For two small sherds it was clear that they had not been re-fired, or only partly re-fired. In this aspect, they differ from almost all other sherds that were found in, at or near Unitas 1 and Delfin 190 (see Chapters 4 and 5). The remaining fragments were too small to see if these were also secondarily burned. As a consequence of such re-firing, surfaces and breaks of most sherds were yellowish-pink to grayish-beige in colour, brittle and weathered and some displayed cracks on outer- or inner-surface areas.

The sherds recovered with certainty from the assumed cremation grave were – as stated above – also all re-fired secondarily. For the sherds recovered from the feature (Fig. 8.5, A) and for a sherd presumably of the same vessel recovered during sieving (Fig. 8.5, no 8), the interpretation of interred grave goods burned at the funeral pyre might be forwarded, but then it remains enigmatic why nearly all other sherds recovered (for which it remains unknown whether they originated from either the grave, the mound body or the former surface underneath the mound body) are re-fired secondarily as well. If the assemblage from outside the assumed grave should represent settlement debris, it remains peculiar that (save for one clear exception) no other unburned sherds were recovered. One might speculate whether these sherds represent fragments of goods also burned at the pyre – or during (near-) contemporaneous funerary rites – and that were deliberately *not* placed into the pit in which the cremated remains were placed. Presumably, specific sherds were selected to be interred with the cremation remains, and the sherds recovered during the archaeological fieldwork were almost certainly from a single vessel (although it cannot be excluded that more sherds were originally placed with the cremation remains, as half of the feature had already been disturbed).

8.5 Dating of the finds

Establishing the age of the pottery assemblage is difficult. Pot-morphology, tempering materials used and the firing-environment suggest an Iron Age dating, but assigning these sherds to a sub-period of the Iron Age is complicated. In part, this is a consequence of the fact that there are not many comparative studies of Iron Age pottery from the ice-pushed hills of *Utrecht* and adjacent *Veluwe* district areas (cf. Chapter 4 and 5). The presence of *besmeten* (smitten) pot walls (e.g. Fig. 8.5, nos. 2; 3; 8) in combination with (?) pots of tripartite form with angular well-defined rims (e.g. Fig. 8.5, no 9) and bipartite forms (e.g. Fig. 6, no 4, Dutch; *twee-ledige vormen*) is known from Early Iron Age assemblages, but in that case some grit-tempered sherds may have been expected, as well as fewer (low) s-shaped flanged pots. A later Iron Age date may also be forwarded, although in that case some rims displaying decoration (on their outside) may have been expected (*cf.* Van den Broeke 1987b, 109; Van Heeringen 1989b, 254-269). The sherds were shown to Iron Age pottery expert P. van den Broeke (*Bureau Archeologie, Nijmegen*) who also could not identify unique markers for a specific sub-phase of the Iron Age, but who would opt for a dating around the Middle- to Late Iron Age transition, based on the presence of the raised bottom fragment (foot-ring), but admittedly with low (55%) certainty (pers. comm. Dec. 2008). The presence of *besmeten* (smitten) walls is noteworthy, as this feature is rare among the Late Iron Age pottery found in, at or near the Unitas 1 and Delfin 190 mounds (*cf.* Chapters 4 and 5).

Comparison to other sites is difficult, due to the limited size of the assemblage and absence of well-datable sherds. The roughened finish of some sherds and tempering agents used may be compared to better dated ceramics finds elsewhere. In the southern Netherlands, smitten walls (Dutch; *besmeten*) occur throughout the Iron Age, but are most common around the early to middle, and middle to late Iron Age transitions respectively (Van den Broeke 1987a, 32 fig. 5). For the Late Iron Age to Roman period occupation at *Wijk bij Duurstede-De Horden*, *besmeten* (smitten) lower parts of pots are seldomly observed (Taayke 2002, 205; 207). At the latter site, also trends in the use of tempering materials are discernible. Only for the first phase (50 BC to 25 *AD*), is pot grit tempering dominant, after which organic tempering only increases in importance (*op. cit*, 207-209). At *Jutphaas*, the threshold for distinguishing native Roman period pottery assemblages by percentage of organically tempered sherd is set at 35% (below probably pre-Roman Iron Age, above; Roman period; Van Tent 1978, 218; 237). According to Van den Broeke (1987b, 101), organic matter is used in *Oss-Ussen* from the second half of the Late Iron Age and the Roman period. At the middle Iron Age site of *Kesteren-De Woerd*, organic material was infrequently (*c.* 4%, versus 93% pot grit) used as tempering agent (Wiepking 2001, 161). At *Lage Blok*, tempering with vegetal matter was even more rare (< 0.4%), and roughened/smitten walls were observed with 20-44% of the sherds (Ufkes 2002, 75; 80). Parallels for the foot-ring (fig. 6, no 1) are depicted in Van Heeringen (1989a, 51 no 117; 118, no 110; 1989b, 200; 202, no 14, specimens dated to Middle and Late Iron Age) and Arnoldussen/ Ball (2008, 187 fig. 8, no 7; Late Bronze Age). In the southern Netherlands and central river area, organic tempering occurs only sporadically during the Late Bronze Age and Early Iron Age (Arnoldussen/ Ball 2008, 192).

In conclusion, the presence of *besmeten* sherds and – albeit with low dominance and frequencies – use of organic temper is documented for Middle Iron Age to Late Iron Age ceramic assemblages in neighbouring regions. However, parallels for the shape of several quite distinct sherds (particularly fig 6, nos. 1, 4, 5, 9 & 11) could not yet be identified. Moreover, small assemblage size hampers proper comparison of relevant parameters such as (percentages of) tempering agent and surface finish (*cf.* Van den Broeke 1987a, 34; Van Heeringen 1996, 251). Therefore, a provisional date of transition Middle- to Late Iron Age must be tentatively assumed.

8.6 A (Middle to Late) Iron Age barrow? An interpretation

The stratigraphic position of the charcoal-stained body of soil (Figs. 8.3; Fig. 8.4) underneath the main mound body and the presumed (middle- to late?) Iron Age dating of the sherds recovered with certainty next to the cremated remains, suggest that the main mound body was constructed during or after the Middle Iron Age. This may indicate that barrow Unitas 4 was erected more than a millennium later than those known as Unitas 1 dated to the Early Bronze Age (see Chapter 2) and Delfin 190 (Middle Bronze Age (Chapter 3). To construct a new Middle or Late Iron Age barrow near much older (Early to Middle) Bronze Age barrows is a relatively rare phenomenon (*cf.* Fontijn 1996a, 82-84; Gerritsen 2003, 148-149).

Middle Iron Age cemeteries in the southern Netherlands are in their funerary traditions well comparable to late Urnfield traditions, but are, by contrast, thought to occur more spatially dispersed (Gerritsen 2003, 134). These graves are interpreted as graves forming isolated or small clusters of burials, for which it may be suggested that their distribution seems more bound to that of settlement remains, than that of (much) older graves (Gerritsen 2003, 131-135 esp. table 4.3; 148). In the southern Netherlands, not all graves were accompanied by ditches, but in any case peripheral structures were – unlike in the Northern Netherlands – still dug after the Middle Iron Age (Hessing/ Kooi 2005, 651; Hiddink 2003, 27-28). In the eastern Netherlands, cremation graves without peripheral features are known from the eight century BC up to first century *AD* (Van Beek 2006; 2009, Chapter 13). Middle/Late Iron Age cemeteries are just relatively small, and extensively scattered, like their counterparts from the southern Netherlands (Van Beek 2009, 432).

The ice-pushed hills of *Elst* border a part of the river area where grave fields *with* peripheral features dominate (Hiddink 2003, 29 fig. 8; Gerritsen 2003, 149). The absence of ditches might suggest that no mound body was present (Hiddink 2003, 9), but the observation at *Rhenen-Elsterberg* indicated that this needs not always to have been the case. The discussed assemblage, being a combination of pyre-debris (*i.e.* charcoal, burnt pottery) and burnt human remains, is often interpreted as a coincidental accumulation of pyre remains that is interred (Hiddink 2003, 23; 121; 273). The large size of the sherds in the *Rhenen-Elsterberg* feature and their tight packing, suggests that at least these remains were specifically (rather than unintentionally) selected from the cremation location.

The quoted largest sizes for barrow Unitas 4 (12-18.7 m) are at the larger end of the spectrum of urnfield round barrow sizes (*c.* 1-13 m; Hessing/ Kooi 2005, 636-638; Gerritsen 2003, 125), although some much larger Middle and Late Iron Age barrow ring-ditches are known in the southern Netherlands (*op. cit.*, 651; Gerritsen 2003, 133 (*Lummen-Meldert*; 20 m (Middle Iron Age) / *Oss-Kraaijennest*; 16 m (Late Iron Age))). However, the 8.5 m diameter recorded during the most recent fieldwork may indicate that the barrow was much smaller, but even then is considerably larger than the average Middle/Late Iron Age monument from the south. Large mounds do however occur in the centre of the Netherlands. Van Beek (2009, 437) refers to a large monument (D=17 m) from *Friezenveen*, as well as to one from *Dorper Es, Wierden* (D=11 m). In recent excavations at *Apeldoorn-Echoput*, the Ancestral mounds project excavated a high and large mound (D= 18.5) that was C14-dated to the late Middle or Late Iron Age (Fontijn forthcoming). So, large Middle Iron Age monuments may be a feature of the funeral rites of the Central Netherlands.

Provided that the provisional Middle/ Late Iron Age *terminus post quem* age indicated by the pottery is confirmed by radiocarbon analysis (subduing doubts on a possible earlier Iron Age date for the pottery), the disturbed *Rhenen-Elsterberg* barrow may represent a rare case of later Iron Age re-use of considerably older funerary landscapes. This pattern of barrow construction near older ones is well-known for the Middle Bronze Age B in particular (Bourgeois/ Fontijn 2008, 48-49, esp. fig. 3.5), and several examples of urnfield graves placed into, or close to, older mounds are known as well (Gerritsen 2003, 141-143). For the Middle and Late Iron Age, this is a much rarer occurrence (*op. cit.*, 145, esp. note 127; Hessing 1989; 1990; Hiddink 2003, 9, esp. note 24). Roman period grave fields, however, seem to overlap again more frequently with older (Urnfield) barrow clusters, although the intentionality of this overlap is difficult to establish (Hiddink 2003, 48-49; 67-69). The shift in funerary traditions to inter the deceased in the Middle and Late Iron Age away from older (Bronze Age and Urnfield period) graves is seen as reflecting an ideological change (Fontijn 1996a, 84; Hiddink 2003, 10; Gerritsen 2003, 149, *cf.* Hessing/ Kooi 2005, 650) in which the former importance of ancestors and long-term collectivity changes towards more segregated, more individual and less monumental funerary traditions. The disturbed barrow Unitas 4 however seems to indicate that – similar to Middle Bronze Age B people before them – deliberate links with ancestral burial may have been created through burial proximity even after the Early Iron Age. The excavations at the *Ballooër veld* in the Northern Netherlands show that (later, Middle) Iron Age funerary monuments sometimes specifically spatially referenced older barrows, to which they were orientated (Van Giffen 1935, esp. 72-73). The presence of numerous other (late) Iron Age remains in the direct vicinity of the *Elsterberg* barrow cluster, may however suggest that a quite different (less exclusively funerary?) usage of the barrow cluster may be envisaged for the Middle to Late Iron Age. Nonetheless, before more in-depth analyses of the meaning(s) and representativeness of the *Rhenen-Elsterberg* Iron Age barrow may be undertaken, additional absolute dating and – if possible – more extensive excavation of the area between the barrows, is necessary.

Chapter 9

THE *ELSTERBERG* BARROWS: LIVING NEAR THE DEAD?

D. Fontijn

This chapter seeks to bring together a number of the conclusions reached in chapters 2 to 8. First, I will sum up the results reached on the application of new research methods (9.1). Then, a revised chronology of the investigated barrows will be presented in section 9.2. I will go on to sketch a general outline of the history of the entire *Elsterberg* barrow group on the basis of the new excavations and the research of amateur finds in the environment (9.3). The results will be compared to general theory on the development of barrow groups and the role of barrows in the prehistoric landscape of late prehistory. Finally, suggestions will be done for future research of the *Elsterberg* barrow group (9.4).

9.1 The application of new prospective and excavation methods

The five-day excavation of *Elst* was the first barrow excavation to be carried out for mainly scientific reasons in the Netherlands since the 1980s. We felt that we should also seize the opportunity to experiment with new methods that were not applied to barrow excavations before. The experiments to be discussed are as follows.
1.   The prospection the mound with corings,
2.   Using the penetrologger device to predict whether the mound is of a natural or anthropogenic nature.
3.   The systematic sieving of the mound
4.   The excavation of a barrow by hand on artificial horizontal levels
5.   Using the metaldetector for the detection of other finds than metal.

9.1.1 Using corings to prospect the mound

The *RCE* prospected the mounds and their environment with a number of corings, using standard pedological and lithological criteria for the description of the corings (Chapter 7). This was carried out when the excavation was already in full swing, but it was a "blind" test: the results were done without any reference to the profile sections we prepared during the excavation. On the basis of pedological changes, they determined the location of the original surface underneath the mound, and tried to discern difference among the barrow material. Only a considerable time later, L. Theunissen and the present author met to compare the interpreted profile drawings to conclude that there was a general match between both results. Since the corings were done at a distance of about 50 cm to one meter behind our profile, and thus at a different position of the gentle slope of the ice-pushed ridge on which the mounds were built, a perfect match could not be expected. Allowing for an error margin of 15 to 20 cm, the zone determined as the original surface on the basis of corings is generally the same zone detected by ourselves on the basis of the excavation. Only for the case of the Unitas 1 mound, it should be mentioned that the original soil was extremely hard to observe, even during the excavation (see Chapter 2). The corings did not provide information on an internal subdivision of the mound. The excavation results showed that this is correct: any such division is not observable, both in Unitas 1 and Delfin 190.

In conclusion, it proves to be possible to determine the presence of original prehistoric soils with corings, and with it, to provide us with arguments for an anthropogenic origin of mounds without excavating them. However, it should be borne in mind that these corings were carried out by experienced scientists who both already had a great deal of experience with corings carried out in burial mounds, and are well-trained in the detection of difficult pedological phenomena from core probes. Without any such experience, coring prospection will prove to be very problematic.

9.1.2 Using the penetrologger to recognize anthropogenic mounds

An experiment was carried out using the penetrologger (Chapter 7), which measures differences in soil compaction. The idea was that natural mounds like dunes will have a different compaction than anthropogenic ones. Measurements were taken by the RCE on both mounds.

In both cases, a difference was measured between the ground beyond the mound and the compaction of the mound material itself. This can be explained by the fact that the natural soil, particularly around Unitas 1, consists of very coarse sediment (including pebbles). Such sediment will not have been used for the construction of a mound, as it is inconvenient to collect. Sand is easier to collect and the practical way would be to build a mound by means of stacking sods, as sods are held together by small roots. The use of sods for mound construction is well-documented, also for mounds on ice-pushed ridges[71]. Building a burial mound on an ice-pushed ridge, then, leads to stacking relatively homogeneous material on top of each other, whereas the subsoil of its environment is very variable in lithology. This research should be repeated for burial mounds built in areas where lithological differences between mound construction material and subsoil of the environment are not as great as on ice-pushed ridge (like on loess or cover sand plateaus or in Holocene clayey environments). In retrospect, the number of penetrologger measurements in the area beyond the mound is too low to allow for a substantial testing of the environment. As a first result, however, we are of the opinion that the use of the penetrologger device provides us with an interesting new avenue of prospective barrow research.

9.1.3 The sieving experiment

At Unitas 1, a 50 cm wide section of the mound material from top to bottom was sieved in order to see if this more refined method of find collection delivered better and more useful results than shoveling by hand in the way we did (Chapter 2).

We indeed did find a few tiny artefacts, but objects of similar size were occasionally also found during shoveling. Such very small artefacts did not add to a better dating of the mound: they are simply too small to allow further dating, and, more importantly, they are without context. We are dealing with material that was included in the mound itself, and might both have been part of the material with which it was built (providing a *terminus post quem*-date of the mound), con-

---

71　At the excavation of *Apeldoorn-Echoput*, sods were clearly visible in two mounds (Fontijn in prep.).

temporary (*terminus ad quem*) or later intrusions (*terminus ante quem*). So, even when objects are found, it is still unclear if and how they contribute to a better understanding of the mound as long as the matter of context remains unsolved. Alternatively, the sieving method did help to underline the significance of manual excavation by shoveling as we did here. The fact that large numbers and small sherds and flint splinters were found by the excavation members in itself pleas for excavating burial mounds by hand.

We will nevertheless carry on the sieving experiment on burial mounds where the nature of the mound material can be better assessed (mounds with recognizable sods), in order to further test the applicability of sieving of mound material[72]. At any rate is it advisable to sieve the prehistoric surface beneath the mound: such a sealed-off surface may contain better preserved material than outside the mound.

9.1.4 Excavation of the mound in artificial horizontal levels

At both the Unitas 1 and the Delfin 190 mound we did not try to excavate "stratigraphically", as we attempted to do at the excavation of the *Oss-Zevenbergen* barrows (Fokkens *et al.* 2006), nor did we use a mechanical excavator. We rather chose to create artificial horizontal "slices" through the mound at set distances (usually a new level was 10 to 20 cm lower than the former one), and we created the new levels by manual shoveling (Dutch "*schaven*"). The choice for manual excavation must certainly have contributed to the recovery of the relatively large number of small finds; it is highly unlikely that these small finds would have been recovered if we would have excavated with a mechanical excavator. The match in number and size between the finds done by sieving on the one hand, and manual shoveling on the other (see section 9.1.3) shows that manual shoveling has been accurate. An important result is that by being able to record finds in their original position in the mound construction material, we are now able to see something more on the "palimpsest" character of barrows (section 9.1.6).

In retrospect, the choice for excavation in horizontal levels rather than "stratigraphically" worked out fine. The vague soil discolorations, the invisibility of different construction phases all made it practically impossible to follow clear litho-stratigraphical layers other than the topsoil of Delfin 190 (which was removed "stratigraphically" as one discernable unit). Even the original surface buried underneath the mound proved to be hard to recognize (particularly in the case of Unitas 1). We have continued to use this way of excavation in our later barrow excavations (*Oss-Zevenbergen* Tumulus 7; *Apeldoorn-Echoput*; *Apeldoorn-Wieselse Weg*).

9.1.5 Using a metaldetector to find other materials than metal ones

Throughout the entire excavation, Mr. A. Manders assisted us with his metaldetector. He inspected shoveled levels and spoil heaps at Unitas 1 several times a day, and was present at the Delfin 190 mound all the time. Thus, we are rather sure that no metal objects were missed. Before the excavation started, Mr. Manders also made clear that it was possible to detect non-metal objects like sherds with his detector. In order to test this, Mr. Manders surveyed the surface before it was dug down to a deeper level, and we let him indicate where he noticed a signal. When we continued to excavate, we had special attention to the places marked by him. Many times, his predictions proved adequate. Particularly sherds and fire-cracked

---

72   A similar experiment has been carried out at the large tumulus 7 of *Oss-Zevenbergen* (Fontijn/ Jansen in prep.).

stones were liable to detection by a metal detector. Unfortunately, time pressure made it impossible to adequately quantify the number of correct and false predictions, and keep the excavation running at the same time. The experiment could not proceed. Our experiences so far, however, are promising and we hope they will be continued at future excavations.

9.1.6 The palimpsest character of burial mounds

Recording the position of sherds and flint in the mound construction material itself, brings us to the role of post-depositional processes. Publications from the past sometimes show barrows as multi-period monuments where the different phase of use are easy to be distinguished as different "mound construction phases", each phase "sealed off" from the other (e.g. Van Giffen 1943, Fig. 18, or Van Giffen's reconstruction drawing used in Lohof 1994, Fig. 7). Experienced excavators like Van Giffen probably knew better than that. However, the present generation of archaeologists including ourselves before we started here, who never worked at a barrow excavation, might be easily misled by such clean and clear stratigraphies. The idea is probably also undoubtedly generated by neat excavation photographs of old barrow excavations of relatively easy-to-read mounds with visible sods. This is usually on sites where Humus Podzol soils dominate (for example: Glasbergen 1954). Such easy-to-read stratigraphies do exist (as we experienced ourselves in the case of the Oss-Zevenbergen excavations, cf. Fokkens *et al.* 2006). There are many more examples, however, where mound periods are much harder to recognize and where "sealed-off" construction layers are practically invisible. Such mounds are particularly known from the ice-pushed ridges where soils are much less clearly developed[73]. It might also result from the general neglecting of finds of small sherds in barrows. In old excavation reports one can sometimes read that "some small sherds were found". Usually, not much information was given on such finds in terms of stratigraphical position or 3D-position within the mound. We found a remarkable large number of small prehistoric sherds and worked flint, and the systematic 3D-recording of each individual sherd often shows a confusing scatter of finds throughout the mound.

In both mounds, we found evidence that intrusion of artefacts from above by means of bioturbation (animals and tree roots) was much more important than initially thought (section 5.3). Late Iron Age sherds sometimes penetrated deep into mounds that were built in the Middle Bronze Age (*cf.* section 5.3.4). In such vaguely-shaded and hardly-outspoken matrixes as we encountered in both mounds, these disturbances rarely leave visible traces, but we do know that the mounds were all covered with large trees some 50 years ago. Half-decayed roots we found throughout the mound are clear indications thereof, and so are the traces of gnawing by mice that were detected on several sherds. These also indicate that material was replaced from its original position.

So, one of the unexpected results of paying attention to even the smallest of finds, is that mounds are much more than thought palimpsests, and not "sealed-off time-capsules" . In order to assess the integrity of mounds as chronological

---

73   It should be emphasized that representatives of the older generation of barrow excavators we spoke to, like prof. T. Waterbolk and prof. L. Louwe Kooijmans, also pointed this out. They gave us many examples of barrows where stratigraphy and different phases were very hard to discern. Such barrows, however, are much less likely to enter the text books as examples. Thus, the younger generation is at risk of having a too simplified and even naïve idea on how barrows are to be "read".

units, this calls for new excavations to be carried out with the same attention for detecting and 3D-positioning of small finds. In our view, this can best be arrived at by manual excavation.

9.2 Revising the chronology of the excavated mounds, and some conclusions on their prehistoric environment

9.2.1 Reasons for selecting the Elsterberg barrows

The main aim of this excavation was to get an insight into the long-term history of two barrows of the *Elsterberg* barrow landscape. It was decided to focus on a reconstruction of the vegetation and its development through time by means of analysis of pollen samples. We assumed that evidence on the prehistoric vegetation could serve as a proxy for general developments of the local landscape. Such information is hardly available in the southern and central part of the Netherlands, particularly for the Early Bronze Age and we therefore chose to study a barrow group where evidence from this 'Dark Age' was potentially available for such an investigation. The *Elst-Rhenen* area is one of those rare micro regions in the Low Countries where a concentration of Early Bronze Age barrows is known, as well as mounds dating to the preceding Late Neolithic B Bell Beaker period. A small cluster of loosely scattered burial mounds to the south of the *Elsterberg* and near the flanks of the ice-pushed ridge that overlooks the Rhine valley, seemed to offer the best opportunities for taking such a research. To this end, we selected a burial mound that was considered to date to the Late Neolithic B, Delfin 190 mound at the *Prattenburg* estate, and what seemed to be one of those rare examples of an Early Bronze Age mound associated with Barbed Wire Beaker material, the so-called Unitas 1 mound at the estate of *Staatsbosbeheer*, in the *Amerongsche Bos*. Evidence uncovered in small excavation trenches dug into the mounds in 1971 suggested this dating. Our aim was to check the dating evidence in the field, and if possible, to provide more material for dating purposes. Thus we would prepare profile sections from which to sample pollen, for which the chronostratigraphy was carefully checked. Our main research question can thus be divided into three sub-questions.

1. How are Delfin 190 and Unitas 1 to be dated. Do they indeed date to the Late Neolithic B and to the Early Bronze Age?
2. What can be deduced about environmental development on the basis of pollen that are available in combination with other evidence on finds and features and the revised chronology?
3. What can be concluded on the basis of the newly acquired evidence on the history and development of this barrow group?

As so often, our results were not as expected. Unitas 1 could indeed be dated to the Early Bronze Age but did not yield preserved Early Bronze Age pollen (Chapter 6). The excavated part of Delfin 190 appeared not to be older than Unitas 1 but younger. It dates to the Middle Bronze Age and appears to cover the remains of one of those very rare examples of a Middle Bronze Age A settlement with Hilversum pottery. From this mound, samples with preserved pollen dating to the period just before the construction of the mound could be taken in one sample. However, the other samples did not yield any pollen, just like in the case of Unitas 1 (Chapter 6). On closer inspection, the one sample that did contain preserved pollen appears to be contaminated and therefore of no further use. Unfortunately, our attempts to reconstruct the environment failed entirely. The question to be answered now, is why pollen was not preserved in these mound, whereas it is preserved underneath other barrows on the ice-pushed ridges (like in the *Apeldoorn-Echoput* mounds recently excavated, Fontijn forthcoming). Marieke Doorenbosch, PhD student in our *Ancestral Mounds* project will hopefully find out more about the reasons behind preservation and non-preservation of prehistoric pollen underneath burial mounds.

Another unexpected result was that we found prehistoric artifacts in the mounds in quantities that are remarkably large for burial mound excavations: over one hundred artefacts were found during the excavation of what is approximately 15 to 20 % of the mounds. At the moment that this is written this quantity of finds from different prehistoric periods is still unparalleled, even though the *Ancestral Mound* project has excavated six other burial mounds since on a much larger scale than we did at *Elst-Rhenen*. Investigation of amateur collections stored in the provincial depot of *Utrecht* and in the local *Rhenen* museum *'t Rondeel*, yielded an even larger number of artefacts found by amateurs around these mounds, including the rare partially preserved example of a large Pot Beaker (Chapter 4 and 5). Although the pollen research failed to live up to our expectations, this quantity of finds offered us another opportunity to get insight into the long-term history of land use in this barrow group. For that reason, we tried to retrieve and describe as many of those artefacts as possible.

The 2006 excavation provided us with enough means to adequately assess the chronostratigraphy of the investigated section of both barrows and to reassess the findings of the small 1971 excavation. Two years after our excavation, another mound of the *Elsterberg* group could be investigated: Unitas 4 (Chapter 8). Unfortunately, this research was necessitated by non-archaeological digging activities which destroyed the larger parts of the mound. In a one-day rescue excavation in far from ideal circumstances, the *RCE* was able to investigate the remnants of the mound. The results of all three barrow excavations will be summarized in the following sections.

9.2.2 Revision of chronology: the Unitas 1 mound

-A large Pot Beaker was buried just to the east of the mound during the Late Neolithic or Early Bronze Age. This Pot Beaker dates to the Late Neolithic B or Early Bronze Age (Fig. 4.4). It is unclear whether it was deposited in complete or broken condition. Although known from settlements, such vessels are also known from burial mound contexts. As these large decorated vessels are not very common, its position close to what appears to be an Early Bronze Age mound can hardly be a coincidence. It either shows that significant – ceremonial – practices took place at this site before the construction of the mound. Alternatively, the vessel might have been deposited when the mound was already constructed. In the latter case, its burial may have had a relation to the 'burial' practices.

A mound was built on a surface that was probably leveled or stripped. This can be inferred from the profile section and may explain why no pollen were preserved on the ancient prehistoric surface.

On the surface thus created, sherds of one Barbed Wire Beaker were deposited (Fig. 2.10; 4.2). As this is recorded for more mounds with Barbed Wire Beaker finds, it seems to have been a deliberate deposition which is related to the burial of the deceased for whom the barrow was erected. Of the burial itself, we do not know anything, since we did not excavate the central part of the mound where the grave must be sought. The fact that one of the five sherds is secondarily burnt suggest that we are not dealing here with a deliberate breakage of one vessel on this spot, but rather with a deposition of sherds that were broken earlier. Our findings corroborate the Early Bronze Age dating suggested by the 1971 excavations.

A mound with a diameter of at least 14 m was constructed with material that had a different, finer, lithology than the very coarse surface. This implies that the construction material does not come from the same site where the mound was built. The material, however, is local and might have been collected in the surroundings of the Delfin 190 mound, where a finer/grained sediment surfaces. It might have included one or two Pot Beaker sherds (Fig. 4.3) and four flint flakes (found by us in the mound itself). Such artefacts included in the material with which the mound was constructed, thus evidence previous prehistoric activities nearby. No sods were visible in the profile. It is well possible, though, that the mound was built from stacked sods which remained invisible due to the weak soil formation. A peripheral structure (like a ring ditch, stone or post circle) was not found, but this does not imply that there was not any: due to the dense forest at all sides of the mound we were not able to determine where exactly the mound ended.

There is no evidence for a secondary mound construction phase, but a large and at least 80 cm deep ditch was cut through the mound during the Late Iron Age. The ditch probably defines a rectangular or square area on the flanks of the mound (Fig. 2.11). Because of the coarse sand through which it was dug and its relative steep sides, the ditch must have silted up relatively quickly. The northern side of this ditch was marked with a row of posts, at a moment when the ditch was already partly filled (Fig. 2.9).The ditch fill segment excavated by us contained some twenty finds, mostly pottery sherds, but also fragments of a tephrite quern. The material has all the characteristics of settlement debris. The pottery is similar to finds done at the top of the mound and in its immediate surroundings (particularly to its south), which suggest that the ditch was part of a larger (settlement?) complex. The digging of such a deep ditch through the higher parts of a much older burial mound is remarkable. It defies a functional explanation as field, farmyard boundary, or drainage ditch. A rectangular ditch around a much older barrow has some parallels with (near-)square Iron Age enclosures that are interpreted as "ritualized" space or even entire "sanctuaries" focusing on much older monuments (Slofstra/Van der Sanden 1987; Fontijn 2002). However, these usually are dug *around* older barrows and not, as happened here, in them.

9.2.3 Revision of chronology: the Delfin 190-mound

Before the construction of a mound, this area bordering a dry valley was used. It probably was the site of a settlement during the Middle Bronze Age A-*Hilversum* pottery phase. This is evidenced by a cluster of pits and posts containing many artefacts found underneath the flank of the mound excavated by us (Fig. 3.12 and 3.13; Fig. 5.4 and 5.6). Middle Bronze Age A settlement sites are rare in the archaeological record of the Low Countries. A stray find of sherd(s?) a kilometer to the north provides another indication for Middle Bronze Age activities. Although reliable pollen evidence is not available, the implication is that this area was open. The extent of the probable settlement site cannot be determined, however.

Later on, but still during the Middle Bronze Age, a mound was constructed on the area of this settlement site. The mound covers a weakly developed, not-leveled Moder Podzol soil. The moment of construction cannot be determined with precision, but the burial of a Middle Bronze Age pot with cremation remains in the top of the mound provides a *terminus ante quem* date (Fig. 3.10 and Fig. 5.2). As in the case of Unitas 1, no sods were visible, but as explained there, this may relate to the relatively weakly developed soils. Several Middle Bronze Age pottery sherds and flint flakes in the mound are probably inclusions in the construction material/ sods. This implies that the construction material was collected on a former settlement site, probably the same site to which the pits covered by the mound belong. The similarity between the sediment of the mound and its immediate environment suggests that sods/sand was collected in the immediate surroundings of the place where the mound was built.

There is no evidence which supports the dating of this mound in the Late Neolithic as suggested by previous fieldwork. The evidence we have shows that a barrow was constructed in the Middle Bronze Age, late in the Middle Bronze Age A or in the Middle Bronze Age B. As our excavation was confined to the western flank, our conclusions only apply to that part. In our view, there is also no firm evidence to support a Late Neolithic date on the basis of the data of the 1971 excavation, however. Theoretically, the mound may contain a small Late Neolithic core barrow that was untouched by both excavations. As we did not penetrate into the central area of the mound, we cannot make a definite statement on this.

This mound was probably defined by a ring ditch. Traces of the same ditch were also observed during the 1971 excavation at the eastern flank (Figs. 3.3, 3.11, 3.12).

Activities took place at and around the mound during the Late Iron Age or Roman Period, possibly relating to the presence of a settlement at this place. The top of the mound was scattered with pottery sherds dating to these periods. Some ended up deep in the mound. This can be explained by bioturbation (mice that left their marks on several sherds as gnawing traces and roots). The light, poorly developed soils prevent such bioturbation activities from leaving traces discernible by color differences. Pits were dug into the top of that mound, possibly related to these Late Iron Age/Roman Period activities.

9.2.4 The destroyed Unitas 4 barrow

The Unitas 4 barrow, to the northwest of Unitas 1, was never investigated before. In 2008 the centre of the barrow was severely destroyed by a 2.7 m wide, 4.4 m long and some 40 cm deep pit in the centre of the mound. This pit was probably dug by people who wanted to make a shelter. The *RCE* was able to collect some finds (Fig. 8.5), to document the profiles of the walls of the pit and describe some stratigraphical details, be it under unfavorable conditions (Figs. 8.3-8.4). Pollen samples were taken but unfortunately contained no pollen. Like in the case of the other mounds, no sods were visible and soils were only lightly developed. The prehistoric surface underneath the mound is very similar to that underneath Unitas 1. It remains unclear whether the surface was leveled or truncated as has been argued for the case of Unitas 1. The excavators have argued that the remains of a pit with cremation remains, charcoal and pottery sherds (pyre gifts) represents the (central?) interment. On the basis of the pottery, this grave should be dated in the Middle to Late Iron Age. This means that Unitas 4 was built more than 1000 years after Unitas 1.

9.3 The Elsterberg barrows: tentative outline of the long-term history of a barrow landscape

Our research focused on data that were provided by our own fieldwork, but we also tried to combine our findings with other evidence on the barrow group. Due to the work of amateur archaeologists like Ms Ch. Delfin, H. Reusink and J.

Elevation in
metres NAP

Fig. 9.1 Elevation model of the ice-pushed ridge of the Utrechtse Heuvelrug with sites mentioned in the text. 1. The Elsterberg barrows; 2. Elst 't Bosje; 3. Rhenen-Remmerden; 4. Rhenen-Larikshof; 5. Remmerdse Laan/ Reumersweg; 6. Donderberg; 7. Koerheuvel. A. Ice-pushed ridge; B. Fluvioglacial sandr plain. Map based on the AHN, used with permission under license of the Province of Utrecht.

Mom, this proved to be possible, though many of the broader ideas on the developments of the barrow group as a whole remain tentative. It should be emphasized that further field work is badly needed to check some of the hypotheses outlined here. As much as possible, I will compare the *Elsterberg* data with contemporary evidence from published excavations nearby. Particularly the excavations from *Elst 't Bosje*, *Rhenen-Remmerden*, *Rhenen-Larikshof* and the N225 bicycle road excavations provided relevant evidence (Fig. 9.1)[74].

9.3.1 Was the Elsterberg a separate "funerary landscape"?

A question of central importance for barrow research that I would like to answer is whether the barrows of the *Elsterberg* group represent a separate "ritual" landscape. To this end, the comparison with the evidence from the excavations at the low-lying *sandr* are crucial. Most of these sites are within a range of two kilometers from our barrow group, and *Elst 't Bosje* is even situated at the lower area to the south at a distance of less than one kilometer away. The large-scale excavations at the ice-pushed ridge of *Nijmegen* gave rise to the hypothesis that Neolithic and Bronze Age barrows were preferably situated at the higher parts of the hills, whereas the settlements were mainly built on the lower sites (Fontijn/Cuijpers 2002). The excavation results showed that we were dealing with a separate funerary landscape *sui generis*. At *Rhenen*, the *Remmerden* site seemed to support that theory: here the traces of several Middle Bronze Age houses were recognized, whereas graves were lacking (Fig. 9.4 to 9.6). A barrow group is known to be situated at some distance from this settlement. Although it is not proven that the barrows and the settlement are contemporary, the spatial separation of settlement and barrows at

---

74   *Elst 't Bosje*: Meurkens 2006 and 2009a; *Rhenen-Remmerden*: Jongste 2001; Meurkens/Van Hoof 2005 and 2007; *Rhenen-Larikshof*: Meurkens 2009b; N225 road: Schute 2009.

THE ELSTERBERG BARROWS: LIVING NEAR THE DEAD?   139

least suggests that we are dealing with something comparable to the *Nijmegen* situation. At the *Oss-Zevenbergen* site, the notion of "separate funerary landscapes" could be further substantiated, when not only all barrows were investigated but also large areas around it (Fokkens *et al.* 2006; De Leeuwe 2007). This proved that there were no traces of settlement activity here, but the remnants of several constructions were found that may relate exclusively to the funerary and ceremonial activities carried out here. In the next outline, I will try to investigate whether there was a similar dichotomy between "higher" funerary, "ritual", landscapes (the *Elsterberg* barrows) and "lower" domestic areas (the sites on the fluvioglacial *sandr* deposits).

Before I start this comparison, it is important to realize that all the excavations of prehistoric sites in the *Elst-Rhenen* area mentioned before are situated to the south of the ice-pushed ridge on the fluvioglacial *sandr* plain below the ice-pushed ridge (Fig. 9.1). Both are biased in a different way.

The fluvioglacial plain situated between the south of the ice-pushed ridge and north of the Rhine has seen a long history of agricultural use up until today. The *Elsterberg* , however, was mainly an uninhabited heath since the Late Medieval Period. This means that the archaeological record of the *Elsterberg* ice-pushed ridge has a very different character from that of the strip of lower fluvioglacial sediment just to the south of it. Due to the long and intensive agricultural use, we may expect that most barrows on the fluvioglacial *sandr* plain between the ice-pushed ridge and the river Rhine were leveled in the course of time. At the heaths of the higher ice-pushed ridge, however, chances that prehistoric mounds were leveled or destroyed for cultivation purposes are much lower. As a matter of fact, most burial mounds that survived until today are situated in the forests which grew on the former heath areas of the ice-pushed ridge since the early 20th century. On the other hand, large excavations that allow us to see anything on the nature of prehistoric cultural landscapes practically only took place on the – of old cultivated – lower-lying fluvioglacial plain. Such information is hardly available for the ice-pushed ridge itself.

9.3.2 Late Neolithic B to Early Bronze Age (2500-2000 BC cal): the Pot Beaker evidence

At the nearby ice-pushed ridges of *Oosterbeek-Arnhem* and *Nijmegen-Ubbergen*, the history of barrow groups starts in the Late Neolithic (Houkes/Mittendorf 1996; Louwe Kooijmans 1973). In both regions, Late Neolithic barrows were built along the dry valleys which provide natural causeways to often steep ice-pushed ridges. With this in mind, we expected that the Delfin 190 mound would also be an example of such a Late Neolithic "founder's grave" .

However, our excavation of this mound and our survey of the available data of other barrows in museums and the Provincial Depot did not give us any hint that the history of this particular barrow group started as early as the Late Neolithic.

The only evidence we have of a possible Late Neolithic B use phase may be represented by the find of a largely complete Pot Beaker, buried close to the site of the Unitas 1 mound. However, as argued before, even this Late Neolithic dating is open to doubt. As set out before (section 4.6) these finds cannot be precisely dated (Late Neolithic B *or* Early Bronze Age). If we assume the earlier date (Late Neolithic B) to be correct, then the Pot Beaker find may reflect activities during a pre-barrow phase.

There are reasons to think that these were not everyday, domestic activities. As argued in more detail in section 4.6, the lavishly decorated Pot Beaker pottery may have had a special significance to prehistoric communities and could fulfill special roles. In particular, there is evidence that Pot Beakers played a role in funerary practices, and were – in a more general sense – often associated with burial mounds (and possibly with the rites enacted at such places). It is very unlikely that the presence of (sherds of) a Pot Beaker vessel close to the Unitas 1 barrow is just a coincidence. It probably represents a deliberate deposition of a special vessel (with content?), or sherds of one such a vessel, as part of funerary ceremonies and the preparation for barrow construction at this site (in the scenario where the Pot Beaker pre-dates the mound). The Pot Beaker deposition would then reflect the special nature of the location prior to barrow building. Alternatively – if it dates to the Early Bronze Age rather than to the Late Neolithic B – the Pot Beaker (sherds) might have been deposited once the Unitas 1 barrow was already there. In that scenario, it reflects the significance attached to the barrow as a landscape monument (and/or of the deceased buried in it).

At the nearby lower-lying site of *Elst 't Bosje*, none of the many traces found there could be dated to the Late Neolithic with certainty, although a few Pot Beaker-related[75] sherds were found (Meurkens 2009a,73-4; Fig. 6.1). A few kilometers southeast of our barrow group, another example of a deliberately deposited Pot Beaker sherds were found (site 5 of the N225; Schute 2009, 69-74).

In all, the available evidence is too scanty to allow any conclusion on a possible special (ritual) use of the ice-pushed ridge prior to the erection of the first barrows.

9.3.3 Early Bronze Age (2000-1800 BC): the first barrows

It is only for the Early Bronze Age that the first burial mound seems to have been built: Unitas 1. This was probably done on a leveled terrain. It is unclear if the first act of barrow-building took place in a pristine, "uncultivated" environment. The lack of pollen evidence and excavations around the burial mound preclude any conclusion on the rate of reclamation. It is important to note that a situation where an Early Bronze Age mound is the first mound to be erected is quite rare. As a matter of fact, Early Bronze Age mounds are rarely found south of the river Rhine, which makes the *Elsterberg* case rather special.

This time, there are indications that the lower-lying *Elst' t Bosje* location was also used during the Early Bronze Age. There is a stray find of a sherd with Barbed Wire decoration found by an amateur during building activities (Meurkens 2009a, 24-5, Fig. 3.7)[76]. The excavators found the traces of a ring ditch (diameter of the enclosed area 7 by 6 m; Fig. 9.2). It probably represents the remnants of a barrow that was completely leveled during later agricultural activities at the *sandr* plain (Meurkens 2009a, 58-9). Although a central burial was not found (the centre of the mound was disturbed), charcoal from the ditch fill could be C14-dated

---

75 Meurkens (2009a, 73-4) speaks of "Beaker Pot", rather than "Pot Beaker". He interprets "Pot Beakers" as a separate category among the main category of coarse ware vessels which he indicates as "Beaker Pots" (idem, 73). Like our sherds, they are thick-walled, tempered with stone grit and some are decorated with horizontal lines and fingertip impressions in ways comparable to what we have called "Pot Beaker"; *cf* Meurkens 2009a, Fig. 6.1: V187 and 249.

76 Meurkens also interprets V167 as a Barbed Wire pottery sherd, but the drawing at his Fig. 6.1 suggests that we are dealing here with rope impressions rather than with impressions of a Barbed Wire stamp.

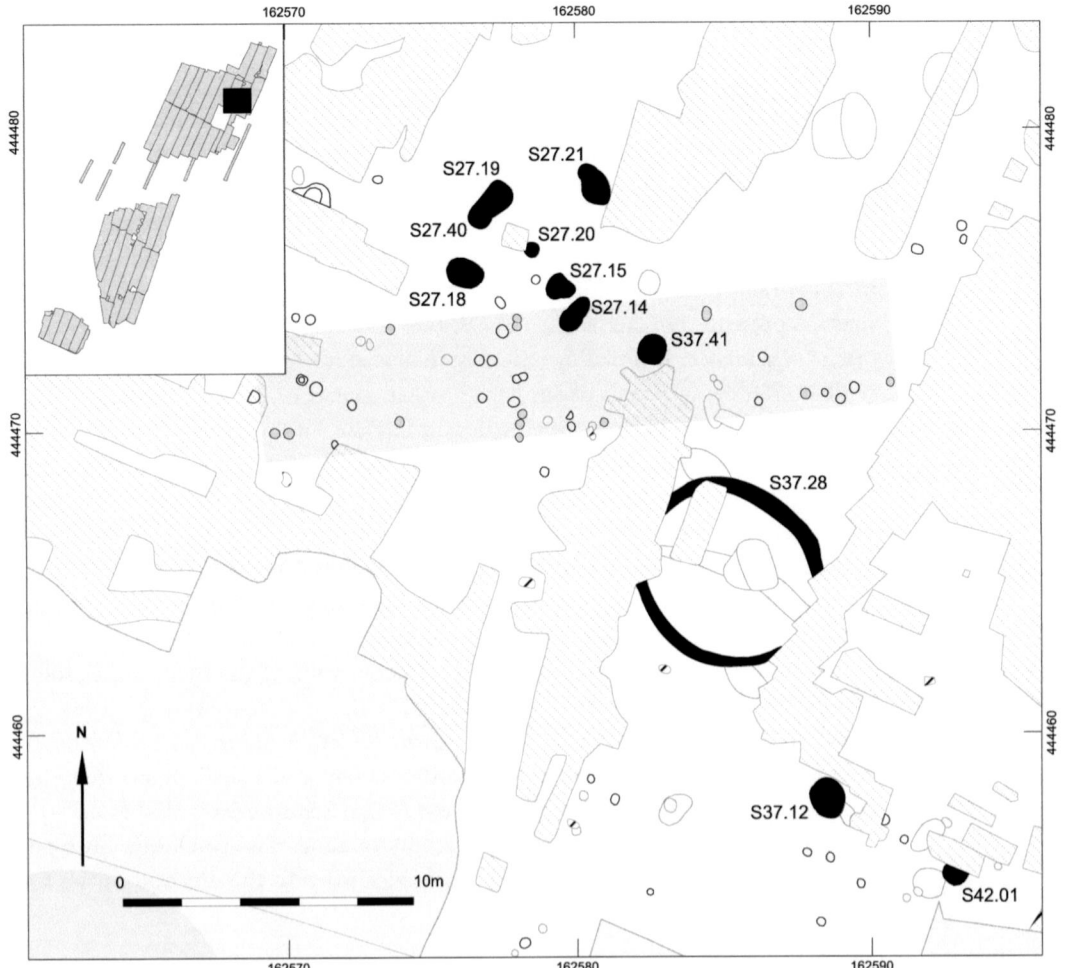

between 1890 and 1690 (at the two sigma-range). It might thus well be possible that during the Early Bronze Age, a barrow was built at the lower-lying site of *Elst 't Bosje* (a later date cannot be excluded though). Unfortunately, no pollen was preserved in the ditch fill, just like in the case of our barrows (Bakels 2009 and Chapter 6 in the present book). At any rate, the presence of a ring ditch monument at *Elst 't Bosje* indicates that is there no compelling reason to think that the higher *Elsterberg* was by that time the only area where barrows were built. Close to the ring ditch, there is a remarkable cluster of pits (Meurkens 2009a, 51-2; Fig. 5.16) which may well have been related to activities carried out at or around the ring ditch barrow. In the fill of six of them a small number of Pot Beaker sherds were found. This is in line with the Early Bronze Age dating of the ring ditch proposed by Meurkens[77] (Fig. 9.2). Pit clusters around (remnants of) barrows are known from a Middle Bronze Age structure found at *Nijmegen-Kops Plateau* (Fontijn/Cuijpers 1999, Fig. 7).

Since Early Bronze Age sites are relatively rare, it is remarkable to find a concentration of both Early Bronze Age burial and settlement sites in this *Elst-Rhenen* area. Only a few km to the east of the *Elsterberg*, amateurs did another find of Barbed Wire Beaker pottery sherds close to the *Remmerdse Laan/Reumersweg*[78]. Unfortunately, further inspection did not yield any information on the context of

Fig. 9.2 Traces of a ring ditch and pit cluster at Elst 't Bosje, dated to the Early Bronze Age/Middle Bronze Age. After Meurkens 2009a, Fig. 5.16. Reproduced with kind permission of Archol BV.

---

77   Three small Late Bronze Age/Iron Age sherds were also found in two of those pits, but Meurkens suggests that these represent a determination error or material from the higher parts of the pit fill (2009a, 52).

78   *Archis CAA* no: 39-E-079; monument no. 11549. Coordinates: 166403 / 443304.

these finds. At *Remmerden*, less than a kilometer to its south, more information could be gathered on the context of Barbed Wire pottery sherds (Jongste 2001; Meurkens/Van Hoof 2007). An excavation uncovered traces of pits and postholes which the excavators interpreted as remains of an Early Bronze Age settlement. A large vessel with Barbed Wire decoration was probably intentionally deposited at this site. Another remarkable Early Bronze Age find is the bronze low-flanged axe of the *Neyruz* Type that was allegedly found at the *Donderberg* near Rhenen (Butler 1995/1996, cat. No. 40; Fig. 13). Such rare finds are unlikely to represent lost axes, and it is well possible that it represents a deliberate deposition as well, as demonstrated for Early Bronze Age axes from all over the Low Countries (*cf.* Fontijn 2002, Chapter 5).

So, the available evidence so far suggests that people started to build barrows in the *Elst* area during the Early Bronze Age. Of course, this is no more than a tentative conclusion, as we lack information on the dating of so many barrows around the *Elsterberg*. More important, however, is that the Early Bronze Age evidence does show that barrow construction in this formative period was certainly not restricted to the ice-pushed hills of the *Elsterberg*, but took place in the lower-lying *sandr* plain as well.

9.3.4 Middle Bronze Age-A (c. 1800-1600 BC): a Hilversum-period settlement

With the construction of the first barrow at the *Elsterberg*, one might expect that at least from that period onwards, an exclusive funerary landscape started to develop at the hills[79]. However, the excavation results show that this is not the case. At the *Elsterberg*, some 90 m to the southeast of the Unitas 1 mound, there now appears to have been a settlement during the Middle Bronze Age A *Hilversum* pottery phase. This is at the place where later Delfin 190 would be built. A cluster of pits, containing many pottery fragments and what probably is a dump of cooking stones indicates domestic activities that were carried out in the immediate vicinity. This settlement was thus located close to an older burial mound : the Unitas 1 mound. This implies that domestic activities and burial mounds were in that period not spatially segregated. A stray find containing Middle Bronze Age pottery at c. one km to the north of this location in the present *Prattenburg* estate (section 5.7.7) may indicate that the Middle Bronze Age domestic area extended further to the north and was not confined to the immediate surroundings of the Delfin 190 location.

Hilversum pottery sherds were also found at *Elst 't Bosje*, and there are even several Middle Bronze Age A features there (Meurkens 2009a, 49-52). The pits show a remarkable clustering which recalls the concentration of the Delfin 190 pits (Fig. 9.3). This pit cluster represents a clear, functional structuring of a settlement area. Like the pits underneath Delfin 190, we are dealing with rectangular deep pits that were secondarily used as refuse pit. It was very close to the place where the remains of a ring ditch indicate the Early Bronze Age-Middle Bronze Age-A barrow (discussed above). So, we have here a comparable situation to what we saw at Delfin 190: a cluster of comparable, contemporary pits, very close to a burial mound. Another Middle Bronze Age A group of pits shows the same tight clustering (Fig. 9.3), evidencing something of the ordering of the Middle Bronze Age A settlement space. Separate Middle Bronze Age clusters of contemporary pit

---

79 This is, after all, what happened at sites like *Nijmegen-Kops Plateau* and *Oss-Zevenbergen* (resp. Fontijn 1996 and Fokkens *et al.* 2006).

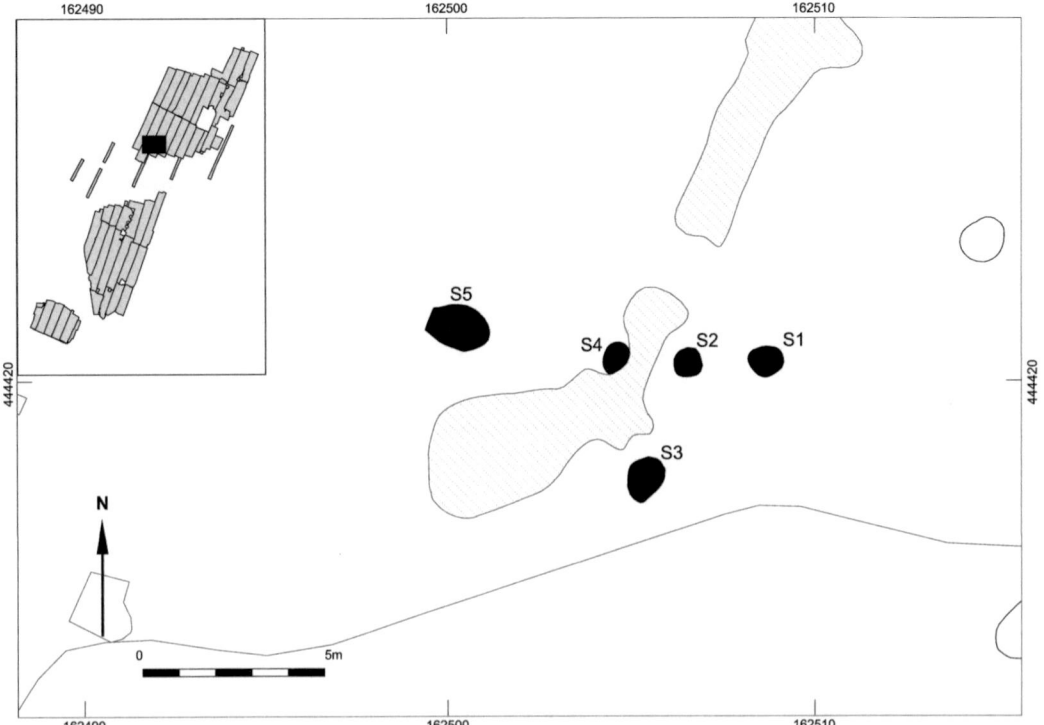

and posts were found nearby at the *Remmerden* site as well. Here, however, there was no evidence for burial monuments in their immediate surroundings (Van Hoof/Meurkens 2005, 29; Fig. 5.4)[80].

Summing up, for the Middle Bronze Age A, there is no evidence for any separation between burial and other activity areas. The domestic activities at the Delfin 190 site took place close to the Unitas 1 barrow, and closer to the river Rhine, at *'t Bosje*, there might have been a similar situation: in the Middle Bronze Age A, people were living close to the dead.

Fig. 9.3 A Middle Bronze Age pit cluster at Elst 't Bosje. After Meurkens 2009a, Fig. 5.14. Reproduced with kind permission of Archol BV.

9.3.5 Later Middle Bronze Age: a domestic site transformed into a funerary area?

At some moment in the Middle Bronze Age A, people decided to construct a Middle Bronze Age burial mound (Delfin 190) over a part of the settlement site. Such a conversion of terrain from domestic to funerary is not something which seems to have taken place very regularly. An inventory of traces preserved underneath barrows does not indicate that Middle Bronze Age mounds were as a rule built on settlement terrains (Bourgeois/ Fontijn 2008, Table 3.1). In the Netherlands, there are occasional examples of barrows constructed on sites with fences (*Toterfout-Halve Mijl* mound 21; Glasbergen 1954a, 77-8; Fig. 30) or barrows built on ploughed, agricultural fields (example *Oostwoud*, Van Giffen 1962). In one case, a Bronze Age mound appears to have been built over the remains of a house (*De Bogen*; Meijlink 2001; Bourgeois/Fontijn 2008, 45-7, 51-4). In the case of barrows over house and agricultural fields, there is a considerable debate in European archaeology on the question whether such a location was chosen for ideological reasons (Svanberg 2005). It has for example been argued that there

---

80 A Hilversum pottery sherd was also found in the pit fill of a site close to Remmerden: *Rhenen-Larikshof* (Meurkens 2009b). This cluster of finds from the otherwise elusive Early Bronze Age (Barbed Wire pottery) and Middle Bronze Age A (*Hilversum* pottery) periods in *Rhenen* is remarkable and deserves further examination.

was a relationship between the original inhabitants of the house or settlement buried under the mound, and the barrow built on top of it. There is also a discussion whether the plough traces underneath barrows represent ritual ploughing for funerary purposes rather than purely agricultural activities (Bradley 2005, 23-8). Given the fact that such a concentration of pits under such a small part of a mound is very rare, we may ask ourselves whether some of the activities of which the remains are buried in these pits, may actually have related to funerary practices, or whether the plot of land buried underneath the mound belonged to the group that used the Delfin 190 mound as burial ground? Such ideas are easily said than proven and as there is no evidence on the traces elsewhere under the mound, nor in its immediate environment, we must leave it at that.

As the centre of the mound has not been excavated, we do not know the nature of the primary burial, the dead for which the mound was raised in the first place. We do know, however, that the monument was used later on in the Middle Bronze Age: an urned Middle Bronze Age cremation grave was dug into the mound flank that we excavated. If by that time people were still living in the immediate environment of the mounds is unknown, but remains a possibility (in view of the find of Middle Bronze Age sherds further north at the *Prattenburg* estate, see section 5.7.7).

With regard to our discussion on the spatial relationship between burial mounds and settlements, the situation for the Middle Bronze Age B remains unclear. Traces of settlements are known from the low-lying zones. At *Elst 't Bosje* the traces of a small four-post building were found, which probably date to the Middle Bronze Age B (Meurkens 2009a, 46). This building probably burnt down, with the grain stored in it. Examination of charred remains shows that *Triticum dicoccum*, *Hordeum vulgare nudum*, *Cerealia*, and *Panicum miliacum* were stored in this building (Kuijper 2009, 101-3). It suggests that the environment of *Elst 't Bosje* was an agrarian area.

Somewhat further to the west in *Elst* "traces and remains" of a Middle Bronze Age settlement were discovered in 1968 by Ms Ch. Delfin. Allegedly, pits, one or more ditches and a post hole were discovered. One of the pits contained sherds of Middle Bronze Age pottery and fragments of burnt loam (Hulst 1969, 275-7; Fig. 4). The sherds are undecorated and the remarkable tri-partite form of one of the pots (idem, Fig. 4: no. 9) suggests a date late in the Middle Bronze Age. Interestingly, Hulst also discusses the possible relationship between this settlement find and the barrows in the hills nearby. The barrows closest to this settlement are three barrows at the southwest flank of the *Elsterberg*, which are somewhat removed from the group of barrows that is central in this book (Fig. 1.3). As a Middle

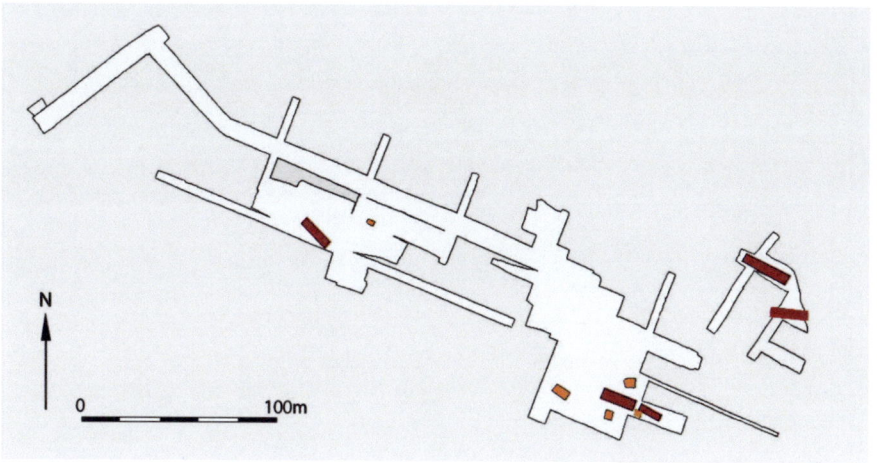

Fig. 9.4 Schematized plan of the excavations at Rhenen-Remmerden. Indicated are the locations where traces of Middle Bronze Age houses have been recognized. Large rectangles represent Middle/Late Bronze Age house plans, small rectangles represents remnants of other buildings. After Van Hoof/Meurkens 2007, Fig.15.8a. Reproduced with kind permission of Archol BV.

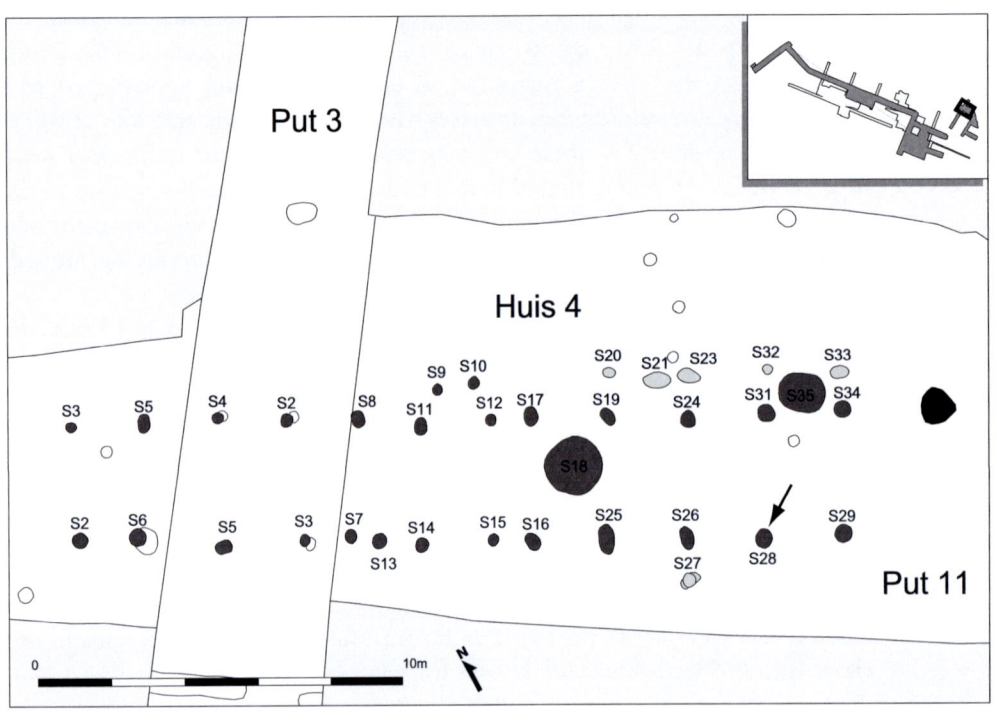

Put 3

Huis 4

S9 S10 S20 S21 S23 S32 S33
S3 S5 S4 S2 S8 S11 S12 S17 S19 S24 S31 S35 S34
S18
S2 S6 S5 S3 S7 S14 S15 S16 S25 S26 S29
S13 S27 S28

Put 11

0   10m   N

Bronze Age ("*Hilversum* or *Drakestein*") sherd was found in one of those barrows (the northernmost), at least one of them was used during the Middle Bronze Age (idem, 277). In retrospect, a closer inspection of this find is needed as *Hilversum* pottery is characteristic for the Middle Bronze Age-A, whereas *Drakestein* pottery is known from the entire Middle Bronze Age (*cf.* Theunissen 1999, 205). A link between this settlement and the use of the barrow on the hills can therefore not be convincingly demonstrated.

One of the better known settlement areas of the Middle Bronze Age B is situated a few kilometer to the east of the *Elsterberg* , at *Rhenen-Remmerden*. Here, the traces of several Middle Bronze Age B longhouses were uncovered at the *sandr* plain (Fig. 9.4-9.6; Van Hoof/Meurkens 2005 and 2007). It is interesting to note that no traces of burial mounds were found during this excavation, whereas a group of mounds existed nearby at the higher grounds (Van Hoof/Meurkens 2005 and 2007). This again suggests the existence of a separation of settlements and barrows during the later Middle Bronze Age. However, just like in the case of the other barrow group to the west of *Elst*, we lack the means to adequately date those mounds: they might just as well be much older or younger than the settlement on which they command such a fine view.

Fig. 9.5 Traces of Middle Bronze Age house 4 at Rhenen-Remmerden. After Van Hoof/Meurkens 2007, Fig. 5.12. Reproduced with kind permission of Archol BV.

In conclusion, there are in the *Elsterberg* sites no positive indications that post-*Hilversum* phase Middle Bronze Age burial mounds were built or used in a separate, "funerary" zone, away from the place where people lived. However, it can certainly not be excluded that such zones emerged during the post-*Hilversum* period around the *Elsterberg*. What we do know is that a part of a domestic site was used to build a burial monument. Systematic excavation of the environment of these mounds will be the only way to check whether this was part of a more encompassing transformation of the *Elsterberg* into an funerary landscape during the post-*Hilversum* Middle Bronze Age.

9.3.6 The elusive Late Bronze Age-Early Iron Age (1100-500 BC)

With the available data, it is difficult to reconstruct what happened at the *Elsterberg* site around the Late Bronze Age-Early Iron Age. There are no finds available that can be clearly dated to that period. What often happened around barrow sites, is that these locations became foci for urnfield interments in the Late Bronze Age or Early Iron Age (Fontijn 1996; Gerritsen 2003). Such urnfields are the best known example of exclusive, even nucleated cemeteries in Dutch late prehistory (Gerritsen 2003). It is possible that such a development took place here as well. There is a 45 m and 10 m wide long barrow with intact mound with a height between 1 and 2 m: the Unitas 5 mound (Fig. 1.3; Fig. 9.7). It is situated some 80 m to the southwest of Unitas 1. When the *AWN* dug small trenches through this mound, they found pottery sherds at the prehistoric surface covered by the mound as well as a cremation burial without urn. Unfortunately, we could not retrieve any of those finds in the *Provinciaal Depot*. Reading the notes on the finds, a cautious conclusion might be that the long barrow dates to the Iron Age rather than Bronze Age[81]. Long barrows are known from the Middle Bronze Age B (Bourgeois/Fontijn 2008, Table 3.2), but typical for the Late Bronze Age or Early Iron Age. The largest examples are exclusively known from the Early Iron

Fig. 9.6 The excavation of the Rhenen-Remmerden site took place under harsh conditions. Holes in the snow covered excavation trench indicate the traces of posts of one of the Middle Bronze Age houses. Photograph by R. de Leeuwe.

---

81 See the section 4.7 and the data in the student report *Uitwerkingsverslag "Barrow-landscapes project"* by N. van Rijswijk and A. van Weerelt (2007), Leiden University. They discovered that charcoal from this grave was collected for C14-dating, but it was never sent to the laboratory. Unfortunately, the sample could also not be retrieved.

Age (Roymans/Kortlang 1999). It is not probable that this long barrow is the only monument that is likely to date to the Early Iron Age. Unfortunately, nothing is known on the (primary) dating of the mounds Unitas 2 and 3[82].

Evidence from the recently destroyed mound Unitas 4 shows that this mound was built during the Middle or Late Iron Age. This suggests that the by then already ancient burial mound group was still in use for funerals. Its relative late dating – Middle/ Late Iron Age barrows are not very common – is noteworthy and so is its large size. Middle and Late Iron Age graves in the Southern Netherlands are usually small, non-monumental or even flat grave cemeteries (Fontijn 1996a; Gerritsen 2003; Hiddink 2003). The Unitas 4 barrow, however, clearly is a large monument and this makes one wonder whether developments in Middle and Late Iron burial practices north of the Rhine took a somewhat different course. A recent study by Roy van Beek (2009, 438) on the Eastern Netherlands, indeed shows that large Middle Iron Age mounds are more common there than in the region south of the Rhine.

The relative dearth of Late Bronze Age and Early Iron Age finds on the *Elsterberg* site is in marked contrast to the large number of sites at the nearby lower fluvioglacial *sandr* plain. There is ample evidence that people were living at the *Elst 't Bosje* site during the second part of the Late Bronze Age and the earliest phases of the Early Iron Age (9th-8th centuries BC; Meurkens 2009a). Close to 'Bosje, Early Iron Age cremation graves were discovered by amateurs of the *WAR* at the *Tabaksweg* (Meurkens 2006, 20-2). It is only one of many known Early Iron

Fig. 9.7 Long barrow Unitas 5 in its recent state (entirely surrounded by forestation and practically invisible from the road. People standing on its top give an impression of the considerable size of the still remaining barrow mound. Photograph by D. Fontijn.

---

82   The only find known from Unitas 3 are Late Iron Age/Roman Period pottery sherds without clear context, described in section 4.7.

Age urnfields in the Rhenen area, both situated at the *sandr* (*Rhenen-Larikshof*; Meurkens 2009b) and on the higher ice-pushed ridge (*Rhenen-Koerheuvel*; Van Heeringen 1998/1999). The latter was the site where the rich "chiefly" Hallstatt C grave was situated. It clearly makes the point how urnfields became pivotal places in the ritual landscape, which could become the scene for conspicuous funeral rites and monumental graves. Although Late Bronze Age/Early Iron Age finds are at present hardly known here, the construction of a 45 m long, 10 m wide and over 1.5 m high long barrow at the *Elsterberg* would well fit within this picture.

9.3.7 The Later Iron Age (500 BC-earliest decades AD): a funerary landscape reshaped?

One of the most significant changes in the *Elsterberg* landscape must have taken place in the Late Iron Age. The large amount of Iron Age sherds found on top of both mounds, and around them is impressive. As set out in chapters 4 and 5, most of them are comparable and can be dated to the later part of the Iron Age or in the earliest part of the Roman Period. The fragmentary, worn state of the sherds suggests that we are dealing with material which was scattered as debris around the site, like one may expect at a settlement site. The fact that also fragments of tephrite querns were found (section 4.1 and 4.2) is also suggestive of this. Excavations of the environment of the barrows are badly needed to shed more light onto the use to which this barrow area was put. If the area became the site of an agrarian settlement, it is interesting to see that the barrows themselves remained untouched. The amount of debris on top of them rather suggests that activities were taking place right on top of the mounds themselves. There is reason to believe that these were not the sort of activities one would expect on an average agrarian settlement. The digging of a deep, probably, rectangular ditch in the Unitas 1 mound cannot have been done for purely agrarian or defensive reasons. Rather it seems to relate to the significance that was attached to the by then already age-old mound. Parallels for rectangular Iron Age ditches around ancient burial mounds suggest that the digging of such ditches relates to renewed funeral use of such old monuments, or to veneration of (claimed) ancestors (Slofstra/Van der Sanden 1987). The presence of such rectangular/square structures is known from settlement sites (For example: *Oss-Ussen*; Van der Sanden 1998).

Only excavation of the environment of the mounds can help us to understand how the *Elsterberg* barrows were incorporated in the Late Iron Age landscape. A survey of evidence from nearby sites suggests that both the entire *sandr* and higher ice-pushed ridge of *Elst-Rhenen* were part of one continuous cultural agrarian landscape in which old and new burial monuments had their place within a landscape marked by farmsteads, and agricultural fields. *Elst 't Bosje* was probably not inhabited during the Middle Iron Age (500-250 BC), but loosely distributed on the former settlement area, human cremation remains were buried. Just like at the Unitas 1, a rectangular ditched enclosure was built. Here, there is no direct spatial link with an older monument or with the contemporary graves. Yet, in view of the fact that the only other contemporary features are graves, a relation between this structure and burial rites is well possible (*cf.* Gerritsen 2003, 150-66 for more examples). *Elst 't Bosje* once again became the site of a settlement during the Late Iron Age (Meurkens 2009a, 38-9). Soil discoloration on air photographs of the modern agricultural fields immediately south of the southern ridge of the *Elsterberg* barrow group – in between *'t Bosje* and our barrow group – show a remarkable pattern of rectangular plots. It is possible that we are dealing with the remains of a "Celtic field" here[83]. A more convincing example of another Celtic field-site on the *sandr* is known from western Elst, only a few kilometers from *'t Bosje* and our barrow group: *Amerongen-Elsterstraatweg*[84]. A convincing examples of a Celtic field are also known from the highest parts of the ice-pushed ridge (*Rhenen-Achterberg*[85]), suggesting that both the higher and lower parts of the landscapes were incorporated in similar system of prehistoric land use. Celtic fields are an Iron Age-Roman Period system of agricultural land use (Fokkens 1998, 119-21). It is at present not possible, however, to say anything on their chronological development or to give a more detailed account on the system of land use and its spatial extension in the later Iron Age. (Late) Iron Age sites are very numerous on the entire eastern part of the *Utrechtse Heuvelrug*, and apart from the Celtic fields, they provide other examples for a landscape that was divided, cultivated and ordered in a way unseen before. A case in point is the large, deep and extensive Iron Age ditch that was found by the RAAP company in *Leersum-Wilhelminalaan* (Tol 2008). It has a depth of c. 1 m and a width of 4 m, and could be followed for over 80 m length. It is another example of an unusually large and wide ditch, the function of which is not easy to explain from a purely agrarian perspective. This ditch, however, deserves some special interest. Tol argues that it was a main element in the prehistoric cultural landscape, which extended over a considerable distance to end up at a group of (still-existing) barrows (personal comment A. Tol).

At any rate: the broad swathe of late Iron Age finds in the zone between the river Rhine in the south up until the highest peaks of the ice-pushed ridge of *Rhenen-Elst*, then, suggest a densely inhabited landscape, in which all types of sandy soils and all types of relief were cultivated and used. This is in contrast to the main division that is visible in the land use now, where the present-day town of *Elst* is situated on the cultivated lower grounds, and where the higher parts of the landscape are now forested natural reserves (*Amerongsche Bos*, the *Prattenburg* estate and the *Remmerstein* estate to its east). How this later Iron Age cultural landscape was used and divided by the many local communities living here is an intriguing, yet hard to answer question.

9.3.8 The barrows in historical times

Remarkably, we found very few indications for activities that were carried out at or around the barrow group during later, historical period. As a matter of fact, even finds from the largest part of the Roman Period, when imported pottery is common, does not seem to be represented here. Mention was made of the find of a native Roman Period pot or urn in Unitas 3, but this pot could not be retrieved in the provincial depot, so we cannot check whether this determination is correct. The only sherds we retrieved that should have been found in that mound may both date to the Iron Age or to the Roman Period (see section 4.7). Neither is there any indication that the barrows were used in the Early Medieval Period, even though the environment of *Elst-Rhenen* was a relatively densely settled, important centre of regional power by then (Heidinga 1988). An important Early Medieval cemetery was, for example, at the fluvioglacial deposits situated close to the river Rhine (*Elst 't Woud*[86]). For the later Medieval Period up until the start of the 20th century, large parts of the area were used as a heath, and such land-use usually does not involve an intensive re-structuring of an area, apart from vegetation man-

---

83   Personal communication drs. R. Kok, (province of *Utrecht*). This Celtic field hypothesis has not yet been tested by field work.
84   *Archis* Monument no. 4859.
85   *Archis* Monument no. 4867.
86   *Archeologische Kroniek Provincie Utrecht* 1980-1984, 9-13.

agement and sod-cutting. The barrows, then, appear to have been left alone. We did not find indications that Unitas 1 and Delfin 190 were severely damaged by heath cutting. This happened only in relatively recent times: part of the west flank of the Delfin 190 was cut away when people dug a larg ditch, probably for water supply to the tobacco industry situated to the lower-lying south of the *Elsterberg*. The sand-extraction in 1983 is another activity that left its marks, particularly on the Delfin 190-mound: parts of the mound were dug away, and only due to the indispensable activities of amateurs archaeologists of the *WAR* , at least some archaeological evidence could be documented. Forest-ploughing (documented to have disturbed archaeological remains to the immediate south of Unitas 1 and a part of Unitas 3), and recent digging activities by unknown people (Unitas 4) are other recent activities that had a profound impact on the archaeological record.

9.3.9 Conclusion: separate funerary landscapes or living near the dead?

A general question for the late prehistoric usage of the *Elst-Rhenen* landscape was to find out whether our barrow group at the higher ice-pushed ridge of the *Elsterberg* was at any time in its history a separate "ritual" funerary area as we know them from some other barrow sites. The evidence from sites on the higher and the lower grounds is often biased, and it is not possible to provide an answer to this question for every use phase (*e.g.* Late Neolithic). It is possible that the higher ice-pushed ridge was exclusively a funerary area during the Middle Bronze Age B, but it should be borne in mind that the lack of evidence of settlements on the higher grounds on the one hand, and for graves on the lower grounds on the other, is not necessarily *evidence of absence*. For all other prehistoric periods discussed in the sections above, we rather have evidence to the contrary. For all these periods, there are positive indications that there was not any clear separation in land use between high and land grounds. Most of the times, people were living close to burial sites. This is not to say that burial sites did not have a place of their own in the cultivated landscape. Rather, it seems as if burial monuments were situated within existing land orderings for particular reasons of social ties and tenure (which unfortunately must remain hidden for us): the Delfin 190 mound on top of a former settlement, the Middle Iron Age graves of 't Bosje on a plot of land that was formerly inhabited but no longer used, to be used again one phase later (in the Late Iron Age). Particularly for the Iron Age, the entire system of land allotment that Celtic fields represent suggests widely-shared ideas on tenure, land ordering and necessary land divisions. The small scale of our excavations, and the lack of an overarching, systematic attempt to synthesize all data from the *Elst-Rhenen* area, precludes further discussion on its nature and logic. The phrase that characterizes the long-term essence of this barrow group, however, would be that all the time people were *living near the dead*.

9.4 The *Elsterberg* group and the phenomenon of extensively dispersed barrow groups

The aims of our excavations were modest, and there is no pretention that we have solved the problem of the characteristic remarkable loose spatial patterning of burial mounds that we see reflected in the *Elsterberg* group. If we want to know more about the reasons behind such orderings, several conditions should be met

9.4.1 How representative are our results?

First, we should have a better understanding how representative the present spread of barrows is for the situation in prehistory. As we have seen, it is only due to systematic surveys of amateur archaeologists that we know of these barrows in the first place. The barrow discoveries of Ms Ch. Delfin have already been referred to many times, but it is important to note that even recently new barrows are being found in the forests of the *Utrechtse Heuvelrug*, particularly by Mr H. van het Loo. On the other hand, the destruction of the largest part of Unitas 4 in 2008, and of parts of Delfin 190 is probably not the first time, but are at least instances where destruction was noticed by interested laymen and (amateur) archaeologists . We can only guess as to how many barrows have disappeared without anyone knowing.

Second, a representative insight into the chronological development of the barrow group is necessary. As the incomplete and tentative account in 9.2 shows, this is a very difficult task to do on the basis of old, small excavations.

9.4.2 Explaining barrow location: why there?

Third, monuments of which the construction requires a considerable input of human labour were not built at a particular place without a reason. The decision to build a barrow at a specific site will have been motivated by characteristics of the environment. Combining amateur survey material and excavation data, we have already seen that for both the Unitas 1 mound and the Delfin 190 mound, there are indications that the place where they were built had an added significance. If we want to make more sense of the reasons behind site preferences, we will have to take into account many aspects: specific characteristics of the natural environment (vegetation), visibility patterns, but also the existing ordering of the local cultural landscape. Such a research requires not only a systematic sampling program of pollen analyses (*cf.* Casparie/Groenman-Van Waateringe 1980), but also viewshed-analyses (cf. Lagerås 2002). Within the framework of our *Ancestral mounds* project, M. Doorenbosch and Q. Bourgeois have started to systematically deal with such questions for their PhD. theses at Leiden University. What is particularly needed, are excavations of the surroundings of burial mounds. The stray finds of the *WAR* surveys, done under difficult circumstances in the unfavorable context of a dense forest, in themselves already show there is ample reason to do this. The presence of large parts of a Pot Beaker, Middle Bronze Age material and so many (contemporary) finds of Iron Age/Roman Period pottery in the forest (chapter 4 and 5) evidence activities, and often past orderings of the landscape. The excavations described in this book prove that all those categories that were only represented by amateur stray finds, are matched by contextualized finds in the barrow excavations. At this moment, however, it is very difficult to link survey observations with those from such limited excavations as we did. Clearly, more extensive excavation – for examples with trial trenches – are needed.

9.5 Significance of the *Elsterberg* barrow group and suggestions for further research

The above shows that our excavations were able to answer some questions, but raised even more new ones. Of course, this is common practice in archaeology, and before we suggest new lines of research, we should first say some words on the question how important this barrow group is after having processed all the excavation data.

There are still large numbers of burial mounds available for research, and many show comparable loose orderings as the one discussed in this book. This means that for a proper research of this phenomenon of extensively dispersed barrow groups (9.4), potentially many options. As it is vital to excavate a representative part of the environment (see section 9.4), barrows situated in a forest like the *Elsterberg* are not the obvious candidates, although more recent excavations of the *Ancestral mound project* have shown that excavation in forests is possible. Also, pollen were not preserved, and features were extremely hard to read owing to the *holtpodsol* soil, the comparatively dry environment and the heterogeneous lithology.

Chapter 1 already gave a number of characteristics that showed the special nature of this group. These are the presence of an Early Bronze Age burial mound, a long barrow with preserved mound, and the presence of a great number of finds indicating Iron Age activities. On the basis of our excavations we can now give more, and better arguments. These are as follows.

Features show that the area on which the Delfin 190 mound was built, just to the west of the dry valley, was the location of a Middle Bronze Age A *Hilversum* period settlement. We found indirect evidence (the several Pot Beakers and the Barbed Wire sherds in or underneath Unitas 1) that the area of the *Elsterberg* may have been inhabited even before that time, during the Early Bronze Age. A *Hilversum* period settlement is very rare, and so far, no reliable structures (house plans, byres, farmyards) have been documented in the Low Countries (Arnoldussen/Fontijn 2006). It is unknown how severely the site was damaged by forest ploughing and sand extraction. A prospective research campaign with small trial trenches is suitable to detect the rate of disturbances and the boundaries of the feature cluster. A better understanding of the nature of the settlement site is only possible by a larger excavation of the entire mound and its surroundings. Since the forest is a natural reserve, this is not an option at this site.

The *Elsterberg* group shows a remarkable, uncommon development throughout the Iron Age. The likely dating of the large, but now destroyed barrow Unitas 4 in the Middle/Late Iron Age is different from the typical development of barrow and urnfields south of the Rhine. The other mounds of the group ought to be dated anew in order to provide a more adequate picture of its chronological development. This should be done in a combination with a non-destructive field survey (coring), that may give us a better insight in which parts of the forested have been destroyed by ploughing or more sand-extraction. As for the barrows, dating evidence can be supplied by modest excavation as those described in this book. Owing to the visible detection of old surfaces (not always easy at this site, see chapter 2), OSL-dating is an option[87]. Such excavations can often be carried out using the – sometimes severely – damaged sides of a number of mounds.

Part of the seemingly uncommon history of the *Elsterberg* barrow group, is the remarkable concentration of Late Iron Age/Roman Period activities at and around the mounds. We have argued in this book that many amateur finds are genuine reflections of prehistoric activities in this area. The Late Iron Age features we found, like the deep ditch cut through Unitas 1, are highly unusual but can unfortunately not be totally understood due to the limited size of our excavation. The presence of so many Iron Age material on top of both mounds is very rare. After the excavations at *Rhenen*, we have excavated barrows and their environment at *Oss-Zevenbergen*, *Apeldoorn-Echoput* and *Apeldoorn-Wieselse Weg* at a much larger scale with comparable methods (manual excavation, sieving). We found nothing in the way of the large quantity of objects we found at *Elsterberg*, and what was found

---

87 See Wallinga *et al.* in prep. for good results with the OSL-dating of Tumulus 7 of *Oss-Zevenbergen*.

can all be attributed to funerary traces, certainly not to Iron Age settlements. Given the now widely surveyed concentration of Celtic fields and settlements in the *Elst-Rhenen* area, it is vital to get to grips with these remarkable Late Iron Age features around the *Elsterberg* barrows. Again, a general systematic field survey, where possible aided by trial trenches is badly needed. It should particularly be tried to link this barrow group to the Iron Age settlement and urnfield excavated only 1 km to the south, at *Elst 't Bosje*.

Finally, new excavations of these mounds should include systematic samples of profile sections for thin section analysis (to find evidence for the presence or absence of sods and of old – decapitated – surfaces). Adequate pedological descriptions of the soils are also needed in order to get a better understanding in soil formation, and particularly why relatively late features like the deep Iron Age ditch S19 are so badly visible.

Chapter 10

THE FUTURE OF THE *ELSTERBERG* BARROWS

D. Fontijn, R. Kok, L. Theunissen

The previous chapter ended by emphasizing the special significance of the *Elsterberg* barrow group. We described opportunities for new research that may have an important offspin for our knowledge on barrow landscapes in particular. However, throughout the chapters of this book, we have also several times pointed to the destruction of parts of those barrows and of their immediate environment. Only due to the active role of amateur archaeologists of the *WAR*, like Ch. Delfin, the late J. Mom (†), H. Reusink(†), E. van Hagen and H. van het Loo something could be written on this environment at all. It is very sad to see how in the 1980s parts of the Delfin 190 mound could simply have been dug out for sand extraction. A change for the better was the fact that the then *ROB*, later *RACM* and now *RCE*, took care of the mounds, restored them in 1987 and registered the mounds as 'of very high value'. But even then, we have seen how recently, in 2008 an entire never before excavated burial mound, Unitas 4, could be destroyed without anyone able to intervene in time. Even greater worries concern the environment of the barrows. As early as in 1991, J. Mom, H. Reusink and other members of the *WAR* already showed that the environment around barrows may have an important archaeological value. Their follow-up of the forest ploughing just south of Unitas 1 in the 1980s showed this again, but at the same time it made painfully clear how the ploughing must have destroyed an important part of the archaeological record here.

Considering the results of our research, we will now first give an overview of the still remaining archaeological value of the excavated mound Unitas 1 and Delfin 190, and then say some more on the future of the archaeological heritage of the site.

10.1 The remaining archaeological value of the excavated barrows

No systematic coring was done in order to assess the damage done to the Delfin 190 and Unitas 1 mound. We have to base our conclusions on the results of our excavation and the observations done by the *ROB* (now *RCE*) during the restoration in 1987 (laid down in a hand-drawn map sketching the extension of depressions that were filled with white sand).

10.1.1 Unitas 1

Basing ourselves on the 1987 *ROB* map, the top soil of the southern part of the mound is damaged in places. Iron Age features (think of the 'footpath finds' done during this restoration; section 4.5.2) situated in the top soil will have been damaged or disappeared. Unfortunately, it was not established how deep the depressions were. In the future, it is recommended that restorations are only to be carried out after careful and precise registration of the damage done to the barrow.

We expect the damage to be local only: we do not have any indication that a part of the mound was dug away, as happened with part of the Delfin 190 mound.

It may be expected that the central grave, the Iron Age ditch S19, as well as the post row flanking it are all still preserved. Trees are however growing on the northern flank of the mound. Our observations on the vertical movement of artefacts (see especially 5.3.4) shows that tree roots will continue to distort the archaeological record: it is advised that trees are cleared from its flank. For the archaeological record, they are best sawn down instead of pulled with roots and all. The remaining trunk can stay where it was; it will not damage the archaeological record any further.

10.1.2 Delfin 190

As set out before, the western flank of the Delfin 190 mound was dug away: first during the digging of the ditch in the 19th century (possibly in relation to the tobacco industry to the south, and in the 1980s for sand extraction. If we are right in our identification of S9 as a peripheral ditch, then the entire mound west of our excavation trench is gone. However, the remainder of the mound is in a rather good condition. It is very likely that the centre was not disturbed, and the presence of well-preserved and rare Middle Bronze Age A *Hilversum*-phase settlement features underneath it, make the barrow still of great scientific interest.

10.1.3 Special features shared by both barrows

Pollen have not been preserved, unfortunately, and the readability of features is also far from ideal. Barrows from Humus Podzol soils are generally much more informative on both points (*cf.* Glasbergen 1954 or Fokkens *et al.* 2006). However, a feature that is uncommon is the large number of artefacts preserved in the mound. Although our excavation method was sensitive to finding even the smallest of finds, the *Elsterberg* mounds still stand out: in all the excavations we carried out ever since the *Elsterberg* we barely found more than a few sherds or flakes. Clearly, the *Elsterberg* barrows document a special occupation history. This in itself is an argument to try to preserve these mounds for the future.

How this should be done is another question. Despite all good intentions from the part of the estate owners and foresters, in 2008 an entire mound was destroyed . The presence of burial mounds so close to a modern town apparently makes it very hard to prevent this sort of things from happening. Only sealing off of the topsoil with special material seems an option now. Much more important, however, seems to be dissemination of knowledge on these mounds to the wider public. During our excavation we talked to people living in *Elst* who visited the forest daily and never had realized that these "bumps" in the landscape were prehistoric burial mounds. It goes without saying that dissemination of knowledge to the wider public must go hand in hand with reminders on the vulnerability of the burial mounds. Bearing in mind the rapid increase in internet sites selling illegally found ancient artefacts from the Netherlands, it is also important to once more stress that the only "value" to be found in those mounds is of a scientific nature.

10.2 Assessing the archaeological value of the environment of the barrows

The number of stray finds around the barrows, as recorded and described in chapter 4 and 5 suggests that part of the forests around the mound conceals the remains of one or more Middle Bronze Age settlements, and Iron Age inhabitation. The fact that several pottery sherds are stray finds along the paths also shows that the archaeological record has already been disturbed there. It may be expected that forest ploughing will have erased most features. We currently do not have a clue as to the nature of the preservation of features around this barrow group. That is why we propose to carry out a prospective research campaign assessing the quality of the archaeological record around the mounds along the lines set out in section 9.5.

Phase 1: inventory

It should start with an inventory of all known finds. All retrievable finds around the barrows Unitas 1 and Delfin 190 have already been described in this book (Chapter 4 and 5). The *Archis*-database of the *RCE* describes some additional finds further away. These should be retrieved, dated and assessed for the reliability of the information of the precise find spot. Then, the following question should be addressed in order to assess the quality of the archaeological record of the environment around all barrows of the *Elsterberg* group: *in which way does the distribution of archaeological finds inform us on the disturbances of the archaeological record?* Are all the finds from places where trees have fallen down like in the case of our Pot Beaker find (cf. chapter 4), or are they strays found at the surface along the paths through the forest? In other words: do the finds represent a potentially intact (*i.e.* buried in the ground as in the case of the tree fall pits finds) or an already severely destroyed archaeological record (as in the case of stray finds along the paths)? An important question might also be whether there is a relation between archaeological finds (and the presence of surviving barrows) and parcels of old forests that presumably did not undergo the destructive deep forest ploughing of modern times? A recent inventory of patches of old forest on the *Utrechtse Heuvelrug* may be very helpful here (Wildschut *et al.* 2004). A careful analysis of the Digital Elevation Model of the *Elsterberg* area (using the excellent *AHN*-data) may be very helpful for the detecting of other archaeological sites or even new, so far undiscovered barrow sites.

Phase 2: assessment of remaining archaeological value of the environment by coring and trial trenches

A next phase will be the archaeological prospection of those parts of the forest where the inventory gives indications that the archaeological record is relatively well-preserved. It is explicitly stated that this research should be carried out by a combination of trial trenches and corings. Corings are helpful in assessing the profile of barrows (particularly those in Humus Podzols), but *contrary to what seems to be common practice in the Netherlands, we want to emphasize that corings alone are insufficient for detecting the presence/absence of archaeological traces in the environment.*(*cf.* Fokkens 2007). Trial trenches in forests cannot always be carried out that easily, but our experiences at the *Apeldoorn-Echoput* and *Apeldoorn-Wieselse Weg* sites show that much more is possible than is usually thought (*cf,* Fontijn in press; Fontijn/Van der Linde in prep.).

Phase 3: Assessment of remaining archaeological value of all barrows

As was stated above, there is insufficient information on the way in which the *Elsterberg* barrows were destroyed in the past. Generally, we may roughly distinguish between 10 % preserved (only profile sections of a barrow after excavation), 25 % preserved up until 100 % preserved. Existing documentation of barrow restorations carried out in the 1980s must be supplemented with additional corings if necessary. We have already seen that the existing documentation on Unitas 1 and Delfin 190 was insufficient for an adequate assessment of the remaining archaeological value of these mounds. The coring method recently developed by the *RCE* has proven to be useful in this respect (see for example the results in chapter 7).

Phase 4: Making a pragmatic plan for heritage management

Finally, results on the inventory, and assessment of remaining archaeological values should result in a pragmatic plan for heritage management of the *Elsterberg* barrow group.

10.3 How to preserve it

10.3.1 The role of amateur archaeologists

Establishing the value of an archaeological site is one thing, preserving it is another. We cannot go beyond any conclusions of a future prospective research that assesses the value of this sort of environment, except for one point: the indispensable role of amateur archaeologists

As remarked many times in this book, it is due to the active amateurs of *Rhenen* that the mounds became known in the first place, but also that there were always follow-ups to the many local disturbances of the archaeological heritage (Chapter 2 to 5). If it was not for the amateur archaeologists, it is questionable whether we would know of any of the finds described in this book. One of them, Heinz Reusink, also played a part in disseminating something of the archaeological knowledge on barrows to the wider public (Reusink's "barrow trail"; Reusink 1988) With the recent changes in the Dutch Archaeology, the possibility of amateur archaeologist to carry out excavations is subject to stricter regulations than before. However, the possibility to react instantly to threats of the archaeological heritage and to play a critical, pro-active role in such matters is not precluded. Their site observations, reporting of new finds, field surveys are needed more than ever. The *Elsterberg* barrow group is a case in point: knowledgeable amateurs, living in the environment and frequently inspecting the site are indispensable in the meticulous monitoring and surveying of the forest, something that is rarely or never done by professionals. Much of the story told here on the development of the prehistoric landscape was based on all these small and inconspicuous amateur finds, A joint survey project of the University and amateurs might be one possibility to stimulate such an endeavour in a more structural way. The often dramatic destruction of heritage that happened at the *Elsterberg* until very recently, however, once again makes clear that archaeology cannot exist without local archaeologists, who are prepared to spend time to visit sites in their living area time and time again. It is therefore no more than logical that any form of monitoring can only be done in close cooperation with amateurs. Such amateurs might act as "ambassadors" of one particular site, who can act as an important source of information to the local public, but who can also immediately warn heritage instances (the *RCE*, the land owner or municipality) when the site is threatened by destruction. In order to fuel local enthusiasm, professional archaeology should do much more to inform the public on their local heritage than is done now. Apart from the stimulation of cultural tourism by books, barrow trails, and internet sites, attractive archaeology projects at local primary and secondary schools are also indispensable.

10.3.2 The role of estate owners

Amateurs and the wider public are not the owners of the estates on which the *Elsterberg* barrow group is situated. The preservation of the archaeological heritage is primarily the responsibility of the estate owners. At several occasions, we learnt that both estate owners are very much interested in the archaeological sites on their estate and willing to do what is in its interest. It is up to archaeological instances to supply them with information and advice concerning the proper way to deal with the heritage on their land. This might be effected as follows:

The knowledge on the barrows and on other archaeological sites on an estate should result into a <u>pragmatic plan of heritage management</u> (Dutch: *beheersplan*). Such a plan should state which measures should be taken in order to prevent the archaeological sites from being further damaged, which activities are better not to be undertaken at particular sites (e.g. the use of heavy tractors, removal of top soil from heaths, or deep forest ploughing at a site where the archaeological record is still untouched but vulnerable to such disturbances. Ideally, it is the site inventory and quality assessment of the archaeological heritage in place (as suggested in

Fig.10.1 The excavation attracted many visitors and a lot of publicity. Still, it would be better if a more lasting presentation would inform inhabitants of Elst of the barrows in their backyard. Photograph by R. Kok.

section 10.2) that provide the basis for such a plan of heritage management. It is crucial to keep on informing the local foresters on how to act responsibly and to recognize threats to the archaeological heritage.

As a part of the history of their estate, it is also part of their history. It should be their responsibilty to take measures to preserve the archaeological heritage on their estate. It is a responsibility of the archaeologists to inform the estate owners on the value of this heritage. This implies that there is also a heavy responsibility on the part of archaeologists to inform people in an *accessible* way about the past, by means of readable books, folders, websites and to inform and support evocative presentations of heritage at their estates. We, as archaeologists, therefore should certainly not stop with academic books like the one you are reading now. A popular-scientific companion to such books and a good website would be a good starting point. For this site, we refer to www.grafheuvels.nl as well as to the accompanying popular-scientific booklet *Op de Rand van de Rug. Grafheuvels op de Elsterberg bij Rhenen* by Evert van Ginkel and Yuri van Koeveringe (Van Ginkel *et al.* 2010).

References

Anonymus, 1965/1966. De Periodisering van de Nederlandse prehistorie, *Berichten van de Rijksdienst voor Oudheidkundig Bodemonderzoek* 15/16, 7-11.

Anthony, D.W., 2007. *The horse, the wheel and language – how Bronze-Age riders from the Eurasian steppes shaped the modern world*, Princeton.

Arnoldussen, S., 2008. *A living landscape. Bronze Age settlement sites in the Dutch river area (c. 2000-800 BC)*, Ph.D. thesis, Leiden.

Arnoldussen, S./ D.R. Fontijn, 2006. Towards familiar landscapes? On the nature and origin of Middle Bronze Age landscapes in the Netherlands, *Proceedings of the Prehistoric Society* 72, 289-317.

Arnoldussen, S./ E. Ball, 2007. Nederzettingsaardewerk uit de late bronstijd in Noord-Brabant en het rivierengebied. In: R. Jansen/ L.P. Louwe Kooijmans (eds), *Van contract tot wetenschap. Tien jaar archeologisch onderzoek door Archol BV, 1997-2007*, Leiden, 181-203.

Arnoldussen, S./ J. W. de Kort/ Q. Bourgeois, 2009. A barrow for a camp-site? The disturbed barrow of Rhenen - Elsterberg (Unitas 4), *Lunula Archaeologia protohistorica XVII*, 177-188.

Bakels, C.C., 2009. Pollenanalyse van een kringgreppel uit de vroege bronstijd/midden-bronstijd A. In: L.Meurkens (ed), Laat-prehistorische nederzettingssporen en graven op de sandr-vlakte bij Elst, *Archol rapport* 128, 103-104.

Bakker, J.A., 1976. On the possibility of reconstructing roads from the TRB period, *Berichten van de Rijksdienst voor Oudheidkundig Bodemonderzoek* 26, 63-91.

Beek, R. van, 2006. Het grafritueel in Oost-Nederland tussen de Vroege IJzertijd en de tweede eeuw AD (ca. 500 BC-100 AD), *Lunula Archaeologia protohistorica* 14, 61-69.

Beek, R. van, 2009. *Relïef in tijd en ruimte: interdisciplinair onderzoek naar bewoning en landschap van Oost-Nederland tussen vroege prehistorie en middeleeuwen*, Ph.D. thesis, Wageningen.

Beek, Z. van der/ H.Fokkens, 2001. 24 years after Oberried: the 'Dutch' model reconsidered. In F. Nicolis (eds), *Bell beakers today. Pottery, people, culture, symbols in prehistoric Europe. Proceedings of the International Colloquium Riva del Garda (Trento, Italy), 11-16 May 1998*, Trento: Province of Trento, 301-308.

Bertemes, F., 2004. Frühe Metallurgen in der Spätkupfer- und Frühbronzezeit. In: H. Meller (ed), *Die geschmiedete Himmel. Die weite Welt im Herzen Europas vor 3600 Jahren,* Stuttgart, 144-149.

Blijdenstijn, R., 2007. *Tastbare Tijd. Cultuurhistorische atlas van de provincie Utrecht,* Amsterdam.

Bloemers, J.H.F., 1978. Rijswijk-De Bult. Eine Siedlung der Cananefaten, *Nederlandse Oudheden* 8.

Bloo, S.C., 2003. Het prehistorisch aardewerk. In: D.A.Gerrets/ A.H. Schutte (eds), *Schagen, Plangebied "De Hoep Noord"* (ADC-rapport 179), 25-26.

Bogucki, P., 1999. *The origins of Human Society,* Malden.

Bourgeois, J./ J. Semey/ J. van Moerkerke, 1989. Ursel. Rapport provisoire des fouilles 1986-1987. Tombelle de l'âge du bronze et monuments avec nécropole de l'âge du fer, *Scholae Archaeologicae* 11.

Bourgeois, J., 1998. La nécropole laténienne et gallo-romaine d'Ursel-Rozenstraat (Flandre Orientale-Belgique), *Revue Archéologique de Picardie* 1/2, 111-125.

Bourgeois, Q./ S. Arnoldussen, 2006. Expressing monumentality: some observations on the dating of Dutch Bronze Age barrows and houses, *Lunula Archaeologia protohistorica* XIV, 13-25.

Bourgeois, Q./ D.R. Fontijn, 2007. Nieuw onderzoek naar twee grafheuvels op de Utrechtse Heuvelrug, gemeente Rhenen, *Lunula Archaeologia protohistorica* XV, 3-12.

Bourgeois, Q./ D.R. Fontijn, 2008. Houses and barrows in the Low Countries. In: S. Arnoldussen/ H. Fokkens (eds), Bronze Age Settlements in the Low Countries, Oxford, 41-57.

Bourgeois, Q./ D.R. Fontijn, in prep. Diversity in uniformity, uniformity in diversity. Barrow groups in the Netherlands. In: S. Wirth (ed), Grabhügellandschaften-Texten zu der Tagung in Herne 2008, Herne.

Bradley, R., 2005. *Ritual and domestic life in prehistoric Europe*, London.

Broeke, P.W., van den, 1987a. De dateringsmiddelen voor de ijzertijd van Zuid-Nederland. In: W.A.B. van der Sanden/ P.W. van den Broeke (eds), *Getekend Zand. Tien jaararcheologisch onderzoek in Oss-Ussen*, Waalre, 23-43.

Broeke, P.W., van den, 1987b. Oss-Ussen: Het handgemaakte aardewerk. In: W.A.B. van der Sanden/ P.W. van den Broeke (eds), *Getekend Zand. Tien jaar archeologisch onderzoek in Oss-Ussen*, Waalre, 101-119.

Broeke, P.W., van den, 1991. Nederzettingsaardewerk uit de late bronstijd in Zuid-Nederland. In: H. Fokkens/ N. Roymans (eds), *Nederzettingen uit de bronstijd en vroege ijzertijd in de lage landen*, Amersfoort (Nederlandse Archeologische Rapporten 13), 193-211.

Brombacher, A.A./ W. Hoogendoorn, 2000. *Aardkundige Waarden in de provincie Utrecht*, Utrecht.

Brongers, J.A., 1976. Air photography and celtic field research in the Netherlands, *Nederlandse Oudheden* 6, Amersfoort.

Bulten, E./ Y.Boonstra/ S.Bloo, 2008. Hilversum aan Zee. Een midden bronstijd-vindplaats bij Bronovo in Den Haag (Nederland), *Lunula Archaeologia protohistorica* XVI, 3-10.

Bursch, F.C., 1933. *Die Becherkultur in den Niederlanden*, Marburg.

Butler, J.J., 1990. Bronze Age metal and amber in the Netherlands (I), *Palaeohistoria* 32, 47-110.

Butler, J. J., 1995/1996. Bronze Age Metal and Amber in the Netherlands (II:1). Catalogue of the Flat Axes, Flanged Axes and Stopridge Axes', *Palaeohistoria* 37/38, 159-243.

Butler, J./ H. Fokkens, 2005. Van steen naar brons. Technologie en materiële cultuur. In: L.P. Louwe Kooijmans/ P.W. van den Broeke/ H. Fokkens/ A. van Gijn (eds), *Nederland in de Prehistorie*. Amsterdam, 371-399.

Butler, J.J./ J.D. van der Waals, 1966. Bell beakers and early metal-working in the Netherlands, *Palaeohistoria* 12, 41-139.

Butler, J.J./ J.N. Lanting/ J.D. van der Waals 1972. Annertol III: a four-period Bell Beaker and Bronze Age barrow at Schuilingsoord, gem. Zuidlaren, Drente, *Helinium* 12, 225-241.

Casparie, W.A./ W. Groenman-van Waateringe, 1980. Palynological analyses of Dutch barrows, *Palaeohistoria* 22, 7-65.

Cherretté, B./ J. Bourgeois, 2005. Circles for the dead. From aerial photography to excavation of a Bronze Age cemetery in Oedelem (West-Flanders, Belgium). In: J. Bourgeois/ M. Meganck (eds), *Aerial Photography and Archaeology 2003. A Century of Information. Papers presented during the Conference held at Ghent University December 10th-12th*, (Archaeological Reports Ghent University), 255-265.

Drenth, E., 2005. Het Laat-Neolithicum in Nederland. In: J. Deeben/ E. Drenth/ M. Van Oorsouw/ L. Verhart (eds), *De Steentijd van Nederland* (Archeologie 11/12), 333-365.

Drenth, E./ Lohof, E., 2005. Heuvels voor de doden. In: L.P. Louwe Kooijmans/ P.W. van den Broeke/ H. Fokkens/ A.L. van Gijn (eds), *Nederland in de prehistorie*, Amsterdam, 433-454.

Drenth, E./ W. Hogestijn, 1999. De klokbekercultuur in Nederland: de stand van onderzoek anno 1999, *Archeologie 9*, 99-149.

Es, W.A., van, 1968. Handmade Pottery of the Roman Period from Rhenen, *Berichten van der Rijksdienst voor het Oudheidkundig Bodemonderzoek* 18, 267-272.

Es, W.A., van/ M. Miedema/ S.L. Wynia, 1985. Eine Siedlung der römischen Kaiserzeit in Bennekom, Provinz Gelderland, *Berichten van der Rijksdienst voor het Oudheidkundig Bodemonderzoek* 35, 533-652.

Fokkens, H., 1986. From shifting cultivation to short fallow cultivation: Late Neolithic change in the Netherlands reconsidered. In: H. Fokkens/ P.M. Banga/ M. Bierma (eds), *Op zoek naar mens en materiële cultuur. Feestbundel aangeboden aan J.D. van der Waals ter gelegenheid van zijn emiraat*, Groningen, 5-21.

Fokkens, H., 1997. The genesis of urnfields: economic crisis or ideological change?, *Antiquity* 71, 360-373.

Fokkens, H., 1998. *Drowned Landscape. The Occupation of the Western Part of the Frisian-Brentian Plateau, 4400 BC - AD500*, Assen/Amersfoort.

Fokkens, H., 2001. The periodisation of the Dutch Bronze Age: a critical review. In: W.H. Metz/ B.L. van Beek/ H. Steegstra (eds), *Patina: Essays presented to Jay Jordan Butler on the occasion of his 80th birthday*, Groningen/Amsterdam, 241-262.

Fokkens, H., 2007. Sleuven of boren? Archeologische prospectie van oude cultuurlandschappen. In: R. Jansen/ L.P. Louwe Kooijmans (eds), *Van contract tot wetenschap. Tien jaar archeologische onderzoek van Archol BV*, Leiden, 59-68.

Fokkens, H./ R. Jansen, 2004. *Het vorstengraf van Oss. Een archeologische speurtocht naar een prehistorisch grafveld.*, Utrecht.

Fokkens, H./ R. Jansen/ I. M. Van Wijk (eds), 2006. *Het grafveld Oss-Zevenbergen. Een prehistorisch grafveld ontleed*, *Archol Rapport* 50, Leiden.

Fontijn, D.R., 1996a. Socializing landscape. Second thoughts about the cultural biography of urnfields, *Archaeological Dialogues* 3, 77-87.

Fontijn, D.R.,1996b. Aardewerk uit de Late IJzertijd en Romeinse Tijd. In: M. Groothedde (ed), *Leesten en Eme. Archeologisch en historisch onderzoek naar verdwenen buurschappen bij Zutphen*, Zutphen, 56-65.

Fontijn, D.R., 2002. Sacrificial Landscapes. Cultural biographies of persons, objects and 'natural' places in the Bronze Age of the southern Netherlands, c. 2300-600BC, *Analecta Prehistorica Leidensia* 33/34, 1-392.

Fontijn, D.R., 2006. *Programma van Eisen voor Elst, gemeente Rhenen, grafheuvels Elsterberg*, Leiden.

Fontijn, D.R., 2007a. The significance of 'invisible' places, *World Archaeology* 31, 70-83.

Fontijn, D.R., 2007b. *Ancestral mounds. The social and ideological significance of barrows, 2900-1100 BC. Project proposal NWO- programmatic research*, Leiden.

Fontijn, D.R. (ed), *in prep. Echoes from the Past – Late Iron Age barrows at the hilltop near the "Echo-well" in Apeldoorn*, Leiden.

Fontijn, D.R./ A.G.F.M. Cuijpers, 1998/1999. Prehistoric Stone circles, stone platforms and a ritual enclosure from Nijmegen, *Berichten van de Rijksdienst voor Oudheidkundig Bodemonderzoek* 43, 33-67.

Fontijn, D.R./ A.G.F.M. Cuijpers, 2002. Revisiting barrows: a Middle Bronze Age burial group at the Kops Plateau, *Berichten van de Rijksdienst voor het Oudheidkundig Bodemonderzoek* 45, 157-189.

Fontijn, D.R./ H. Fokkens, 2007. The emergence of Early Iron Age 'chieftains' graves in the Southern Netherlands. In: C. Haselgrove/ R. Pope (eds), *The Early Iron Age in Britain and the near continent*, Oxford, 354-373.

Fontijn, D.R./ R. Jansen, *in prep. Tumulus 7: a new Ha C chieftain's grave from Oss-Zevenbergen*, Leiden.

Fontijn, D.R./ C.M. van der Linde, *in prep. The Barrow Landscape of Apeldoorn-Wieselse Weg*, Leiden.

Garwood, P., 2007. Before the hills in order stood: Chronology, time and history in the interpretation of Early Bronze Age round barrows. In: Jonathan Last (ed), *Beyond the grave, new perspectives on barrows*, Oxford, 30-52.

Gerritsen, F., 2003. *Local identities. Landscape and community in the late prehistoric Meuse-Demer-Scheldt region*, Amsterdam, (*Amsterdam Archaeological Studies 9*).

Giffen, A.E. van, 1930. *Die Bauart der Einzelgräber: Beitrag zur Kenntnis der alteren individuellen Grabhügelstrukturen in den Niederlanden*, Leipzig.

Giffen, A.E. van, 1935. Oudheidkundige aanteekeningen over Drentsche vondsten (II), *Nieuwe Drentse Volksalmanak* 53, 67-121.

Giffen, A.E. van, 1937. Bouwstenen voor de Brabantsche Oergeschiedenis, *Werken van het provinciaal genootschap van kunsten en wetenschappen in Noord-Brabant* 30, 7-46.

Giffen, A.E. van, 1939. Tumulus 43 in het Hijkerveld, gem. Beilen, *Nieuw Drentsche Volksalmanak* 1938/1939, 12-13.

Giffen, A.E. van, 1943. Opgravingen in Drenthe tot 1941. In: J. Poortman (ed), *Drenthe, een handboek voor het verkennen van het Drentsche leven in voorbije eeuwen*, Meppel, 393-564.

Giffen, A.E. van, 1961. Settlement traces of the Early Bell Beaker Culture at Oostwoud (N.H.). *Helinium* 1, 223-228.

Gijn, A.L. van, 1990. The Wear and Tear of Flint: Principles of Functional Analysis Applied to Dutch Neolithic Assemblages, *Analecta Praehistorica Leidensia* 22, Leiden.

Ginkel, E. van/ Y. van Koeveringe/ D.R. Fontijn 2010. *Op de rand van de rug. Grafheuvels op de Elsterberg bij Rhenen*, Sidestone Press, Leiden.

Ginkel, E. van/ R. Jansen/ D.R. Fontijn/ H. Fokkens, 2009. *Prins Onder Plaggen, Vorstengrafheuvels op de Maashorst bij Oss*, Sidestone Press, Leiden.

Glasbergen, W., 1954. *Barrow excavations in the Eight Beatitudes, the Bronze Age cemetery between Toterfout & Halve Mijl, North Brabant*, Ph.D. thesis, Groningen.

Glasbergen, W., 1962. De Hilversum-pot van Budel/Weert (Ned. Limburg), *Helinium* 2, 260-265.

Glasbergen, W., 1969. Nogmaals HVS/DKS, *Haarlemse Voordrachten* XXVIII.

Glasbergen, W./ J.J. Butler 1959. The Late Neolithic Gold Ornament from Bennekom, *Palaeohistoria* V, 53-71.

Harding, A. F., 2000. *European societies in the Bronze Age*, (Cambridge World Archaeology), Cambridge.

Harsema, O.H.,1991. De bronstijd-bewoning op het Hijkerveld bij Hijken. In: H. Fokkens/ N. Roymans (eds), *Nederzettingen uit de bronstijd en de vroege ijzertijd in de Lage Landen*, Amersfoort (Nederlandsche Archeologische Rapporten 13), 21-29.

Heeringen, R.M. van, 1985. Typologie, Zeitstellung und Verbreitung der in die Niederlande importierten vorgeschichtlichen Mahlsteine aus Tephrit, *Archäologisches Korrespondenzblatt* 15, 371-383.

Heeringen, R.M. van, 1989a. The Iron Age in the Western Netherlands IV: Site catalogue and pottery description, Map sheet 3, *Berichten van de Rijksdienst voor het Oudheidkundig Bodemonderzoek* 39, 69(153)-156(240).

Heeringen, R.M. van, 1989b. The Iron Age in the Western Netherlands V: Synthesis, *Berichten van de Rijksdienst voor het Oudheidkundig Bodemonderzoek* 39, 157(241)-255(339).

Heeringen, R.M. van, 1992. *The Iron Age in the western Netherlands*, Ph.D. thesis, Amsterdam.

Heeringen, R.M. van, 1998/1999. Burial with a Rhine view: the Hallstatt situla grave on the Koerheuvel at Rhenen, *Berichten van de Rijksdienst voor het Oudheidkundig Bodemonderzoek* 43, 69-92.

Heidinga, H.A., 1988. From Kootwijk to Rhenen: in search of the elite in the Central Netherlands in the Early Middle Ages. In: J.C. Besteman/ J.M. Bos/ H.A. Heidinga (eds), *Medieval Archaeology in the Netherlands*. Assen/Maastricht, 9-40.

Hessing, W.A.M., 1989. Wijk bij Duurstede 'De Horden': Besiedlung und Bestattungen aus der frühen Eisenzeit, *Berichten van de Rijksdienst voor het Oudheidkundig Bodemonderzoek* 39, 297-344.

Hessing, W.A.M., 1991. Bewoningssporen uit de midden-bronstijd en de vroege ijzertijd op 'De Horden' te Wijk bij Duurstede. In: H. Fokkens/ N. Roymans (eds), *Nederzettingen uit de bronstijd en de vroege ijzertijd in de Lage Landen*, Amersfoort (Nederlandsche Archeologische Rapporten 13), 41-52.

Hessing W.A.M./ P.B. Kooi, 2005. Urnenvelden en brandheuvels. Begraving en grafritueel in late bronstijd en ijzertijd. In: L.P. Louwe Kooijmans/ P.W. van den Broeke/ H. Fokkens/ A.L. van Gijn (eds), *Nederland in de prehistorie*, Amsterdam, 631-654.

Hiddink, H., 2003. Het grafritueel in de Late IJzertijd en Romeinse Tijd in het Maas-Demer-Scheldegebied, in het bijzonder van twee grafvelden bij Weert, *Zuidnederlandse Archeologische Rapporten* 11, Amsterdam.

Hielkema, J.B./ T. Hamburg, 2008. Bronze Age settlements in Tiel-Medel. In: S. Arnoldussen/ H. Fokkens (eds), *Bronze Age Settlements in the Low Countries*, Oxford, 127-136.

Hoof, L.G.L., van/ L. Meurkens (eds), 2005. Vluchtige huisplattegronden. Erven uit de midden-bronstijd B en nederzettingssporen uit de vroege bronstijd en midden-bronstijd A (verslag van een tweede opgravingscampagne te Rhenen-Remmerden), *Archol Rapport* 51, Leiden.

Hoof, L. G.L., van/ L. Meurkens, 2008. Rhenen-Remmerden revisited: some comments regarding site structure and the visibility of Bronze Age house plans. In: S. Arnoldussen/ H. Fokkens (eds), *Bronze Age Settlements in the Low Countries*, Oxford, 83-95.

Houkes, M.J./ D. Mittendorf, 1996. *Onderzoek naar relaties in de verspreiding van grafheuvels uit het laat neolithicum en de bronstijd in het gebied Arnhem-Renkum Kaartblad 40A Noordelijk deel*, Arnhem.

Hulst, R.S., 1965/66. A pot beaker from Velp, prov. of Gelderland, *Berichten van de Rijksdienst voor het Oudheidkundig Bodemonderzoek* 15/16, 231-232.

Hulst, R.S., 1969. A Bronze Age settlement at Elst, prov. Utrecht, *Berichten van de Rijksdienst voor het Oudheidkundig Bodemonderzoek* 19, 275-278.

Hulst, R.S., 1970. Archeologische kroniek van Gelderland 1966-1977, *Bijdragen en Mededelingen der Vereniging 'Gelre'* 64, 26-48.

Hulst, R.S., 1981. Einheimische Keramik des 1. Jahrhunderts nach Chr. aus Aalten (Gelderland), *Berichten van de Rijksdienst voor het Oudheidkundig Bodemonderzoek* 31, 365-367.

Jongste, P. F. B, 2001. Rhenen - Rhemmerden, AAO en DO, *ADC Rapport 92*, Bunschoten.

Kok, T., 2007. *Grafheuvel 'De Dijnselburg.' Nieuwe interpretaties van een oude grafheuvel*, Ba-thesis, Leiden.

Kort, J.W., de, 2002. Schapen op de heide. Een vegetatiereconstructie van de omgeving van het vorstengraf van Oss in de Vroege Ijzertijd. In: H.Fokkens/ R.Jansen (eds), *2000 jaar bewoningsdynamiek, Brons en ijzertijdbewoning in het Maas-Demer-Scheldegebied*, Oss, 341-353.

Kort, J.W., de, 2008. De vegetatieontwikkeling rondom de Zevenbergen bij Oss, circa 1800-500 BC. In: R. Jansen/ L.P. Louwe Kooijmans (eds), *Van contract tot wetenschap. Tien jaar archeologisch onderzoek door Archol BV, 1997-2007*, Leiden, 221-234.

Kortlang, F., 1999. The Iron Age urnfield and settlement of Someren-'Waterdael'. In: F. Theuws/ N. Roymans (eds), *Land and Ancestors. Cultural dynamics in the urnfield period and the middle ages in the southern Netherlands*, Amsterdam (Amsterdam Archaeological Studies 4), 133-197.

Kuijper, W.J., 2009. Botanische macroresten. In: L. Meurkens (ed), Laat-prehistorische nederzettingssporen en graven op de sandr-vlakte bij Elst, *Archol rapport* 128, 101-102.

Lagerås, K.E., 2002. Visible intentions? Viewshed analysis of Bronze Age burial in western Scania. Sweden. In: C. Scarre (ed): *Monuments and Landscape in Atlantic Europe. Perception and society during the Neolithic and Early Bronze Age*, London/ New York, 177-191.

Lanting, J. N, 1969. Verspreiding en datering van wikkeldraadaardewerk. *Nieuwe Drentse Volksalmanak* 87, 191-210.

Lanting, J.N., 1973. Laat-neolithicum en vroege bronstijd in Nederland en N.W.-Duitsland: continue ontwikkelingen, *Palaeohistoria* 15, 216-317.

Lanting, J.N., 2007/2008. De NO-Nederlandse/NW-Duitse klokbekergroep: Culturele achtergrond, typologie van het aardewerk, datering, verspreiding en grafritueel. *Palaeohistoria* 49/50, 11-326.

Lanting, J.N./ W.G. Mook, W.G.,1977. *The pre- and protohistory of the Netherlands in terms of radiocarbon dates*, Groningen.

Lanting, J.N./ J. van der Plicht, 2001/2002. De ^{14}C chronologie van de Nederlandse Pre- en Protohistorie IV: Bronstijd en Vroege IJzertijd, *Palaeohistoria* 43/44, 117-261.

Lanting, J.N./ J.D. van der Waals, 1971. Laat-neolithische grafheuvels bij Vaasen en Maarsbergen. *Oudheidkundige Mededelingen uit het Rijksmuseum van Oudheden te Leiden* 52, 93-127.

Lanting, J.N./ J.D. van der Waals, 1976. Beaker cultures in the Lower Rhine Basin. In: J.N. Lanting/ J.D. van der Waals (eds), *Glockenbecher Symposium Oberried 1974*, Haarlem, 1-80.

Leeuwe, R. de, 2007. Twee grafheuvels in het prehistorische dodenlandschap van Oss-Zevenbergen. In: R. Jansen/ L.P. Louwe Kooijmans (eds), *Van contract tot wetenschap. Tien jaar archeologisch onderzoek door Archol BV, 1997-2007*, Leiden, 205-220.

Lehmann, L.Th., 1965. Placing the pot beaker, *Helinium* 5, 3-31.

Lehmann, L. Th., 1967a. New pot beakers from the Veluwe, *Berichten van de Rijksdienst voor het Oudheidkundig Bodemonderzoek* 17, 162-166.

Lehmann, L. Th., 1967b. Pot beaker news, *Helinium* 7, 65-69.

Lohof, E., 1991. *Grafritueel en sociale verandering in de bronstijd van Noordoost-Nederland*, Ph.D. thesis, Amsterdam.

Lohof, E., 1994. Tradition and change. Burial practices in the Late Neolithic and Bronze Age in the north-eastern Netherlands, *Archaeological Dialogues* 1, 98-118.

Louwe Kooijmans, L.P., 1967. Elspeet, gem. Ermelo, *Archeologisch Nieuws*, *35.

Louwe Kooijmans, L.P., 1973. Een grafheuvelgroep uit het laat-neolithicum en de bronstijd in het terrein van de Romeinse castra te Nijmegen. In: W.A. van Es/ A.V.M. Hubrecht/ P. Stuart/ W.C. Mank/ S.L. Wynia (eds), *Archeologie en Historie. Opgedragen aan H. Brunsting bij zijn zeventigste verjaardag*, Bussum, 87-125.

Louwe Kooijmans, L.P., 1974. The Rhine-Meuse delta. Four studies on its prehistoric occupation and Holocene geology, *Analecta Praehistorica Leidensia* 7.

Louwen, A.J., *in prep.* Bathmense potten. Een aardewerk assemblage uit de overgangsperiode Late IJzertijd-Vroeg Romeinse tijd, aangetroffen in een waterkuil op de Bathmer Enk, *Archeologische Kroniek van de Provincie Overijsel*.

Maes, E./ J. Vroemen, 2001. Amateur-archeologe Delfin: Graven zit me in het bloed, *GM Kwadraat* 3, 16-19.

Meijlink, B., 2008. The Bronze Age cultural landscape of De Bogen. In: S. Arnoldussen/ H. Fokkens (eds), *Bronze Age Settlements in the Low Countries*, Oxford, 137-150.

Meurkens, L. 2006. Elst – Het Bosje (gemeente Rhenen). Resultaten van een inventariserend onderzoek, *Archol rapport* 63.

Meurkens, L. 2007. "Ter Afschrick ende Exempele", Het gebruik van prehistorische grafheuvels als galgenbergen. In: R.Jansen/ L.P. Louwe Kooijmans (eds), *Van contract tot wetenschap. Tien jaar archeologisch onderzoek door Archol BV, 1997-2007*, Leiden, 353-372.

Meurkens, L. 2009a. Laat-prehistorische nederzettingssporen en graven op de sandr-vlakte bij Elst, *Archol rapport* 128.

Meurkens, L. 2009b. Een urnenveld en nederzettingssporen uit de late prehistorie bij Remmerden (gemeente Rhenen), *Archol rapport* 114.

Modderman, P.J.R., 1955. Laat bekeraardewerk versierd met indrukken van een wikkeldraadstempel, *Berichten van de Rijksdienst voor het Oudheidkundig Bodemonderzoek* 6, 32-43.

Modderman, P. J. R., 1957. Een dodenhuis op de Gelpenberg bij Aalden. *Nieuwe Drentse Volksalmanak* 75, 19-22.

Modderman, P.J.R., 1959. Een 'Hilversum'pot met wikkeldraadstempel versierd en een bronzen naald uit Vorstenbosch (Noord-Brabant), *Berichten van de Rijksdienst voor het Oudheidkundig Bodemonderzoek* 9, 288-289.

Modderman, P.J.R., 1974. Een opgeofferde grafheuvel op de Groevenbeekse Heide bij Ermelo. *Westerheem* 23, 10-14.

Modderman, P.J.R., 1975. Bodemvorming in grafheuvels, *Analecta Praehistorica Leidensia* VIII, 11-21.

Modderman, P.J.R., 1982. Ermelo, grafheuvels op de heide, *Archeologische Monumenten in Nederland* 10, Zutphen.

Reusink, H.J., 1988. Leersum, Grafheuvels op de Zuilensteinsche Kop. *Archeologische monumenten in Nederland* 11, Amersfoort/ Zutphen.

Roymans, N., 1991. 'Late urnfield societies in the Northwest European Plain and the expanding networks of Central European Hallstatt groups'. In: N. Roymans/ F. Theuws (eds), *Images of the past. Studies on ancient societies in Northwestern Europe*, Amsterdam (Studies in prae- en protohistorie 7), 9-89.

Roymans, N. 1995. The cultural biography of urnfields and the long-term history of a mythical landscape. *Archaeological Dialogues* 2, 2-24.

Roymans, N./ F. Kortlang, 1999. Urnfield symbolism, ancestors, and the land in the Lower Rhine region. In: Theuws, F. and N. Roymans (eds), *Land and Ancestors. Cultural dynamics in the urnfield period and the middle ages in the southern Netherlands*, Amsterdam (Amsterdam Archaeological Studies 4), 33-61.

Roymans, N./ H. Fokkens, 1991. Een overzicht van veertig jaar nederzettingsonderzoek in de Lage Landen. In: H. Fokkens/ N. Roymans (eds), *Nederzettingen uit de bronstijd en de vroege ijzertijd in de Lage Landen*, Amersfoort (Nederlandsche Archeologische Rapporten 13), 1-19.

Sanden, W.A.B. van der, 1998. Funerary and related structures at Oss-Ussen. In: H.Fokkens (ed), *The Ussen Project. The first decade of excavations at Oss, Analecta Praehistorica Leidensia* 30, 307-336.

Scholte Lubberink, H.B.G., 2006. Plangebied Bornsche Maten-Zuid Esch, gemeente Borne. Een nederzetting uit de Late IJzertijd en Vroeg Romeinse tijd, *RAAP-rapport* 1432.

Schutte, I.A., 2009. Plangebied Fietspad N225 gemeente Rhenen. Archeologische vooronderzoek: een inventariserend veldonderzoek (kartering en waardering), *RAAP-rapport* 1864.

Slofstra, J./ W.A.B, van der Sanden, 1987. Rurale cultusplaatsen uit de Romeinse tijd in het Maas-Demer-Scheldegebied, *Analecta Praehistorica Leidensia* 20, 125-168.

Smits, L., 2009. *Het fysisch-antropologisch onderzoek van de crematieresten van de grafheuvel te Rhenen – Elsterberg* (unpublished report), Amsterdam.

Sprang, A. van, 1993. *Wat Aarde Bewaarde. Uit de voorgeschiedenis van Ermelo en omgeving*, Ermelo.

Svanberg, F. 2005. House Symbolism in Aristocratic Death Rituals of the Bronze Age. In: T. Artelius/ F. Svandberg (eds), *Dealing with the Dead. Archaeological Perspectives on Prehistoric Scandinavian Burial Ritual*, Ödeshög, Riksantikvarieämbetet, 73-98.

Taayke, E., 2002. Handmade pottery from a Roman period settlement at Wijk bij Duurstede-De Horden, *Berichten van de Rijksdienst voor het Oudheidkundig Bodemonderzoek* 45, 189-218.

Tent, W.J. van, 1976. *Archeologische Kroniek van de Provincie Utrecht over de jaren 1970-1971*, 71-74.

Tent, W.J. van, 1978. A Native Settlement at Jutphaas, Municipality of Nieuwegein, *Berichten van de Rijksdienst voor het Oudheidkundig Bodemonderzoek* 28, 199-239

Tent, W.J. van, 1989. Inheems aardwerk. In: L.R.P. Ozinga/ T.J. Hoekstra/ M.D. de Weerd/ S.L. Wynia (eds), *Het Romeinse castellum te Utrecht*, Utrecht, 154-155.

Tent, W.J. van, 1997. Rhenen-Elst. In: D.H. Kok/ S.G. van Dockum/ F. Vogelzang (eds), *Archeologische Kroniek. Provincie Utrecht 1990-1991*, De Boer-Coperus, Utrecht, 58.

Theunissen, E.M., 1993. Once again Toterfout-Halve Mijl. An attempt to demonstrate vertical stratification in the burial evidence of a Bronze Age cemetery, *Analecta Praehistorica Leidensia* 26, 29-43.

Theunissen, E.M., 1999. *Midden-bronstijdsamenlevingen in het zuiden van de Lage Landen. Een evaluatie van het begrip 'Hilversum-cultuur'*, Ph.D. thesis, Leiden.

Theunissen, E.M., 2001. 'The Kwaalburg', a Bronze Age barrow near Alphen –new results from old remains. In: W.H. Metz/ B.L. van Beek/ H. Steegstra (eds), *Patina. Essays presented to Jay Jordan Butler on the occasion of his 80th birthday*, Groningen/ Amsterdam, 539-549.

Theunissen, E.M., 2006. Burial practices in the south of the Low Countries: the symbolic meaning of the Bronze Age barrow. In: L. Šmejda (ed), *Archaeology of Burial Mounds*, Plzeň, 150-162.

Theunissen, L./ M. van den Dries, 2006. Prikken in prehistorische grafmonumenten, *RACM-nieuwsbrief* 1 (september 2006), 12-13.

Theunissen, E.M. *et al.*, *in prep*. De archeologische monumentenzorg van grafheuvels en urnenvelden. Over de identificatie, waardering en duurzaam behoud, *Rapportage Archeologische Monumentenzorg*, Amersfoort.

Tol, A., 2008. Plangebied Koningin Wilhelminalaan Leersum. Gemeente Utrechtse Heuvelrug. Een archeologisch vooronderzoek (proefsleuven), *RAAP-rapport* 1692.

Ufkes, A., 2002. Aardewerk. In: J. Milojkovic/ E. Smits (eds), *Archeologie in de Betuweroute: Lage Blok. Een nederzettingsterrein uit de Midden-IJzertijd bij Meteren (gemeente Geldermalsen)*. Amersfoort (Rapportage Archeologische Monumentenzorg 90), 69-103

Veen, M. Van der/ J.N.Lanting, 1991. A group of tumuli on the Hooghalen estate near Hijken, municipality of Beilen, prov. Drenthe, NL, *Palaeohistoria* 31, 191-234.

Velde, H.M. van de/ E. Taayke, 2000. Archeologisch onderzoek op de Eelinkes te Winterswijk, Bunschoten, *ADC-Rapport* 20.

Verbraeck, A., 1984. *Geologische kaart van Nederland, kaartblad Tiel (Oost)*. Rijks Geologische Dienst, Haarlem.

Verhart, L., 2005. Vuursteenbewerking. In: J. Deeben/ E. Drenth/ M.F. van Oorsouw/ L. Verhart (eds), *De Steentijd van Nederland*, Meppel (Archeologie 11/12), 81-90.

Verwers, G.J., 1966. Tumuli at the Zevenbergen near Oss, Gem. Berghem, Prov. Noord-Brabant, *Analecta Praehistorica Leidensia* 2, Leiden, 27-32.

Verwers, W.J.H., 1980. Goirle, grafheuvels op de Rechte Heide, *Archeologische Monumenten in Nederland* 8, Fibula-Van Dishoeck, Bussum.

Wallinga, J./ P. Lemmers/ D. Fontijn/ R. Jansen, in prep. Optical dating of a burial mound constructed of stacked sods. A feasibility study of non-destructive age prospection.

Waterbolk, H.T., 1954. *De praehistorische mens en zijn milieu*. Van Gorcum, Assen.

Waterbolk, H. T, 1957. Grafheuvelopgraving in de gemeente Anlo. *Nieuwe Drentse Volksalmanak* 75, 23-34.

Waterbolk, H.T., 1964. The Bronze Age settlement of Elp. *Helinium* 4, 97-131.

Waterbolk, H.T., 1980. Hoe oud zijn de Drentse dorpen? Problemen van nederzettingscontinuïteit van de bronstijd tot de middeleeuwen. In: J.M. Bos/ C.A. Kalee/ Tj. Pot/ O.J. Wittewaal (eds), *Nederzettingsarcheologie in Nederland*, (Westerheem 29), 190-212.

Wegewitz, W., 1960. Eine Schädelbestattung der Einzelgrabkultur, *Nachrichten aus Niedersachsens Urgeschichte* 29, 6-17.

Wegewitz, W., 1967. Bedeutende Funde aus dem Arbeitsgebiet des Helms-Museum, *Führer Mainz* 7, 24-61.

Wiepking, C.G., 2001. Aardewerk. In: M.M. Sier/ C.W. Koot (eds), *Archeologie in de Betuweroute. Kesteren-De Woerd: bewoningssporen uit de IJzertijd en de Romeinse tijd*, Amersfoort (Rapportage Archeologische Monumentenzorg 82), 113-170.

Woltering, P.J., 1994. Texel. Landschap en bewoning van Midden Bronstijd tot Vroege Middeleeuwen. In: M. Rappol/ C.M. Soonius (eds), *In de bodem van Noord-Holland, Geologie en archeologie*, Amsterdam, 189-217.

Woltering, P.J., 2000. Occupation History of Texel, III: Middle Bronze-Middle Iron Age, *Berichten van de Rijksdienst voor Oudheidkundig Bodemonderzoek* 44, 22-28.

Appendix

by P. Valentijn

Pot Beakers in the Netherlands: contextual associations

The following Appendix lists examples of (complete) Pot Beaker finds where there is evidence on deposition context, including the finds from the excavations at Unitas 1 and Delfin 190. The focus is on possible relationships between Pot Beakers and burial mounds

Near a barrow

Ede, 1930	Although Lehmann (1965, pot number 3) remarks that pot number 3 was found within a barrow, a reinterpretation by Lanting (1973, 257) has shown that it was found outside the barrow.	Lehmann 1965, pot number 3; Lanting 1973, 257.
Hunneschans, municipality of Apeldoorn, 1909		Lehmann 1965, pot number 11; Louwe Kooijmans 1974, note 134 & 135.
Driesche Berg, near the hamlet of Drie, municipality of Ermelo, 1967	Two meters from the Pot Beaker, which was placed upside down in a pit, a Bell Beaker was found, also placed upside down in the top layer of a pit.	Lehmann 1967a, 162-4; Hulst 1970, 28.
Unitas 1, Elst, municipality of Rhenen, 1990	Pot Beaker 35 sherds of 1 pot found at a few m distance from the Early Bronze Age barrow Unitas 1	This book, section 2.4.2, section 4.6, Fig. 4.4
Nijmegen-Hunerberg	Pot Beaker sherds found in a pit lined to a ditch of a barrow	Louwe Kooijmans 1973

In a barrow – On the old surface beneath a barrow

Hanendorp, municipality of Epe, 1911	A reinterpretation by Lanting (1973, 257-8) showed that the Pot Beaker was placed in excentrical position on the old surface beneath the barrow.	Lehmann 1965, pot number 1; Lanting 1973, 257-8.

In a barrow – Entered a barrow along with the sods or as a later intrusion

Ginkelse Heide, south of Ede, municipality of Ede, 1957/1958	Sherds of a Pot Beaker were found in the flank of a barrow, mixed with sherds of a large Protruding Foot Beaker-like vessel, just underneath the present surface of a Protruding Foot Beaker barrow.	Lehmann 1967b, 66 (fig. 4).

Vries, municipality of Vries, 1939	One fragment of a Pot Beaker was found of which the stratigraphic position could not be established during excavation. Since only one sherd is found, it is probably that it entered the barrow along with the sods (Lanting 2007/08, appendix 2, e 7.	Lanting 2007/08, appendix 2, e 7.
Unitas 1, Elst, municipality of Rhenen, 2006 find	Pot Beaker sherd found in an Early Bronze Age barrow. Precise stratigraphical position unclear, probably part of the sods.	This book, section 4.4, Fig. 4.3
Unitas 1, Elst, municipality of Rhenen, 1971 find	Pot Beaker sherd found in an Early Bronze Age barrow. Precise stratigraphical position unclear, probably part of the sods although it might also have been deposited at the old surface (AWN find)	This book, section 4.4, Fig. 4.3
Delfin 190, Elst, municipality of Rhenen, 1971	Two Pot Beaker sherds, probably included in the sods of a Middle Bronze Age mound	This book, section 5.6, Fig. 5.8
Delfin 190, Elst, municipality of Rhenen, year of find unknown	One Pot Beaker sherd, stored together with other finds that were done at Delfin 190, a number of which comes from this Middle Bronze Age mound after it was partly damaged due to sand extraction	This book, section 5.7.3, Fig. 5.9

In a barrow – In a pit beneath a barrow

Nutterveld, municipality of Denekamp, 1942	A reinterpretation by Lanting (2007/08, appendix 2, a 42) has shown that the Pot Beaker was found in a pit beneath the barrow and not in a grave, as was earlier stated by Lanting (1973, 259). According to Lanting (2007/08, appendix 2, a 42) the pit predates the erection of the barrow and is probably a remnant of a settlement site.	Lehmann 1965, pot number 19; Lanting 1973, 259; Lanting 2007/08, appendix 2, a 42.
Nijmegen	In a pit beneath a (levelled) barrow were found fragments of both a Neck Pot Beaker and a Veluvian Bell Beaker. The pit probably belongs to the first period of the barrow.	Louwe Kooijmans 1973, grafheuvel VII & pit number 99.

In a megalith grave

Hunebed D9, Annen, municipality of Anlo, 1952		Lanting 2007/08, appendix 2, b 2.
Hunebed D21, Bronneger, municipality of Borgerm 1918	Found in a burial chamber with Beaker- and TRB pottery.	Lehmann 1965, pot number 6; Drenth & Hogestijn 1999, appendix 1, hunebed D21; Lanting 2007/08, appendix 2, b9.
Hunebed D21, Bronneger, municipality of Borgerm 1918	Found in a burial chamber with Beaker- and TRB pottery.	Lehmann 1965, pot number 7; Drenth & Hogestijn 1999, appendix 1, hunebed D21; Lanting 2007/08, appendix 2, b9.

Hunebed D32c, Odoorn, municipality of Borger-Odoorn		Drenth & Hogestijn 1999, appendix 1, hunebed D32c.
Hunebed G1, Glimmer Esch, municipality of Haren, 1957	Decorated fragment of Pot Beaker-like pottery.	Drenth & Hogestijn 1999, appendix 1, hunebed G1
Hunebed O2, Mander, municipality of Tubbergenm 1957	A fragment of a possible large Pot Beaker was found in a levelled megalith grave.	Drenth & Hogestijn 1999, appendix 1, hunebed O2

Isolated finds (no clear relation with burial mounds, megaliths or settlements)

Velp, municipality of Rheden, 1966		Hulst 1965/66; Hulst 1970, 29.
Venenberg, Elspeet, municipality of Ermelo, 1939		Lehmann 1965, pot number 18; Louwe Kooijmans 1967; Hulst 1970, 29.
Poolse Driesten, south of Putten, municipality of Putten		Lehmann 1967a, fig. 6
Poolse Driesten, south of Putten, municipality of Putten		Lehmann 1967a, fig. 7
Poolse Driesten, south of Putten, municipality of Putten		Lehmann 1967a, fig. 8:1
Poolse Driesten, south of Putten, municipality of Putten		Lehmann 1967a, fig. 8:2
Poolse Driesten, south of Putten, municipality of Putten		Lehmann 1967a, fig. 8:3
Poolse Driesten, south of Putten, municipality of Putten		Lehmann 1967a, fig. 9
Rhenen, N225 site 5	Deposition of individual Pot Beaker sherds in a pit	Schute 2009, 65-74
Ermelo	Scatter of Pot Beaker sherds. No features were found during the subsequent excavation of the find spot	Van Sprang 1993, 81-5

Context of (fragments of) Pot Beakers

Near a barrow	5
In a barrow – On the old surface beneath a barrow	1
In a barrow – Entered a barrow along with the sods or as a later intrusion	6
In a barrow – In a pit beneath a barrow	2
In a megalith grave	6
Apparently isolated finds	10
Total	30

Acknowledgements

This book would never have been possible without the extensive help of many people. First and foremost we would like to thank Coert Donker and Jelle Bais (Staatsbosbeheer), Gerard van Heijningen and Miss V.M.G. Van Asch van Wijck Von Papen (Prattenburg Estate) for allowing us to excavate on their property and assisting us with material, information and help. Ton van Rooijen, Bert Huiskens and Mirella de Jong for helping us to recover the finds in the depots and musea. Very important were the students who moved countless cubic metres by hand! We would especially like to thank Yvonne Achterkamp, Nadine Conradi, Pascal Flohr, Pepijn van de Geer, Ade Porreij, Mark Rikkers and Karin Schuitema. Equally helpful during the excavation were the amateur-archaeologists André Manders, Henk van het Loo and Gerard Smits.

This publication was also made possible with the extensive support and discussions with colleagues and fellow archaeologists. We would especially like to thank prof. Harry Fokkens, Eric Van Driel and Lou Jacobs (Leiden University), Eric Lohof (ADC), Ivar Schute (RAAP), Lucas Meurkens (Archol BV), Leon van Hoof (Berlin) ,José Schreurs (RCE) and Edwin van Hagen (Rhenen). We would also like to thank Claire Schnyder (Berlin), prof. Svend Hansen (Berlin-Eurasien Abteilung DAI), Evert van Ginkel (TGV), Olav Odé, Simone Lemmers (Leiden), Stijn Arnoldussen (RCE). And finally we would also like to thank Karsten Wentink and Corné van Woerdekom in helping us produce this beautiful book.

Address of the authors

Ancestral Mounds team:

Prof. dr C.C. Bakels (C.C.Bakels@Arch.LeidenUniv.nl)
Drs Quentin Bourgeois (Q.P.J.Bourgeois@Arch.LeidenUniv.nl)
Dr David Fontijn (D.R.Fontijn@Arch.LeidenUniv.nl)
Arjan Louwen MA (arjanlouwen@hotmail.com)
Patrick Valentijn BA (p.j.c.valentijn@umail.leidenuniv.nl)
Drs Cristian van der Linde (C.vanderLinde@archol.nl)
Karsten Wentink Mphil (K.Wentink@Arch.LeidenUniv.nl)

All: Faculty of Archaeology
University of Leiden
PO Box 9515
2300 RA Leiden
The Netherlands

National Heritage Agency

Dr Stijn Arnoldussen (S.Arnoldussen@cultureelerfgoed.nl)
Drs Jan-Willem de Kort (J.W.de.Kort@cultureelerfgoed.nl)
Drs Axel Müller (A.Muller@cultureelerfgoed.nl)
Dr Liesbeth Theunissen (L.Theunissen@cultureelerfgoed.nl)

All: Rijksdienst voor het Cultureel Erfgoed (RCE)
Postbus 1600
3800 BP Amersfoort
The Netherlands

Province of Utrecht

Drs Ruurd Kok (R.Kok@Raap.nl)

provincie Utrecht
afdeling Economie, Cultuur en Vrije Tijd
Postbus 80300
3508 TH UTRECHT
The Netherlands